Dareen Tatour

MY THREATENING POEM

The Memoir of a Poet in Occupation Prisons

GW00676296

Drunk Muse Press

Translated from Arabic to English by Terrie Dawood
'Resist, my people, resist them' translated by Anon
Cover photographs by Dareen Tatour

Edited by Neil Young

Published by Drunk Muse Press drunkmusepress.com

Printed by Book Printing UK bookprintinguk.com

Printed in Great Britain

ISBN 978-1-8384085-0-3

DEDICATION

I dedicate this book to each woman political prisoner, whether released or still waiting for her freedom to knock on the door, who has suffered the chains and constraints of imprisonment and has experienced the cruelty of its injustice. To each woman who is lying in the ground and enwrapped in the soil of this country after she has screamed, suffered silently, has been killed or has been forgotten, I say, I remember you; I remember you; I remember you...

To all the women who wrote a new feminist history, a history of freedom, equality and equity.

To all my female friends who stood by me during the most difficult times and darkest moments, those who had the greatest impact on unleashing this novel from the darkness of prison to the spaces of light: Ofra Yashua-Lyth, Einat Weizman and Sameera Jamaa't.

To my friend and brother, Yoav Haifawi, for whom this dedication cannot be enough, yet it is the least I could offer him after his devotion and sacrifice for the sake of this case.

To my dad who drew the outlines of my picture; to my mum who coloured it in with the colours of life. To those who suffered greatly during my detention period, yet of whom nobody heard. To my grandma, Khadija, may she rest in peace, who taught me what it meant to be Palestinian. Thanks to her I will, forever, preserve my identity.

INTRODUCTION

This story began from the first letter of an alphabet which emerged while in prison and under arrest. This alphabet was invaded by the emotions and events that changed my life and controlled my sensations, as they were more violent and weightier than any natural disaster, be it an earthquake or a volcano. Thus, it remained stuck deep within me – the memories that played with my heart and rearranged the details of my thoughts, knitted that story.

In this book, I write about a world gone mad and a world exploited by justice leeches and the monsters of authority, racism and occupation as well as political tyrants and oppressors who bear a grudge against humanity, with one outcome: the imprisonment of a female poet after charging her with composing the threatening poem.

With this memoir, I experienced many kinds of constraints, chains and restrictions and, because of that suffering, I challenged, defied and decided to break them all. I decided to expel their darkness from my life and put out their fires. My journey started at the Israeli authorities' prisons, and it soon became the prison of society, its customs and its traditions. After that, I was an inmate in the prisons of my family and the male domination exercised over women, depriving them of their self-determination and keeping them under the control of men.

With this book, I entered yet another stage of a different struggle within myself, primarily, which is how a true struggle should be, in my opinion. I addressed myself saying, "My struggle must not end here in this prison, for when a struggle starts, it should never end, no matter the circumstances. My mission now is not to succumb to despair. I must not to let the birds of my letters abandon the nests of creativity; the birds sing the most splendid songs in cages. All I have to do is adopt a different perceptive of my surroundings, and to transform my previously-held interpretations of everything around me and redefine them.

During the days of detention, the dark prison was transformed into a woman's revelation, and the bleak wall turned into a blank sheet waiting for me to write my feelings on it, and pour the ink of my memoirs out during the very tough circumstances and under the tight restrictions and bitter events I faced, and which lived on with me.

It was not easy for me to take the decision to write and publish my memoirs that reveal the details of experiences I had been through, and to be ready to expose myself and draw out my feelings in public, especially given the attempts of many people to restrict me, break my will and bury my writing alive. Their efforts settled the matter, so I wrote this book and decided to publish it at any cost. Nothing, in my eyes, is more precious than feeling free; and in writing, I find my freedom.

With the first letter I wrote and until the very last letter, as well as a poetry collection I composed during this period, all the handcuffs and chains were destroyed before my eyes, and I witnessed my victory over everything, for, by writing them, I have achieved self-sufficiency and broken free from all the chains, restrictions and prisons by which they wanted to lock me up forever. I ruined all their attempts to have my mouth shut and my voice amputated, especially since I was prohibited from publishing my writings throughout this period.

Another reason that contributed to my persistence in writing this book is that there are very few writings about the experience of women political prisoners, and women in general in the Arab world. By contrast, many male political prisoners have told and published their stories. This entirely absents, silences and pushes the female voice into the background. Women political prisoners do not write about their experience in prison and detention, either because of censorship, fear or shame. This blocks them from discussing the wounds and pains of their experiences. So, the experiences remain unrevealed or in wait for someone else to bring them up as they see fit, only from a male perspective, or as they would want to address the issues and according to the conventions, customs, beliefs and traditions that suit them. Thus, I decided that my bitter experience in prison should not be just a memory soon to be forgotten, and I wrote about it, bearing in mind that my goal was not to shed light on an individual, or an exceptional story, as some might claim, but to be set free from those chains that shackled and still shackle many of us, women political prisoners. Perhaps, through this memoir, I would be able to break down that wall of silence for Palestinian and Arab women so they could see the space of freedom, and enjoy the flight towards it without fear of hitting a wall of any kind.

Having the awareness of writing as a woman in general, and a Palestinian woman in particular, is to be aware of the potential of our inner selves. When a woman writes, not only does she achieve victory over the prison and the prisoner, but she can also end the siege of silence dictated by male authority, or any other authorities.

My writing of these memoirs and the feminisation of language and memory along with it, is the restoration of my being and inner self as a detained woman, being transferred from one prison to another. Furthermore, it is a state of existence which is different from what they wanted for me; it is liberation from the prison of an authoritarian male cultural and social occupation.

I would also like to note that this is not an autobiography, as much as it is a memoir about the period of imprisonment and the feelings I have experienced. I have not discussed certain situations and events because revealing them would not affect myself alone but my relationships as well with people with whom I have severed ties forever, and people with whom my relationship is still intact. I also kept to myself some other events for legal reasons and/or implications.

Resist, my people, resist them

In my Quds I dressed my wounds,
Recounted my sorrows to God
And put my soul in my palm
For an Arab Palestine.
I will not agree to a peace solution
As long as the poison is spreading
And killing flowers from my country,

I will never lower my flags
Until I take them out of my homeland,
I will defeat them when the time comes.
Resist, my people, resist them,
Resist the settler's greed,
Shred the shameful constitution
Which carried the depressing humiliation
And prevented us from reclaiming our rights.

Resist them, my people, resist
And follow the caravan of martyrs.
They burned the innocent children
And they sniped at Hadil in public,
Murdered her in broad daylight,
They plucked Muhammad's eyes,
Crucified him and drew pain on his body,
They poured hatred on Ali,
Set fire
And burned hopes in a cradle.
Resist the Mista'arev's evil
And do not listen to the collaborators
Who tied us to the illusion of peace,
Do not fear the fire tongues of the Merkava tank

For the belief in your heart is stronger
As long as you resist in a homeland
Which experienced invasions and did tire
For Ali is calling from his grave.
Resist, my rebellious people,
Write me as parts of the incense branch
And you become the response to my remains.

CHAPTER 1

As slow as molasses in January, time drags on for the prisoner. I still think about it all, even the tiniest things that happened to me. Everything I was surrounded by was worthy of being addressed. All of it. Closely, I had started watching my only 'cell-mates' and companions – cockroaches and bedbugs and their movements – at al-Jalameh Prison Centre, so as to keep them off my clothes, let alone my body. Suddenly and without thinking twice about whether or not I would one day put it on paper, I was simply acting on it and making it part of my everlasting journals.

The restlessness of these cockroaches, unruffled by cold winters, intrigued me. These constantly moving bugs were the only certain sign of life in this gloomy prison cell. My growing estrangement pushed me to redefine the tiniest details surrounding me, perhaps in unprecedented ways. I thrived on discovering some novel emotional philosophy. Prisons truly have such a philosophy which triggers visual memories, prompting any prisoner to become an artist, a cultured human, a writer or a poet.

I will always remember that night. In fact, the thought of the moment when the police, unexpectedly, raided my room is sufficient to chill me to the bone. They didn't only enter my room at that moment; they penetrated my memory, my papers and my pieces of writing.

It was the night of October 11, 2015. I had barely fallen asleep after turning off my computer. My mind was racing with thoughts, news clips and images of soldiers shooting the young Nazareth woman, Israa' al-Abed, in Afula; a stream of images portraying violence, racism and the tyranny spreading in the country and all over the region rushed through my mind. The echoes of swear words and my cousin's screams hurling at me still haunted me as I tried to sleep. I fell asleep while I was still processing and trying to wrap my head around what had been happening within and around me. How easy it had become for one human to kill and humiliate another.

The rampant violence, those events and screams, made me picture and relive some cruel moments from childhood which had haunted me for

1

years. I went to bed dragging along those pitiful and disgusting details while attempting to get some rest. And with that cumulative burden of a lifetime holding me back from falling into deep sleep, it was almost 3.30 in the morning when I woke up to the cries of my mum and dad: "They are here to arrest you!" Panic-stricken, I got up, opened my room's door wide and looked around to find policemen encircling me and about to arrest me. "Are you Dareen?" four of them enquired as they approached. The way they got into our house this time was a first. I could easily sense the fear of everyone in my family at that moment as I looked at their faces; their eyes said it all. They showed nothing but fear and worry. In a blink of an eye, my whole family, even my siblings who lived on the highest floor of the apartment building, gathered around me inside the house. They all witnessed that scene. Until this very day, I still have no clue how that happened and how they learned about it. It could have been my dad; one phone call in the midst of that gloomy noise would have been enough.

Despite the surprise and fear that invaded me at those moments, I somehow managed to peer at their facial expressions and hear the words they uttered with such concentration that they are burned on my mind to this day.

Combat helmets on heads, military uniforms, rifles and sophisticated weapons, fingers on triggers. Four of them drew closer and closer to my bedroom and stood still at its door watching every move I made, their giant bodies mirroring me. Their eyes sparkled with fear, right and left their eyes darted constantly. I had no idea what they were getting at, or what they were searching for and expecting to find in my room. I could not comprehend what they would want from me to begin with. I was certain I had done nothing against the law. Had they come because I had taken part in protests? I had so many questions but they had yet to answer. As though in a battlefield, everything around me was a mixture of surprise and strangeness. Only two officers entered my bedroom. They looked at its corners, eyeing each inch of my room. Astonished, one of them raised his eyebrows while the other turned his head left and right while maintaining eye contact with his comrade who then asked: "Does this guitar belong to you?"

"Yes, it is mine," I replied.

A few seconds passed. The surprise grew on his face as he reworded his question. "Do you play the guitar?" he asked. Keeping my smile, "yes," I answered sternly. He could not help but raise his eyebrows as his comrade asked me three questions at once: "How so? Are you sure? You play the guitar?" Without hesitation, I said: "Sure, art is my whole life."

At a glance, I could tell my room did not appeal to them; I could feel it in my bones as I observed their expressions and their first reactions as they entered it. What might they spot to begin with? A picture of me and my grandma while I was embracing her before she passed away, hung on one of its walls, and two others of the poets Fadwa Tuqan and Nazik al-Malaika? A picture of myself when I was a child? Or that big picture I had once taken during one of the annual return marches which later on turned into an emblematic picture for those demonstrations? This room did not match their expectations; it was full of artwork scattered all over the place: pens, drawing books, a camera and its equipment, a guitar, an oud, photographs, hanged paintings, crowded bookcases, French perfumes as well as two Persian cats lying in bed.

The moment I stood right before them in my room watching their facial expressions, and despite the fact they seemed to be perplexed during the first few minutes as if they felt they were in the wrong place and had a person who did not match their mental specifications, I smiled.

One of them demanded my computer, my phone and my ID card. They held me and hand-cuffed me tightly and demanded I go with them towards the car. Careless to all of the power surrounding me, I left the room assured of the fact I had done nothing to be afraid of. I assured my mother in an attempt to calm my family down and ease their worries: "Don't worry. I'm coming back."

Hand-cuffed and leg-cuffed, they got me into a Toyota police car, and off we started. Through the window glass, I noticed a big transit vehicle leaving my neighbourhood from the other end of the street. The car went on for a mile or so until it was joined by another. That convoy arrived on the main street only to be joined by a fourth vehicle. 'What an arrest! All that force was set up and deployed to get me arrested,' I couldn't help but think with astonishment. They drove me to al Mascobiyeh Detention

Centre[1] (Al-Muscovite) in Nazareth, and I was oblivious as to why I had been arrested or the type of arrest.

CHAPTER 2

The clock was about to strike 5am. I was standing helplessly in the yard. I'd roamed the streets of Nazareth so many times. I'd organised several tours to familiarise tourists with the city and its history. Often, I spoke of the origin of this building and stones which encapsulated the history and the uniqueness of the city. Many times I'd captured the alleys and old neighbourhoods as memories on my camera. A pigeon standing on one of the windowsills of this very building, the one right in front of me, was the last picture I took of the place. I still remember that moment; I still remember how that scene caught my eye. What a twist of fate! The moment I captured that scene and this moment were worlds apart. I was now under arrest in that very building. There was nowhere to sit in the yard. It was just a parking lot for police and special unit vehicles which were everywhere. Policemen in groups, leaning on their cars, muttered while looking at me, smiling and laughing. Now, this place was the Nazareth Police Office and I, hand and leg-cuffed, was and surrounded by about fifteen policemen from the *Yasam Unit* [2] hurling curses and racist remarks at me. As anyone passed, they would show their prowess by using racist language; it seemed like an achievement to them. I listened but did not get carried away by their provocations or their frivolous discussions about me. While I was relatively calm yet worried, I wondered what sign this morning would offer me.

"You want a weapon to kill me? There. My gun. You, subversive. Terrorist. Arab trash. You look like a subversive. You seem like a subversive."

These words came with many others like them. I was present in that extraordinary scene. I couldn't deny feeling scared and truly anxious, yet the situation was enough to stir my courage and spirit to challenge them. I sensed their cowardice, wretchedness and helplessness as they held their weapons against me, the hand and leg-cuffed. "Who is the weak among us?" I wondered.

Despite the absurdity of the unknown, I started to train my emotions to face various scenarios so as not to be shocked and get carried away to a place where I did not want to be. I kept my cool, and I did not give them

5

what they had been after – that is, for me to unleash my anger or anything that could later be used against me.

I stood still in the same spot for an hour; it was the longest hour I had ever waited in my life. It was incessant. I let my soul wander off to befriend loss and confusion; to look for the secret behind the harmonious fusion between suffering and strength; to digest what these chains that shackled me meant; to come up with a composure that transcended the limits of this reality and reached the unimaginable; it might, perhaps, recognise the secret behind everything that was happening to me.

Nothing changed until a female soldier turned up unexpectedly and demanded that I move along as she escorted me. A woman dragging another along. I started taking my first heavy and bound steps, confined to the length of the chains. She began to walk at a faster pace, pulling me along, which caused my feet to ache; groups of policemen followed her down that long hallway. Afterwards, it was time for us to walk up the stairs. I had to stop as the chains were very tight and causing unbearable pain. Chains against my skin, rubbing and pressing hard. I was covered in scratch marks. The more I moved, the more the pain grew and the deeper those chains dug into my skin. I asked her if she could loosen them, but she utterly rejected that. She ignored my agonised cry for help. Instead, "Go on! Silently!" she cried.

As I walked along, I listened to their discussions, which boiled down to the fact that the detainee reception office had no registration employees or an interrogator to start the interrogation process. Anger and confusion covered their faces, and they exchanged yells and curses. They were clueless as to where they wanted to take me. They would arrive at an office, one of them would enter to ask a few questions but in vain, and again they would take me back to the deserted reception office; back to another room. It was an endless cycle of toing and froing which lasted for thirty minutes.

The receptionist finally arrived and recorded some details, and then one officer came into the room through the door. Later, I realised he was the interrogator after calling on them to bring me into the room.

My chained feet and wrists throbbed with pain; I went into a room packed with computers, cameras and some other strange-looking equipment that I had never seen in my entire life. I was asked to stand in a place where white plastic bridges irradiated some unnatural beams of light. They forced me to take off my hijab. They took a photo of my eyes. A mugshot, one front-view photo and one side-view; they photographed each side. They demanded that I move my head in all directions. I didn't know where to look or the camera direction; up to that moment, I had never before seen that device right before my eyes. They took my fingerprints as well. The former was arduous; a severe electric shock left my left palm covered with lifelong burns, not to mention the lost and forever erased fingerprints. Even those highly-developed machines couldn't identify or record my fingerprint impressions.

The staff couldn't enter the data into the system as they were instructed, which forced them to discuss this issue for about thirty more minutes and call in a specialist to come up with an alternative. He suggested using fingerprint ink. Quickly, they fetched a bottle filled with blue ink, drowned my left hand in it and took my fingerprint impressions, and then I had to put them on every corner of several papers. They tried to enter the data into the computer again, but it was another useless attempt, so they decided to leave it mostly on paper for the time being. I could see my fingerprints being printed on lots of their documents before I was called to the interrogation room.

CHAPTER 3

It was 6am and I was hand and leg-cuffed and sitting in a freezing tiny room. It looked as if it might actually be the interrogation room; the air conditioning vents were aimed at the metal chair where I was sitting and the temperature dropped with every second. "I'm sitting in an ice mould, not a chair!" I thought to myself.

These sudden cold sensations that take over a detainee's body while waiting for their testimonies in interrogation rooms were not new to me; I'd familiarised myself with that through intensive reading. I had always thought that the descriptions of this stage were beyond exaggeration. From my perspective, they were inevitable reactions that instantly arose due to the stress a detainee was undergoing. At the time, I assumed that no external factors played a role in producing those harsh sensations. Still, that cold feeling was invading my body, and I came to realise why. My doubts were removed as I found out that I had been wrong all along. The position of the air-conditioner? Aiming it at the detainee? Well, that would explain the cold eating away at my bones, affecting my mental state and wearing away at my patience and tolerance.

The air-conditioners were invented to ensure people's comfort and to ease any suffering that may result from changes in weather or temperature. Now that useful tool was exploited and abused; it was turned into a pressure strategy. I was reduced to a body bound with metallic chains, sitting in a bitterly cold room, fearing the unknown and surrounded by policemen.

A few minutes passed and the quivering of my body worsened. My mind was filled with questions and bitter conclusions. A policeman approached me, sat on a nearby bench, put his phone in front of him, and played a voice recording or a movie, perhaps. I knew that he turned up the volume to the max as I watched his fingers moving against his phone screen; it was within earshot and recognised it. It was one of Hassan Nasrallah's speeches. After a few seconds, he addressed me directly saying:

"You're happy to hear this, aren't you? You must love this voice. You love terrorism, just like he does. No wonder. You're a terrorist just like he is. Would you like to see him? Take the phone and look at him. You're very much alike and terrorism shows itself in you."

He redirected the phone screen towards my eyes to force me into watching it, but I brushed it off. I simply had a look in my eyes of utter indifference and I gazed at his shirt to try to work out his name. 'Maybe he has a name tag right above his pocket,' I thought. It was a fruitless search. He hid it with a sly move of his second arm. I stayed indifferent, calm and collected.

The voice coming out of the phone speakers vanished. A man wearing civilian clothes and a winter jacket which radiated sensations of warmth came into the room. I didn't give it much thought because I soon realised these were prearranged and calculated steps. This man was yet another one.

"You are charged with incitement, violence and terrorism," he said. "Well, your Facebook posts indicate this," he added. "You wrote that you wished to be a martyr, and you posted a picture of that subversive woman in Afula. So, what do you say? What's your take on these charges?" he demanded.

"I won't utter a word without talking to a lawyer," I said sternly.

"Alright, give me the lawyer's phone number and I will call them," he said.

"It's on my contacts list," I replied.

He turned on my confiscated phone and asked me to give him the names, and I did. Attempting to find the name I requested, he started to scroll down my contact list. Unexpectedly, my phone's ringtone started playing "The most beautiful feeling in the universe is when you're crazy in love." It was a ringtone from one of the Lebanese singer Elissa's songs. A text message. Astonished and perplexed, the interrogator asked: "What kind of song is this? I don't see how you have such a ringtone?" Question left unanswered. He proceeded with his search. I had a female lawyer friend, so he dialled her number first. She was completely shocked. I could sense pain and nervousness in the sound of her voice. Surprisingly, she was literally in pain at some hospital – in the delivery room, to be more specific. She couldn't offer any help and, in turn, I didn't say anything, but I wished her a safe delivery and I congratulated her in advance on her new baby.

I admit I couldn't help but laugh at the awkwardness of that situation and this fate that would leave its unexpected marks on my life. I dug into my memory, trying to find my next option, and I decided to go for the Law Firm Office of Justice and Legal Advice, but no one picked up. I started to question everything after I felt as if the whole universe had conspired against me. I felt as if I had been part of a conspiracy theory and that fate was against my will. What a frustrating start! Finding a lawyer seemed to be unattainable, mission impossible. Everything was getting more complicated for me.

These were my odds, omens of a different kind, I believe. I thought of a third option, and my last ray of hope was calling an activist to help me to find a lawyer, and that was what happened. I was determined I wouldn't break my silence until I'd sought legal advice from my lawyer. My first interrogation was adjourned.

CHAPTER 4

Two hours has passed and here I was in a room unfit for humans. It was indeed a mortuary cabinet, especially with the low temperatures I had had to bear until ordered to move to another room.

It was 9 am. I was surrounded by policemen who forced me to stay fixed at the room's entrance, waiting until I was called in to face questioning by an interrogator.

A wooden door stood right in front of me and on one of its panels a small golden sign was hung with the words, written in black, reading 'interrogation room' in Arabic and Hebrew. My foot pain was growing worse because of the tight chains. Again, I asked them for them to be loosened slightly, and the response was adamantly unchanged – my request was rejected. "You are detained. These are the rules, and we have to abide by them," they replied. Soon they sent me into the room.

For the first time since my arrest at dawn, my hands were un-cuffed. I sat in the chair and looked around, exploring and discovering my surroundings. I could see a room packed with equipment. It was diametrically opposed to the former one which was filled with computers, cameras, a scanner, printers and numerous phones.

There was just one interrogator. He was sitting at his desk, facing me. Then he introduced himself and began to talk while arranging some documents. My body had almost reached its average temperature and I started to get warmer. However, that didn't last for long as he turned on the AC. I asked him to turn it off or down but he refused explaining that he felt hot and needed it.

It wasn't long before he grabbed his winter jacket which was hung on the back of his chair, and put it on. This drew a sarcastic smile to my face. I thought of the meanness, cruelty and inhumanity of some people. I knew for sure that I was in a real battle with the contradictions that surrounded me. After thinking what had been happening and replaying the day's incidents in my head, I decided to tell the truth and to expose their accusations as false. I would tell them about what actually happened and what my intentions were to begin with. 'There is nothing to fear, and I

11

know that I haven't done anything wrong or anything that I would hide or deny,' I reflected.

I was reassured after arriving at this decision and the only thing that was still distressing me were those leg-cuffs after my handcuffs were removed. Initially, the process of questioning consisted of a casual conversation as my accusations – none of which I could recall – were explained to me. and I, for my part, was responsive. I forgot about my lawyer since, frankly, it no longer mattered to me; I was confident of my decision.

Then, I responded to his questions concerning the picture of the Palestinian woman. I told him I couldn't exactly recall whether I had posted it or not and that it all seemed blurry. I only remembered watching that video a few times, especially the moment when she got shot. I also remembered some brutal childhood memory which started at the age of seven and lasted for five more years. I might have posted that then removed it. I struggled to recall details. It was all obscure. I explained to him that sometimes I suffered from disassociation as a result of post-traumatic stress and dissociative disorders; some moments simply went blank as a result of this trauma. It was childhood trauma, after all. I gave him the names of three people who had contributed to that as I attempted to clarify the nature of the crime committed against me in the past. He assured me that he wrote those names down and he would take care of it and refer it to a specialised investigator.

As for the 'I want to be a martyr' post, I said that I had never written anything of this sort before, and I didn't recall this matter. A man entered the room, gave the interrogator a handshake and introduced himself as the lawyer who would defend and represent me in court. Shortly, after a quick discussion between the two men, which I wasn't able to catch or comprehend, the lawyer asked me to consult with him. I reckoned it was about my accusations. On a bench outside the interrogation room and under the watch of the interrogator, we sat together and talked more freely, yet he addressed me:

"In legal terms, you may receive a six-year sentence for these charges. There is a young Nazareth woman who is imprisoned in an anonymous place; nobody knows what has happened to her. Visits are not allowed at that prison. At the beginning she received a six-month administrative detention because of her Facebook posts. In other words, you will have to deny everything; simply say that your Facebook account has been hacked and that you don't know what has happened."

He shook my hand and said: "Goodbye for now; see you in court later today." We'd barely spent any time together; in a two-minute meeting, he rapidly recited his speech and left me even more befuddled. He also made me feel extremely nervous to the point of fear. Meeting my lawyer was supposed to bring me a sense of peace and confidence, but this produced the opposite. Actually, meeting him distracted all my senses, as if I was at a crossroads in my car only to realise the brakes didn't work. I wasn't in control any more, and I was at a loss for direction. Perhaps that would lead me to a safer place. In my case, crashing into something was inevitable; it would happen eventually without a doubt.

I couldn't rationalise things as I'd done before; that rationality that helped me before meeting the lawyer. Everything I had in mind evaporated, and all I could remember were his words. Every bit of me now was wondering 'How will I start to practise waiting? How come I can't let out a sigh loud enough to uncover what is happening deep down inside?' I returned to the interrogation chair while talking to myself. Despite this, I was hoping that the interrogator's questions wouldn't overwhelm me. At that moment, I felt defeated.

We stayed there, but the interrogator asked me to take a different seat. The interrogation started; he asked and I replied. He turned on my phone, logged into my Facebook account and demanded that I look at it. Then he asked whether that was my profile or not. It all went black at once, and I was shocked by that sight. I didn't understand what was happening. I couldn't recognise it, and I didn't know how it went blank.

My name was there, but both my profile and cover pictures were blacked out. I couldn't remember that happening; was I really disconnected from reality and had I deleted it? Was my account actually hacked as the lawyer had said? I had been through that experience before. I knew of another account with the same name, but I didn't know who managed it. A stranger had been impersonating me and updating that account until this day. I had tried to delete that account and reported it several times, all of which had been dismissed.

13

With each moment, my bewilderment showed more clearly and everything became more confusing; all these situations and words were tangled up. The lawyer's words "six years" echoed in my head. I cursed this situation I found myself in. I was so wrapped up in it that I would have follow my lawyer's advice and deny it all. My mind went blank. All I wanted was an explanation for what had happened to me. Was it a curse? Bad luck? A conspiracy?

The papers were printed out and the policemen were called into the interrogation room again. They handcuffed me and took me back to the car. Black glass. That's all I remember. We arrived at the courthouse and they put me back in a prison cell to wait for my hearing.

CHAPTER 5

A tiny square cell, a 15cm blue chain-link-fenced metal door, freezing cold, a big hole in the wall where an AC was placed, red concrete flooring, and dirty walls – too dirty to look at – empty plastic bottles scattered all over the floor. Leftovers piled in front of the door. It was not a prison cell as much as a landfill. Opposite the door there was an old metal in-cell toilet and a faucet – both of which were disgusting, not to mention the accumulated grime, mould and rust with which covered them. They were surrounded by two 1.5m walls and two blue cubes of molded concrete which were used as seats.

Watched and exposed. The unscreened, door-less toilet entrance could easily be seen from the main metal cell door. A surveillance camera hung on the ceiling. One would go to the toilet well aware of the fact of being watched either through the camera, the cell door or both. Time passed while I'm sitting here in this stuffy cell; a mixture of stinky and musty smells filled the air. Sitting on a piece of concrete in this cold stinking room caused my body to stiffen, so I tried to readjust my position every now and then. I used each inch of my body to try to relieve myself from the cold and rough feelings of concrete. Spasms. I couldn't move any more. All I could do was wait; 'Patience, it is what it is' was my mantra for this time.

I was extremely thirsty yet I didn't drink a drop of water. And going thirsty was easier than using that toilet; I would rather be self-tortured by thirst than use that dirty unscreened toilet. One soldier brought me lunch; he handed it to me through a tiny rectangular cuff port. He also said that it would be the only meal I would get that day. The way it looked and felt indicated it had been left in the fridge for two days at least. I knew it was a pie stuffed with 'mortadella' when I smelled it. I took it and put it on the second concrete seat right next to me. I did not feel hungry at all. There were two more reasons why I refused to eat it. First, I'm vegetarian, so I don't eat such food. Second, I was trying to avoid using that toilet at all costs.

This cell was becoming bone-chilling and my body was worn out. I had just been informed that my hearing was drawing closer. A female soldier approached the door and demanded that I stick my hands out through the small port from which I received my meal. My hands were shackled. She opened the door and directed me to stand opposite the wall. Now that I was facing the wall, she shackled my ankles. A male soldier joined in and they both escorted me along that seemingly endless hallway to the courtroom.

. Red-painted, narrow stairs; there was barely any room for the soles of my shackled feet. There were ten of them at least and they led to a wooden door. I had to walk down those stairs while leg-cuffed. The design and the colour choice suggested that psychology of torture was deployed to make it more difficult for detainees and weaken them mentally.

We stood by the door for a few moments. She unshackled my wrists again. While the female soldier's colleague rushed into the room to inspect it and ensure the absence of any suspicious or forbidden things, she remained there with me. I entered a wooden cage and I started exploring the place. Around me, there were wooden seats intended for those in attendance. Right before my eyes, I saw a glass wall through which I could see the sky. I stood opposite the bench, which was an elevated desk area, placed higher than the rest of the seats. The judge was sitting there and another employee was sitting on another right below it. I looked around trying to find my parents. No one.

After a few minutes, my lawyer came in, shook my hand and sat on his designated seat. A policeman in blue uniform sat beside him as he represented the Public Prosecution. It didn't take too long. My detention would be extended for two more weeks until the investigation was complete. The lawyer had to approve. Wasn't that his intended role? I wasn't surprised that he did; I saw that coming after all I had gone through so far.

The view of the sky outside the window was enchanting. I longed for natural pure colours which would provide me with the 'resilience opium' I needed over the days ahead. I looked out of that wide window and briefly enjoyed watching the colours of the sunset in the sky right before they let me out of that hall. Wrists shackled. Back to the same cell.

CHAPTER 6

It was 8pm. Time dragged so slowly in this cell that I couldn't tell if it passed at all. If not for my watch, I'd have completely lost track. I couldn't tell the difference between day and night; it was all the same to me. My watch was the only truthful thing here.

Clanging chains, door knocks, exchanged curses among the *Nahshon Unit*[3] members themselves on the one hand or the detainees, on the other, and growing, expanding and immeasurable pains triggered all that was buried deep inside of me. Patience. It was my last resort. Hands out through the tiny cuff-ports, handcuffed, door was open, repeat. An endless cycle. And now, the female recruit held my handcuffs and pulled me along, so I asked her: "Now what?" She replied: "Inspection then Kishon[4] (*al-Jalameh* prison centre)."

She moved me from one room to another. The first room had a table and two chairs intended for meetings between the accused and their lawyer, while the other was for inspection. Inside I went. The female soldier asked me to put my hands up and passed the body scanner over the lower part of my body. Then she un-cuffed me and demanded that I remove my accessories and put them on the table, and so I did. Taking my grandma's ring off my finger was tough. We had never been apart, not for a passing second. The moment I had to pull it, to remove it, felt as though my soul had been pulled out of me. I kept my watch, though, as I was familiar with the rights of detainees and prisoners after following up on some political prisoners' cases. First she asked me to take it off, but I told her that I had the right to keep it. "Okay, you can keep it," she said.

She put on some plastic gloves, and once again she used the scanner but this time it touched every part of my body multiple times. She demanded that I take off my shoes and put them aside, on a table. She inserted the scanner into my shoes, took off the laces and got rid of them. "Extend both arms out straight to your sides," she ordered. Up and down my arms she passed that detection wand. The device was passed between my legs at an obtuse angle, over my neck, tummy, my chest, my inner and outer

17

thighs. The wand did not seem to be enough for her, she had her hands on me. She demanded that I take off my hijab, undo my braid, take my hair tie off and wear my hair down, open my mouth and stick my tongue out and let it move in all directions; move my head. When I lifted my head up, she examined my nose. Closer. Touching my ears, sticking her finger into them. My body felt like a maze, from an entrance to a goal, without diversion, and she had to go through every point. She saw nothing but my body. The soles of my feet moved up towards her to spare her the trouble of bending down; she inspected them. Her hands were moving closer to me and she placed them on me. I felt suffocated, and I couldn't stand it, so I backed away a little. I tried my best to control my body's reactions; I tried not to resist or to push her hands off of me. I didn't want to be accused of hitting her or getting in the way of her duties. But all this had brought on traumatic flashbacks from childhood. I backed away until I hit the room's wall. Fate. History was repeating itself, but the details were different. I wanted to let it all out and tell her how that made me feel. Instead, I couldn't utter a word. Speechless. A second later, she demanded I take off my clothes. I refused but she insisted and said she had to do it; those were the rules. She said she couldn't break the rules and I had to obey whatever she asked of me. "If you don't take off your clothes by consent, I will do that for you by force and against your will," she said.

My soul sank in the pool of my broken dignity. My thoughts froze. Thinking was futile now. I'd entered a nightmare, hoping to see the light at the end of the tunnel while stuck in the darkness of the unknown. I couldn't even recall how I carried out her command. I took off one clothing item at a time until I had nothing left on my body. Strip-searched. All I remember was entering a maze of disorientation, noise and emotional chaos. I was struck by an awareness of living in times of violence, power and inhumanity; a time in which I was born to fight against wars and invasions; a time when nobody's cries would be heard, nobody would empathise with the misery of another. This was the world of the 'I' and mere selfishness.

This pain crushed everything within me, and all that was left were the killing screams of silence, and a smile that I had just started to search for in this new reality; a reality invaded by hyenas and feral dogs to tear down human dignity. I had decided to be steadfast despite everything I had been through. Maybe, just maybe I would find a miracle soon among these nightmares.

When she finally finished offensively touching my body and toying with my emotions, she demanded that I put my clothes back on and get myself together so she could re-cuff my hands and ankles. Then she opened the door and asked someone to fetch a deposit bag. One soldier joined in as witness of her act. She took a picture of my belongings with her phone while he wrote down a list of the items: a gold ring, a silver ring, a gold necklace with a heart-shaped pendant, a key, an elephant and a bird pendant. All of a sudden, he was tongue-tied, confusion all over his face. He stopped writing, abruptly. He didn't know what he should say or write down when he saw the map of Palestine pendant or that of Handhala (the symbol of Palestinian resistance). He said: "A chain with a map which I'm not familiar with. It's similar to the map of Israel but coloured red, green and white. And some male figure pendant."

I belly-laughed; it was the first time I'd laughed since my arrest; I was ecstatic. Envelope closed. I signed it then we left.

I went with her and walked through three electric gates before coming to an area where there were three white vehicles with 'Prison Service' on them in blue bold font. These vehicles were intended for transferring detainees from courts to prisons and vice- versa. For Palestinian detainees, it was known as the 'bosta'. A newly-manufactured Mercedes-Benz, it was clean and nice-looking from the outside at least. The back doors were opened and a Nahshon Unit soldier climbed in to check the seats. After he got out he ordered me in. I was told to sit silently.

Once I boarded the vehicle he slammed the door shut and locked it. Pitch black. I was in a metal cage with a 90cm wide metal seat covered with tough stiff leather; it was as long as any typical rear bench seat and as high as a typical car seat's distance from its ceiling. The fact that I couldn't see anything round me heightened three of my other senses. A rediscovery of the effectiveness of my smell, hearing and touch.

A vehicle divided into five sections: three cages, a compartment for soldiers in the back seat and a driver's compartment in the front seat. If I'd seen it beforehand, I wouldn't have guessed it was meant for human transfer.

The vehicle started off while I was in the cage. It was very similar to those cruel cages in which where animals were kept. It would be better to describe it as a moving tomb which had a small, chain-linked, metal window which couldn't be opened at the top, and it had very tiny holes. Ice-cold air was coming from the AC vents which couldn't be closed or redirected. I swung about. The direction of my swings matched those of the car. I couldn't stand still; my wrists and ankles were cuffed. The most agonising part was when the driver hits the brakes; my body pushed against the walls of this cage. When the driver mad a sharp turn, I either swing to that direction or fell down. With every road bump my body bounced, and I felt as if my bones were falling apart.

I was anguished, but I tried to alleviate some of this agony by knocking on the door using my cuffs and asking for the AC to be turned off, at least. They turned a deaf ear. Most of what I did in that tomb was try to clutch onto the seat or wait for a beam of streetlights to shine through the window so I could keep track of time.

It took five hours to get to al-Jalameh prison centre, although a trip from the courthouse in Nazareth to the prison centre should only take thirty-forty minutes. The vehicle made several stops during this arduous journey to drop off some detainees at detention centres. At each stop, the soldiers of the Nahshon Unit would rest, and the screams of detainees would rise from the vehicle opposite the one in which I was caged. Sometimes, they would ask to go to the bathroom, and other times they would bang the cage doors with their cuffs so that the vehicle started to jiggle and might flip over. Vain attempts. The soldiers would be drinking coffee, eating and giggling. They would go to the bathroom and smoke their cigarettes in their own time. And all we got was their silence. They didn't consider us as humans; we deserved nothing but to wait in silence for them.

CHAPTER 7

These heart-wrenching and shocking incidents were not the first and certainly wouldn't be the last. My heart aches for human injustice; its pounding filled with such sadness and moaning that the sounds penetrate my ears. How could a human be so unjust to other human beings? I did not yet know what lay ahead for me. It was 1am, the vehicle was moving fast, yet it slowed down unexpectedly. It went over speed bumps and stopped once. The soldiers got out after banging on the doors. I breathed a sigh of relief when I heard them say al-Jalameh Prison Centre. Ironic. Arriving at the prison excited me simply because the bosta suffering was finally over.

Cage doors opened at last. I filled my lungs with fresh air and lifted my head up with wonder to the starry sky. I smiled and at the sight of the sky, I awaited breezes of hope despite the harshness of life. I plodded, my steps were heavy. I was drained. And as I plodded, all of these unbearable incidents, as dust, piled up in my mind. In spite of this pain, I had a strong comforting feeling deep down which reassured me that life would eventually shine through the cracks of my brokenness, a special unprecedented light that I would still find, even if I had no reason to smile. I found myself marvelling at my ability to smile amidst the severity of circumstances.

Escorted by four soldiers, including one female, I went inside the prison through a huge metal gate. She had taken on the task of holding and pulling me towards the building. We stood in a big metal cage and waited for the duty officer to receive the new arrivals, like me. A few minutes later, one officer arrived, received my papers and ordered me to accompany him to a side room to take booking photographs (mugshots) and register me in the 'prisoner' file. It wasn't more than a reception room for detainees and prisoners, yet it was divided into cages. The big cage was where detainees were held until the end of the registration process while the second cage was intended for the waiting Nahshon Unit forces. Added to this, there was a small registration room and a photo booth for detainees. The two cages were separated by a large gate for post-registration processes. They

21

demanded that I stand at the entrance of the photography room, look into the camera, a small webcam, ordinary and old. They photographed my face and entered my data. From that moment on, I had a number. I became a political prisoner holding number 9022438.

Paperwork was completed. The papers and photos were printed out and I walked along with the same female soldier along the prison hallways. We entered the doctor's room for a quick check-up after which he recorded some data, such as my height and weight, in my new file. And then I entered ward 8, which was for women; the warden received my papers and confirmed my identity. In a small corner, she un-cuffed me. Door closed. She strip-searched me despite my efforts to explain to her that a colleague of hers had just finished searching me. Another vain attempt. They came up with such ways to humiliate human beings! She followed through with the strip-searching in the same manner, which aroused the same difficult emotions in me as before. She opened the giant blue door. I entered the cell and my eyes wandered around that new place to explore it. I entered the cell; foul odour emanated from those walls. My eyes went on a journey to inspect this new place.

It was a tiny, narrow square-shaped cell which contained six beige-painted metal two-tier bunk beds. On each bed, there was a dark brown mattress; most of the mattresses were worn out with light green stuffing poking through. The mattresses were covered with grey blankets which were rough to the touch.

Exhausted, I sat on one of the beds and I could feel its springs. I looked up and I saw several surveillance cameras hung on all four corners. I was almost suffocated by foul-smelling odours of smoke as well as the musty smell coming from the toilet which was only separated from the cell by an aluminum half-height door. The toilet was uncovered and there was no sign of cleanliness or hygiene. To top it off, there was no window or even a small hole that would allow some fresh air in.

It was late at night and I couldn't stand staying in that place any longer while it stank, so I called the warden to explain. At first she refused to listen to my complaints. I bet on my persistence. After a conversation which lasted for a few minutes, she told me she would do her best. She also told me that she would give me cleaning supplies and equipment, only I would have to clean the cell myself. Even though I was physically drained, I didn't reject her idea; on the contrary, I welcomed it as I would be the one sleeping in that cell. I could adapt to almost any condition except filth and bad smells, so I reckoned it would be one of the best solutions to help me cope with what lay ahead.

The warden entered with all the cleaning supplies I needed. I cleaned the cell thoroughly and let it soak in soapy water for over half an hour; I was trying to get rid of that smell. Luckily, it worked. The warden then returned to the cell and took all the equipment back. She handed a towel to me, small shampoo bags, toothpaste and a handle-less toothbrush, which was barely the length of a finger. The way that toothbrush looked made me laugh again.

After those tasks, I could at least go to the bathroom while feeling safer. I felt a little relieved, especially after Wudu (partial ablution) and performing my prayers. I desperately needed to pray. Even though only one day had passed without my performing prayers, it felt as though it had been ages. I had always considered prayers as a haven of peace and quiet. The moments spent performing prayers had always been exceptional; I lived them in solitude, with myself and God practising my faith the way I loved. I had to make up for the prayers I had missed during that long, tough day, the five of them. I began searching for a clean surface that would replace my prayer mat, yet I couldn't find a thing. Everything there was hopelessly filthy. I decided, then, to pray without one as I had just cleaned the floor by my own hands. I tried to work out the direction of the qiblah (the Kaaba in Mecca). It was impossible. The pitch-black cell would never let me find the qibla direction or any other. I followed my heart and prayed to God that my prayers would be accepted under such circumstances.

At first – and with the lack of normal sleep essentials including having a clean bed, pillow and blanket – I couldn't sleep. I decided to try, so I chose the best and the cleanest mattress available. Then I pushed the grey blankets off me; they were disgusting. I folded the towel multiple times and used it as a pillow. I put it underneath my head – and started to have flashbacks.

It was the end of 2014 when I started writing about my childhood trauma, and through that I was able to break the silence that had accompanied me throughout that period of time. I wrote poetry. Still, that was not enough to fulfill my need and desire to express my pain, so I wrote a short story in which I recounted the first time I was physically and sexually assaulted, harassed and abused as a child. I spread the word on social media and in print media. Many people showed interest and started sharing and reposting my story until it was all before the criminal's very eyes, my cousin. He started his fight against me by all kinds of ways; he even incited my siblings and parents against me. One of my siblings beat me up and pressured me to delete what I had posted on my online accounts. Despite all of the pressure and the increasing agony, I stood against everyone. I did not take down my story. Rather, I would repost it every now and then. I also posted more poems which dealt with the same issue.

On the night of my arrest, I heard that person shouting, cursing, swearing and threatening revenge on me. He was there, right in front of my window. He also told me that I would regret the day I wrote that story and those poems. It's true that I shut the window and I didn't pay any attention to his shouts, but now I was in prison. Did he act on his threats? It seemed to me that he actually did and that he was the one who told on me to the police so he could do away with my writing which threatened his reputation as well as his position.

With all of these bitter memories, I was able to connect the dots and come to the realisation that what had been happening was not simply a number of random coincidences. I was almost certain that my cousin had played a pivotal role in my arrest. Emotionally and physically drained, I can't remember how I managed to calm my racing thoughts and get my mind off them. How did I sleep in this weird cell and this dark prison? Lights on, suddenly. I woke up to the sound of my door being unlocked and the warden's voice addressing me: "Count Time, wake up, morning count!"

I opened my eyes and looked at my watch; it was around 5am. I sat on the bed waiting in order to figure out what was meant by 'count'. The door was opened and four guards (detention officers) looked around the cell. One of them then said: "Why are you sitting down? Stand up for the count." I laughed. "How am I supposed to know that I must stand up? I'm new here. I'm not familiar with the rules. This is my first time in prison," I replied, expressing my astonishment. And so he explained to me that I had to get up and get out of bed. He added that after my name was said, I would have to say "yes" and wait until the count was over, and only then could I sit down. I would face a disciplinary action if I didn't stand up. That was all. I found the process was funny, especially as it was being conducted. Standing up for the count? These were merely manifestations of humiliation. I stood up and I abided by their orders as well as the rules imposed on me.

To a very great degree, prison rules and prisoners' rights were talked about, but that was mere ink on paper. The prison was a whole different world with countless unspoken rules, lacking justice and humanity. I seized the opportunity of waking up early to perform my Fajr prayers (the first of the five daily prayers performed by Muslims at dawn). The exhaustion I felt was agonising. I tried to go back to sleep, but all the noise around me got in the way: screams of women in the neighbouring cell for the sake of acquiring some cigarettes; prisoners calling for the warden; doors banging; chains rattling and dogs barking. Noise. I buried my face in my hands and began to think about my destiny. I contemplated everything; I had many questions but no answers.

Time flew. It was 7am, the warden was calling out my name. It wasn't the voice of the warden I met on my first night here in prison; shifts were rotated, apparently. My breakfast consisted of two slices of toast, a small yogurt cup, a small peach jam container and half a cucumber placed in a plastic plate. She then asked me if I wanted a cup of tea; I declined and thanked her. Then I politely requested a bottle of cold water instead.

A few minutes passed before she brought me that water. Again, I didn't hesitate to thank her. She was a human, just like I was, and deserved respect. It was true that her job as a warden didn't accord with my principles or way of thinking, but how would I not show her respect when I was the one who once wrote "your personality is what makes others, including your enemies, respect you" in one of my articles?

I sat on the bed and ate my breakfast quietly, carefully and contemplatively. I was alone in this prison cell and I couldn't do anything but examine its tiniest details. I had to wander off from this tight spot with my shadow to peek into myself and become nothing more than a shadow of a picture that had unintentionally fallen from its frame, a painter's surrealistic painting where meanings of disappointment are carved and mastered.

I looked around me. Countless words covered the walls. They were fascinating enough for me to examine: a variety of phrases written in Arabic, Hebrew and English, names of people who had passed by, heart drawings, Cupid's arrow, initials, prayers and swear words. As I was reading, a strong wave of mixed emotions hit me; some made me laugh while others made me cry. I empathised with each one of them and I wished that I had my camera so I could capture that unique work of art. I had the urge to write; I was desperate for a pen.

I asked for a pen and a piece of paper but the warden rejected my request. When I asked why, she had one excuse: the rules. I asked her about the wall writings and where they came from, and she looked shocked and surprised. A moment of silence. She repeated the same answer: the rules. She added that it was forbidden to provide detainees with pens. "Especially you," she said before opting out of our discussion. She left me with unanswered questions. I went back to bed. I was furious; her silly answer and use of the rules as an excuse made my blood boil. At the same time, I embraced my anger and controlled it. I realised that I had a different kind of triumph, there and then; I was able to manage my anger. My smile came back and I felt ecstatic. The warden's withdrawal was yet another triumph in the face of this prison system.

The rituals of the count were performed three times throughout the day, making them four as the clock struck 4am. Within a day, I also became acquainted with the method the Israel Prison Service employed to inspect a prison cell; it took place three times a day. Here's how it went. Three or four policemen carrying a backpack and a chest pack entered the cell. One of them held a wooden mallet which he used to bang on the beds, the already shut bathroom window, particular sides of the prison walls and various areas of the tile flooring.

As for lunch, I had one mandarin orange, burnt fusilli pasta, a little rice which had nothing to do with the traditional rice I was familiar with, one small bell pepper and two slices of toast. I had to try the food but I could not really eat it; it was nasty and too dry to swallow. I only ate the mandarin and the bell pepper. The day was almost over. Thinking, reading wall writings, performing my prayers, listening to the prisoners in other cells calling for the warden; those were the things I managed to do today. Night fell. Noise filled the department. I overheard two wardens talking and I understood that there were many prisoners, especially women and minors; there were thirty of them up until that point.

Before long, the cell door was opened; five women entered, two of whom were Jewish whereas the rest were Arabs. The two Jewish women were in their forties. Within fifteen minutes, one of them addressed me directly: "I heard that you wanted to kill the Jews, is that true?" Her words tore me up inside, but I managed to let go of my anger and pain. "Had I been that kind of person, they wouldn't have let you share the cell with me or even sleep here, right?" I replied gently.

She was amazed at my answer as much as I was amazed at the words that came out of her mouth; I never thought that my case was the central topic of discussion between wardens and prisoners, and that it was their way to make me sound intimidating at the same time. She didn't respond and I thought that I'd rather stay silent, too. Each one of them chose her own bed.

As for the three Arab girls, they were somewhere around 19 and 20 years old. They seemed extremely worried; their eyes were red and puffy from crying. I felt instantly that I was responsible for them, yet I made sure I took a cautious approach.

I started a discussion with them and I learned that they were arrested because they were in an area near the protest which was organized in Nazareth. I also learned that they were accused of throwing stones at the police or so-called "disturbance of public order and assault of police officers."

At the time, the atmosphere was tense: numerous protests were organized in many Arab regions because of Israeli soldiers' and police officers' deliberate killing of Palestinians, and the closure of al-Aqsa Mosque as well as banning worshipers from entering it to perform their prayers. Hence the demands for the rights of Muslims to enjoy freedom of worship and perform their prayers.

27

One of the girls was dressed up and was wearing high heels; she was also wearing make-up. It was obvious that she had nothing to do with protests or politics whatsoever; that became evident during our conversation too. She just had a date with her fiancé at one of the restaurants close to the protesters' meeting point. When the police began throwing stun grenades towards the protesters, she ran away, but they arrested her.

As for the other two girls, they were best friends. One of them visited the other at her house which was down the street from a meeting point of protesters. Out of curiosity, they left the house and stood in front of it. As the stun grenades were thrown, they ran off and went back inside. Police officers manoeuvred and arrested them.

That wasn't surprising. Just being present in the protest area could lead to an arrest; this is what police officers did, whether that person was taking part in the protests or not. Coincidences, in that scenario, were out of the question; they were never acknowledged. Such coincidences would be used as a convincing excuse for police to make arbitrary arrests. The stories of these girls made that obvious. And now I could see why there were so many new arrivals in the prison that night.

I didn't give up trying to get a pen and some papers for writing, yet they didn't change their mind. I was deprived of the things I considered dearest to my heart. Time and again, I would ask. The only excuse I heard was "the rules." I was not exactly sure of the nature of those rules. What kind of rules would forbid a human being from holding a pen to write? Where did the problem lie in the first place?

I couldn't just sit back and watch the Arab girls in that state; I couldn't stay silent or neutral. My sense of responsibility for them increased. It was a chance for me to turn my helplessness and uselessness into an act of service. Although it appeared to me that my legal case was far worse than theirs, I somehow managed to alleviate their worry and explain to them some of the aspects of the law I knew about. I convinced them their stay wouldn't exceed two or three days. Every now and then, I would make the atmosphere of the prison more fun. Laughter replaced that sadness.

I cracked a joke to make them laugh; I hugged them for a few moments; I caressed their hair to make them feel safe in this harsh place. Perhaps I would be able to keep them from despair. Having them around made me

28

realise what true sacrifice was. All I sought was to comfort them, which was a great help in showing myself more self-respect.

Dinner arrived. It was similar to what I had for breakfast: yogurt and bread. On the one hand, yogurt was served quite often in prison as it can promote sleep. Serving the same meal on a daily basis, on the other hand, seemed to be part of the punishment. It was a policy to sap the prisoners' and detainees' stamina.

I wasn't annoyed with the two Jewish women's constant shouting or their calling out to the warden for cigarettes, even late at night, as much as I was with their smoking in the prison cell which had no vents to filter this foul air. The rest of us weren't smokers. The smoke I drew into my lungs would cause me violent coughing fits. Despite protesting against smoking inside the cell and complaining about that to the warden and the police officer during cell inspection, and despite explaining to them about my coughing fits, it was all still ineffective. They told me there was no solution to that problem for the time being, so I suggested separating smokers from non-smokers. Turned down. The administration justified their response by telling me that I had no right to discuss such issues since I was nothing but a detainee there. Clearly, health had no value in that prison.

The two women cried out provocatively and ceaselessly for cigarettes. They didn't consider the fact that those cries might disturb us. I wanted to talk to them about it, but on second thought I decided to seize the best opportunity to get my point across indirectly; they might find it more convincing. So I didn't discuss it with those two women as I didn't want them to get me wrong amidst of that tense atmosphere. Bearing in mind what they'd heard about me from the wardens, I made sure that I created an atmosphere of mutual respect. I firmly believed they also had the right to smoke; they weren't to blame for the administration's decision to allow smoking in windowless cells.

They were talking to each other in Hebrew, which I was fairly good at. On other occasions they would exchange some Russian words, which made absolutely no sense to me. I learned that the first woman was accused of drug dealing while the second, robbery. They belonged to a whole different world from the one in which I lived; our principles were poles apart. Helpless. I was destined to wake up, sleep, eat and drink with those people who I would classify as a pathetic state of human beings. All I could do was adapt to this situation.

I never desired to be an eavesdropper, yet I had no other choice since the cell was narrow and the beds were closely spaced as well. I had to accept it; listening to the other women's whispers was part of it by default. In a prisoner's dictionary there was no such word as privacy; it simply didn't exist even in the tiniest daily life routines including using the toilet with its half-height door.

Since privacy constituted a significant part in my lifestyle, I began to think of some ways to reclaim a sense of it. I would listen to every conversation they held and vice versa; they were able to listen to the discussions among the four of us, the Arab detainees. There was only one difference; I was good at Hebrew and I comprehended it quite well. In other words, I understood everything they talked about while they didn't understand a word of what we said. I felt a pang of annoyance at the thought of it. Violating their privacy felt as if I had been crossing the line despite the fact that I had no choice in that matter.

Although I myself was a relatively new arrival, I somehow figured that I had to do something to ease my consciousness. It could be my attempt at seeking a new culture among the prisoners in this cell. I was straightforward and I told them the truth; I told them that I overheard them whenever they talked. I also told them that I could understand the Hebrew language well. I then suggested that they use Russian if they didn't want me to understand what they were talking about, so they could have some privacy. I humbly and respectfully apologised for invading their privacy. I clarified my stance on the topic. Our first conversation happened.

This unexpected conversation struck them with wonder; I was also astounded with myself, my confidence and boldness. A smile spread over their faces which in turn boosted my confidence. I was more relieved and reassured too. Only then did I realise that they got the point.

Prison cells would be unfit for animals, let alone humans. Even farmers took very good care of their livestock; they respected them and kept them in a clean place. The prison's administration, however, didn't take the humanity of its inmates into consideration: no ventilation, no food, no health care or cleanliness. Fundamental human needs did not seem to exist in that place.

In the morning of the second day of my arrest, I bid the Arab girls farewell and wished them luck in their hearings. Over and over again, the hours passed; the same incidents were repeated and my cough got worse. Count, inspection, count, inspection, breakfast, lunch, dinner, non-stop smoking inside the cell, unbearable noise from the outside, knocks on doors and the rattling of chains penetrating my ears all day and all night long.

I remained with the two Jewish women. During daytime hours, they were allowed to go out to the yard, while I had not seen the light even once since I first set foot in that cell. I asked the warden about the yard time I was allocated; all I got in return was the bang of the cell door in my face. They could leave the cell several times each day. I was denied that right. Evidently, I was not treated the way others were in that place.

I was still with the two Jewish women, lighting up their cigarettes through the chain-link-fenced window of the door using the warden's lighter, though now they stood by the door and puffed the smoke towards the door holes. I appreciated their gesture and thanked them for that. One of them told me: "Your positive attitude leaves people with no choice but to show you respect," while the other said: "This is the only solution we have for smoking." On hearing these words and that huge achievement of mine, we exchanged smiles and started discussing different subjects.

Respect is never imposed. Respect is an ever-present and fundamental principle of a person's life; it is acquired through social upbringing in the culture they belong to. 'Humanity for all' defines my cultural identity.

Entering and leaving, I watched the comings and goings of many detainees and prisoners from my bed. Different classes, nationalities, communities, cultures and crimes. Prisoners and detainees left for court in the morning; some were released while others were convicted and sentenced. The files of the latter were then transmitted to one of the official prisons, yet others returned to this prison until the investigation was completed. I lived with these recurrent happenings day and night.

Every day, numerous incidents materialised right before my eyes in this prison. I had seen the unthinkable: all types of people, nationalities and cultures. In spite of this, I trained myself to simply observe from a distance without getting involved in any of it. I decided not to talk to anyone during that period. It must have been a bad case of carelessness and indifference. Observing in silence, thinking and talking to myself about what I saw was enough.

One question lingered in my mind 'What did I know about lay people before I ended up here?' the drunk, thieves, beggars, gamblers, addicts, the un-consoled? In this place, these were the ones who suffered from injustice and despair the most. Was it possible for me to love all of God's creatures? This was the hardest test I'd ever gone through; I wouldn't pass it, no matter how much I tried.

I asked for extra clothing items because I had been wearing the same ones since I was arrested. Rejected. They brought me one item of underwear only. I washed my clothes and put them back on while they were still dripping wet, again and again. One of the Jewish women prisoners, who had been arrested on criminal grounds and with whom I shared that cell, remarked: "You are not turning this cell into a mosque!" when I started performing my prayers. I didn't pay any attention to her comment; I dismissed it and resumed praying.

Her attempt to steal my watch while I was asleep was the last incident I could recall. That was a funny yet worrying situation. Although I laughed a lot at it, I gave up the idea of sleeping, especially late at night.

Generally speaking, al-Jalameh prison centre was a miniature of the environment of every criminal prison in this country. I have seen with my own eyes how drug dealing is spreading among detainees and how drugs are smuggled into prison. I witnessed the ways in which cigarettes were smuggled despite inspection. I have learned about some ways to deceive and outwit the wardens. I have experienced fights and sharp conflicts all day long, the cries of addicts as well as the misery of those who suffered from mental health problems. The justice system itself is yet another unspeakable tragedy, as it is completely out of the picture.

Every now and then, the female and male wardens would force the inmates to scrub the floors of the ward as well as those of the empty cells. They would show up, out of the blue, and announce it was cleaning time.

I was not one of them. It could be because they deemed me dangerous and threatening. For me, that was a plus; I loved it.

I had never been so disappointed. The time I spent in that prison made me realise that it was far from the age-old prison philosophy, and that the mental health of the prisoners as well as their rehabilitation did not exist. All the theories about prison life failed me in no time. I even started wondering about the origins of the creator of the idea of imprisonment, and I wondered who the first one to put that idea into practice was. Now that I saw it for what it was, I realised that prison was a form of slavery, the blunt authority of those who worshiped power. Crime rates increased in communities and so did building prisons, so what was the point? The theory was dismissed outright. I wished there could be some prison reform to make a difference in the world of crime and punishment.

CHAPTER 8

It was 2am, I was sitting on my bed in the cell. Here I was with prisoners accused of criminal acts. They were sound asleep. The warden peeked through the door and, unexpectedly, she called out my name. She told me I would be transferred from this cell. I was thunderstruck and worried: this was a sudden transfer.

"Now? At this hour?" I asked.

"Yes," she replied and opened the door right away. She let me out, searched and handcuffed me. She pulled me along behind her.

"Where to?" I asked.

"Solitary confinement," she said.

"But why?" I asked.

"I have been ordered to do so," she said, "from now on you'll be identified as a 'security prisoner'[5] and you must live under different circumstances."

The moment the word 'security' came out of her mouth, I began to feel that my real experience in prison was about to start and all the anguish I had been through was nothing but a joke.

Down a long hallway we went, further and further away from that ward's cells as I walked with her until we arrived at an isolated cell. It looked different. Unlike the rest of the cells which had blue doors, the new one had a grey one. It was far removed from the cell where I used to stay.

The warden opened the door and I stepped into my new shell. She was about to close the door when I asked her to provide me with cleaning supplies. "There aren't any cleaning supplies," she answered.

It was a cell just like any other yet with harsher conditions. At 3x3, it was much smaller than the rest. It had two beds, grey, smelly and dirty walls and an unscreened door-less toilet. It was extremely humid and placed under surveillance. Windowless. Dark. One dim ray of light could make it into the cell.

I chose a bed and lay my head down on the mattress. I tried to get some sleep; my sleep deprivation had led to accumulated tiredness. I hadn't got a moment of sleep since the theft attempt incident. I couldn't sleep as my sleepiness went with the wind in that new cell.

My days in that stone box dragged by and they felt like years. I would call the warden but she didn't respond; I wouldn't even know whether she heard me or not in the first place. Sometimes, I would have to push my feet against the door for minutes before getting any response from the warden. Even when she heard me and responded, she would delay my requests, such as water or toilet paper until it was meal time. No matter what happened, I got to see her three times a day only.

Even though I longed for some moments of peace and solitude, that prison cell had a different type of silence to it. Gloomy grey walls. An intrusion of cockroaches. I felt as if I was kept inside a horrifying stone box. It was an enclosed gated world, far enough away from everything else so that I couldn't hear any noise outside, not even the cries of the prisoners. Noise vanished. The only present sound was that of the leaking water faucet. Drip drip drip. Day and night, it dripped ceaselessly, adding to my stress. I couldn't stand it any more. I didn't know whether that leaking water faucet was placed intentionally, yet staying there under the weight of that agitating sound was psychological torture.

I started my day with a dire breakfast and I ended it with the humiliating count. Two times a day, three of the criminal-case prisoners showed up out of nowhere and approached my cell door. They smoked, puffed the smoke into the cell while cursing me provocatively and humiliatingly. They left once they'd stubbed out their cigarettes. Musty smell. Smoke smell. That mixture of smells which filled this windowless cell caused me persistent coughing fits while the gnawing pain of ulcers worsened each day. The result was that I now have persistent breathlessness and severe, recurring headaches.

Little by little, I lost my dignity in that cell; I reached ultimate boredom, frustration, despair and anger. Everything that surrounded me was about to drive me crazy as I felt the emptiness of my existence and that my fall and collapse were around the corner. I turned into a whole other person, hallucinating and constantly talking to myself out loud. Sometimes I shouted to ease my agitation about that leaking faucet. At other times, I shouted to forget. I sang to forget about my illness and my cough. I danced or laughed loudly whenever those smokers came near my cell. They saw how careless I was about what they did. I would hear them say "crazy", and when I heard it I sang and danced more. Strangely enough, I had not shed a tear in spite of the pain which took over me whenever I was alone.

I could not endure that humiliation, emptiness and nothingness anymore. My thoughts started pushing back that existence the prison administration imposed on me. I started thinking back to the times when I was free. I contrasted what I would have done at a similar moment had I been free with what I experienced in that solitary cell.

I remembered how much I loved to walk, so I spent my day walking in the cell from the toilet area to the cell door, back and forth. I walked so as not to surrender to the grip of time or to fall apart in despair. I lived in a world of make-believe pretending that the grey walls were the streets along which I loved to walk in Nazareth until I arrived in the old traditional market, i.e. the old souk. I walked back and forth for hours. The warden would stand at the door and ask me: "What's the matter with you?" I would say nothing and continued living in my own world of imagination in Nazareth, so she would hurl the word "crazy" at me and leave.

On another day, I put my finger on the wall and started moving it slowly, pretending to write. And then I started moving it faster and faster. I pressed hard on the wall until I bled. I wrote on the wall with my blood. Every day I would cut my finger on purpose so I could get some blood out to write and express my anger. My writings made no sense; they were just words. Still, I managed to break free from this place and reduce my stress by doing so.

I also did yoga. I ran off towards my beautiful memories. Daydreaming or living in an imaginary world was my only way to escape this reality and beyond the boundaries of the grey cell.

In order to feel alive, my palms would caress every part of my body and stroke my face to make up for all the longing and deprivation of a warm, tender touch. I would tell myself: "I'm in prison for the sake of freedom, yet I feel that freedom itself is imprisoned within me; it lives with and inside of me." Every time sadness, pain or distress got the best of me, I imagined freedom as a woman standing before me. She looked like me. She was wearing bright white clothes. She wanted us to stay together at all times. I would start talking to her and then listen to her words directed to me: "You, Dareen, are free." I sang to her and to myself. I heard her response: "Dareen, you are the voice of freedom. Can you hear the call of freedom? You are the voice of freedom." I talked to her so these draining emotions shrunk while freedom grew bigger and bigger. I even saw my dead grandma, and I felt as if she had been experiencing every moment I spent in this prison with me; we talked the way we did before she passed. My grandma, Khadija, was the woman who taught me all about politics. I imagined her telling me the words which were left unsaid before her passing. I heard her, speaking to me, calling me 'rebellious,' as she always had. Her voice gave me with strength. In her tone, I could tell how proud of my rebelliousness she was. I imagined I was in her house, the house I had always loved and the only place where I would go to feel safe, comfortable and secure. I brushed my hand against my finger and felt deeply the loss of that ring she had asked me to give to the one who would preserve me and keep his love for me. Vividly, I recalled our last embrace in the hospital after everyone had said that she passed. I sat close to her, talked to her and asked her to talk back to me. I felt as if she had had something to say, something to tell me. Khadija was that grandmother I adored so much that I dedicated my first book to her.

CHAPTER 9

They called out my name and told me they had come to take me away.

"Where to?" I asked.

"Another interrogation," they reply.

Searched and shackled, I was led into the moving tomb, the bosta vehicle.

After a two-hour ride, they dropped me off and I walked with six soldiers through a giant building with lots of hallways. I read the sign and realised it was a psychiatric hospital. I asked why I was there, so one of the soldiers replied: "Have you just learned of this? It is ordered you be transferred to this hospital for a mental health assessment, to check whether you can be brought before the judge in the court or not."

I was taken aback by the soldier's response. In those moments I experienced a feeling I had never expected before. I didn't know who came up with that heartless idea, yet I felt hatred towards whoever that person was. Being labelled 'unstable' just to win the case when all I did was express my emotions and opinion! 'This is a silly idea; I completely reject it even if that means spending the rest of my life in prison. I could never accept this,' I thought to myself. That was one of the cruellest incidents I'd had ever been through.

'Yes, I do hit setbacks and this harsh reality makes me feel desperate, because of childhood cruelty; it has scarred me for life and left me with a post traumatic disorder, and I was not offered a real solution. I will not accept this at all costs,' I thought. I focused on the new interrogation which would determine my future. That was my priority.

There were two interrogators in the room. One of them was sitting across from me; he was at his desk and had a computer in front of him. The second one sat on a side seat. The appearance of the room made me realise that it wasn't intended for police interrogation sessions, and that it wasn't well-equipped to serve that purpose either since it was outside both the prison and the police station building. It seemed like a social worker's room; it looked nice, tidy, colourful and lively. It was a room which stimulated optimism and hope, especially after being surrounded by the blackness of al-Jalameh prison centre. A replica of The Starry Night painting by Van Gogh was hung on the wall. I contemplated that painting and the mastery of its rich blues. I also thought about the beauty of art, and I started comparing the beauty and immortality radiating from the painting and its blue colours with the blue colours which accompanied me in my cell. Although they had the same shade of blue, they were drastically different and contradictory. I imagined the developer of the self-discrepancy theory, Edward Tory Higgins; had he been alive or had been in my shoes, he would have enriched his theory with new details which weren't written in his time.

The interrogator took out a camera from his bag to document the interrogation. He turned it on and placed it on a shelf in front of me. Then he took out his laptop. My journey with the colours was over; a new journey of questioning was about to begin.

I asked for my lawyer before the interrogator started conducting the questioning process. The interrogator did't oppose the idea and called him using his cell phone. He handed the phone to me and told me I could stand at the room's door and talk to my lawyer freely.

The lawyer repeated what he'd already told me during the previous interrogation; he asked me to keep denying their accusations and say that my Facebook account was hacked. "I'm in a psychiatric hospital," I responded. "I know," he replied, coldly, so I asked him: "Whose idea was that?" to which he replied: "Your dad's, and I agreed with him." I was furious once I'd heard the truth and I told him: "I do not approve of this. This place and the label you are trying to attach to me do not fit me. I have not done anything to be scared of. I will answer what I see fit and in a very logical manner. That's better than this total joke. I will answer depending on what they present and I will clarify my perspective."

The interrogation began. The interrogator showed me some pictures and numerous documents from my Facebook home page. He finally showed me what they had been accusing me of under the name of incitement to violence and terrorism.

A picture of the young Nazareth woman Israa' al-Abed helped me avoid further doubt and self-questioning; he showed me a picture that confirmed the fact I posted it. I told him I couldn't recall when or how I posted it yet the document he showed me proved I posted it following the incident with Israa' which deeply touched me: the deliberate shooting of her, identifying with her story and showing that she was a victim, as I had become by posting that picture.

He called her "subversive" and insisted she intended to commit a knife crime. He repeated the word subversive enough times to make me say it myself, unfortunately. All of my answers about that picture revolved around the idea that I opposed those acts of violence. If she had really been subversive and wanted to stab someone, then I would've disapproved of that. That didn't reflect my way of thinking; it would be against my principles. In that video, I saw a victim; she didn't intend to harm anyone and she didn't pose any threat.

The second accusation was posting a black picture with a white mourning corner ribbon and a sentence in the corner which read "I'm the next martyr." I explained to him that I used that picture for the first time in June 2014 after the young Palestinian Khair Hamdan was shot by the police and after the death of Mohammed Abu Khdeir in Jerusalem. I told him that it was a picture that was used by hundreds of activists throughout the country; it was a unified message and a means of condemning violence. Each one of us might end up martyred, namely a victim, whether it was at the hands of the police or the settlers.

What the interrogator showed me afterwards came as a complete surprise. It was a poem I once wrote. The poem was titled 'Resist, My People, Resist Them'; it called for resistance to the occupation and putting an end to the injustice practised against Palestinian people. The poem talked about a number of martyrs which were the victims of the Zionist terrorism and violence including the baby martyr Ali Dawabsheh and his family, the child Mohammad Abu Khdeir, Hadeel al-Hashlamoun who was martyred at the hands of some soldiers at a checkpoint simply because she refused to remove her niqab (a piece of clothing which covers the face except the eyes).

"Did you write the poem?" the interrogator asked. I was astonished, and I was about to lose my mind after hearing his question. I rose. "So that's what it's all about. My poem. Is that your problem? Why haven't you made that clear before?" I stormed. I didn't think twice about it, and said instantly: "Yes, it is my poem. I was the one who wrote it."

I was very agitated when I realised I was accused because of my poem; I couldn't hold my nerve any more. I defended this poem, my platform as a poet and my right to write in a democratic country. The interrogator claimed it called for the spreading of violence and terrorism. He bombarded me with questions: "In your poem, you are calling for resistance. Resistance means violence! You want to resist the state? Do you want to harm the Jews and the soldiers? Do you want to be a martyr? Do you want to conduct a terrorist attack?" I rejected all those ugly accusations against me. 'No' was my answer to all his questions.

From that moment on, I became a prisoner per se because I wrote that poem and published it on social media platforms; that was the most unexpected reason for my arrest, especially in the self-named only democratic country in the Middle East. To be deprived of freedom is far better than to be deprived of dignity, so after those accusations I decided to make a new deal with myself and put the core of this case in its right place. I was imprisoned and detained without a criminal charge. It was my poem. And because of my political orientation and opinions which opposed the Israeli occupation policy, I was imprisoned. I was imprisoned for being a Palestinian Arab who decided to keep her identity and nationality. I was imprisoned because I showed my support for my Palestinian people and the Palestinian cause in my writings.

A five-hour war of attrition ensued, during which I was asked about everything: my hobbies, religion, education, the party with which I affiliated, my political inclinations and opinions, my laptop, my phone, the genre of my poems, the poetry readings in which I participated, their locations and times, their number and types as well as the photos I took and their type and the movies which I directed, filmed and produced. He asked me about how I would identify myself. I told him that I was an Arab Palestinian. He looked shocked, so he asked me again: "Wouldn't you present yourself as an Israeli?" I said "No." He brought in some clips that showed stabbing attacks. He made me watch them then asked me what I thought of them and whether I was for or against such attacks. He asked: "You belong to the Northern Branch of the Islamic Movement, don't

41

you?" to which I replied: "I support Balad and this time I voted for the joint list," so he said: "But, why are wearing the hijab? Are you religious?" I told him: "I pray five times a day and I fast during the entire month of Ramadan. I don't use the word 'religious'; I am Muslim and I keep this relationship between God and me." I could no longer stand the questions he posed, so I tried to explain to him that composing poetry was a form of peaceful resistance.

I did my utmost to explain what my intentions were, and I tried to explain the purposes of all of the documents they presented as evidence of conviction. I wanted to clarify that their analysis of my poem and the pictures was just a non-existent misinterpretation and far removed from the truth. There was some misinterpretation and miscalculation. I suggested that I delete those posts if they claimed they were threatening and simply end the discussion. I also suggested that they delete my Facebook account and end the so-called threat. Vain attempts. I couldn't communicate my point. I felt as if I were a prisoner in their hands and that all they were seeking was to pin it on me, frame me, making me a terrorist in any way shape or form.

I often laughed at the silly questions I was asked, yet I wasn't completely surprised. There was nothing stranger than the fact that I was just one of those prisoners who were locked up for exercising freedom of speech and expressing opinions. I was a prisoner and my main accusation was the poem.

At the end of the questioning, the interrogator explained that my childhood trauma case was not overlooked and it was still being processed; a specialised investigator had taken on the case. The information, he continued, would be checked and they would check with me, later, to take my statement in order to carry out the investigation out and gather more data so the police could do their job.

The interrogation was over. The interrogator turned off the computer along with the camera. He approached me. Chains back on. He said: "Dareen, hear me out, I have read all the poems which you have written and saved on your computer. I have also read the novel which you have been working on, the one in which the story of your life unfolds. I have also found many of your other poems online. You write beautifully. What's with the politics? Don't waste your time on it. What a waste! Write about love, peace, kisses, romance and feelings." I answered: "I do write about life, about reality, my experiences, what I see and how I feel. If I ever saw your soldiers planting roses and flowers, I would write about that too." He remained silent.

They put me in one of the hospital's units. I could see clearly where this was leading: if I talked, I would be arrested; if I remained silent, I would infuriate myself, I would die a thousand times while I was still alive because of that torture, while being labelled as mentally-ill, with no control over my actions. A deadly feeling. The question was: 'Which death would be harder?'

I remembered all those years I had to live while being silenced and repressed. The meaning of my existence was killed. I decided not to go back to that time no matter what; the death by imprisonment was preferable to anything else. I turned into a lab mouse which had yet many experiments to come; and my experiences always put my resistance to the test. Prison was the ultimate price I would pay for the sake of moving forward with that experience they forced on me. I decided to reject the version of reality that others imposed on me, to fight for my stance and face it bravely so I didn't lose my self-respect, because if I ever did I would never come to terms with myself again until my very last breath. That would be better than living freely while being locked up in the prison of self-alienation.

Once I arrived at the unit, the nurse put me in one of the rooms; recorded my information and ran some tests. She asked me to take off my hijab. I was astounded at her request and asked her to tell me why. "In this place, everyone is equal. It isn't permitted to show any form of religious expression through clothing," she replied. She reiterated that those were the rules which applied to all patients, with no exception, and they should be respected. I made my response concise; I asked one question: "What is the position within rules with regard to humans' freedom of worship and freedom of religion?" She became furious and didn't answer my question; she just said: "You're here as a patient only. You have to follow the rules without starting any discussions or asking any questions." I didn't get into that; it wasn't because I was afraid. I was indifferent. What was the point of starting a discussion with her, knowing well that it would lead to nowhere? I wasn't convinced by anything she said or her use of the rules as an excuse. I took off my hijab and handed it over to her; I continued filling in my information sheet and returned to the ward.

The unit was crowded with men and women who acted strangely. I was terrified during the first few hours of my stay; I felt uncomfortable, as well. The only thing I could do was withdraw into a corner and sit down; whenever anyone approached me, I would choose a different seat away from them.

While I was sitting there thinking, one man's voice was enough to stop the voices in my head and that negative train of thought. He put out one of his hands in which there was a Walkman, and he addressed me in Hebrew saying: "Do you like music? There, enjoy listening to some music." I thanked him and I was really pleased with his offer, which I accepted unhesitatingly. After hearing the first note, I was reminded how much I loved music; it was as if I had been listening to it for the first time in my life. For days, I only heard rattling chains, door knocks and door lock sounds or profanities which kept echoing in my head. They didn't leave my head until those melodies enraptured me, and I swooned with joy at the beauty of something again.

That incident was an enormous leap, from seeking to finding. It warned me of the danger of falling into the trap of looking for answers to futile questions. I decided not to allow my thoughts affect the way I perceived people who were mentally ill, as a matter of principle. I would never push them away or look down on them; each one of them must have gone through some trauma or tragedy that led them here. If not for that, they might have been artists, scientists or writers. After that incident, all my fears vanished, and I decided to learn more about these people so I would have learned many lessons by the time I left the place.

I used to read books on psychology and sociology, and I learned about many aspects of these never-ending fields of study. Talking with this ward's inpatients brought to my mind one thing, though. It was one of William Burroughs' quotes: "A psychotic is (someone) who has just found out what's going on." Those words touched me deeply, and I started to appreciate that mentally-ill people were much more than the 'crazy' label that society attached to them.

Certainly, this was not where I belonged. I would stay here for a few days; this was the truth that no one could escape. Instead of just sitting there crying over my bad luck, I would have to explore the strange and the unfamiliar. I simply must make the best of this experience despite its cruelty and hideousness; I sought nourishment not poison.

I was amazed at my ability to empathise and adapt. Besides, I was astonished at my ability to overlook many things which seemed too complicated to understand. I was surprised because I wasn't the same person I used to be. I'd changed and become a better version of myself. I used to be too attached, and that attachment wasn't a way of holding onto my identity; rather, I used to be attached to what could have been one of the root causes of my misery.

I let myself be, I went with the flow and I tried to reach safer and more peaceful places. I met the doctor tasked with writing my case report to the judge. I explained everything to him including the facts about why I was there. I wanted to get my message across but not according to anyone else's version, whether it was my dad, my lawyer or whoever wanted to control my fate in a way that didn't correspond with the reality of my situation.

It hadn't been long since I arrived at this psychiatric hospital, yet I had met someone who dreamed about becoming a professional violin player; someone who wanted to be a singer; someone who wanted to be a plastics artist. Some dreamed of becoming teachers, engineers, and heads of household or mothers. They talked about their dreams with great enthusiasm and spontaneity. They looked fine, but suddenly they would start behaving strangely, shouting and panicking. They would fall back into the trap of their past traumas and live yet another shock caused by techniques used by some doctors and nurses which, I believed, were punitive and had nothing to do with treatment. One of the cruellest ones was tying the patient down to a bed in an isolated, dark room followed by parenteral nutrition or electroshock therapy.

I still recall the incident when a girl was transferred to the isolation room where she was strapped down to bed for two days in a row after she opened the bathroom water faucet; her bed and her room were drenched in water.

She wasn't aware of what she was doing. The medical staff, which consisted of five nurses, two females and three males, rushed into the room with an orange wheelchair. Then they left the room and strapped that girl to the wheelchair. Wide orange straps held her down in it. They all went inside, but ten minutes later almost everyone left the room and locked it, leaving that girl behind.

I could not resist my curiosity; I wanted to know what that room contained and what happened to that girl. I walked towards the room. Through a small clear glass door window, I saw her in a psychiatric restraint bed. Hands and feet tied up. There was nothing in that room except the tools required to carry out the so-called physical restraint. Dim light. The room was under surveillance. Arms stretched out and legs spread open.

She was sleeping on her back. That was how she was strapped. A TPN bag was hung there. I wished my curiosity hadn't led me to witness that harsh scene and see how cruel one human being could be to another; it was a movie-like scene taking place before my eyes. Was this the era which the following quotation described? "We live in times when you tell the stone to turn into a human being, and it apologises saying 'I'm not rough enough'."

I could not find any excuse for the so-called 'angels of mercy' after watching them apply that method of torture to mentally-ill people, regardless of the medical law which allowed such a punishment. I could not call it 'treatment,' as it was, from my perspective, devoid of humanity and had nothing to do with mercy or treatment, let alone the miserable state in which the patient was when she left the room after two days of strapping and isolation. Worn-out body and a crushed, desperate soul. The consequences of that experience were written all over her face. I could not get the image of that crucified girl out of my mind. Wherever I turned, I saw another manifestation of human rights abuse. How ironic! I witnessed those acts of abuse in two places where rights and laws were supposed to be most respected. I forgot about myself and what was waiting for me and was preoccupied with the struggle of the forgotten. I wanted to know more about that humiliating treatment, so I asked five patients; that seemed to stir their emotions and they sounded horrified. Three of them had been strapped and isolated during their stay. More than once. When I asked about what they did when they needed to go to the bathroom, their answer was: nappies.

Another incident bewildered me. The medical staff declared an emergency and shortly afterwards announced the death of one of the patients from an acute heart attack while he was asleep that night. The tears of his fellow patients, the way they talked about him and their memories, were extremely moving and striking. As for me and despite the fact that emotions usually controlled my behaviour and my life in general, I was not affected. I was the only one who did not cry or shed a tear over that sudden death and that difficult situation. I wouldn't be exaggerating if I said that I was not moved in the slightest. I was stone cold.

The strangest thing, however, was that when I saw that person, the way he looked, how stout he was, the way he walked, I was reminded of my cousin. I couldn't stand being anywhere near him. And whenever I saw him, I was filled with dread. I never imagined that I would witness his death before my eyes. Whether that was a mere chance or fate, I did not know. He might have wanted to leave his mark on my memory in some different way.

On another day, a Jewish woman was brought to the unit. She was wearing a headscarf (Tichel) which looked very much like the one I was wearing when I first entered the hospital. Her presence made me curious, so I kept watching her to know what would happen to her headscarf. Surprisingly, she was able to enter the unit without having to take it off. What's more surprising was the fact that it was the same nurse. I couldn't hold myself back; I went to the office and asked them to open the window so I could talk to them. That nurse was there together with another who, as I learned later, was the chief nurse.

I wanted to know what her take on that would be; I wanted to know if she was aware of what was going on too. Without any introductions, I asked her to give me my headscarf instantly, within the earshot of the other nurse. She answered: "It's not possible. It's not allowed. The rules forbid this."

The happiness I felt with her response was indescribable. Deep inside, I wanted her to say that, but it was not likely for her to do so. I was just like a hunter waiting for a prey to fall into its trap, and I pointed to the Jewish woman, and said: "What about that woman's headscarf? Do the rules allow her but forbid me from doing so? She looked perplexed and didn't answer my question. She simply closed the window in my face; she started talking to her colleague for about five minutes, and they both looked troubled. She opened a drawer which had my name on it and took out my headscarf. When she gave it back to me, I put it on and left while feeling ecstatic at that achievement.

My insistence on taking my hijab back was not a matter of religion as much as it was about restoring a part of my existence which had been stripped of me and standing against those rules which they pretended applied to everyone, while they were in fact a source of racism and discrimination. That was what I detested the most in life and fought against. I was even happier when an Arab woman saw me wearing my hijab and said she wanted hers back too. I told her: "Go to the office and ask for it." I kept watching her until she took it back and put it on.

My stay at this hospital was very short, yet it left me with many questions and much confusion. Tangled emotions. The untold stories behind the closed doors of that hospital made my heart restless, even as I tried to calm my emotional storm; many conflicted emotions were roused by those stories.

Human dignity and patient rights were totally disrespected. History would never forgive those responsible for such acts. What have we come to when people who shamelessly violated human dignity and patient rights were working in mental health and at psychiatric hospitals? Did human rights organisations know about what went on inside the rooms and the hallways of this place? Were they absent from this? I vowed to speak up and to ask those questions without fear; the voice and cries of those who suffer from injustice, racism and violation must be heard.

During my stay, I had the chance to get changed, which filled me with happiness. Pens were made available too. I would let my fingers hug a pen, and even though I longed for writing and to pour out my feelings of anger and pain because of what I had been enduring, I did not write; I learned that I would not be allowed to keep anything I wrote after leaving the hospital. I managed to borrow two books in Hebrew from one of the patients there: they were two works of Russian literature. One of them discussed spirituality while the other was a detective book. I devoured them not because of their content. I missed books and I missed the letters which formed those words.

My memories of this place were finalised by the time I was taken to court by bosta and as I entered the red and blue holding cells inside the courthouse.

CHAPTER 10

My hearing was scheduled for 11.30am, yet I was surprised how early they arrived; they took me out of the cell at 10.30 instead. It's usually the opposite when it comes to courts. I then realised that, rather than taking me to the courthouse, they were leading me towards al-Moscobiyeh (Moscovia Detention Centre) in Nazareth for questioning.

At around 11, the interrogator came in and was accompanied by another man who, later, sat at a side desk. That was my fourth interrogation, but this time I didn't even ask for my lawyer; I did so based on a personal conviction. Another thing was different this time, the interrogator was constantly yelling at me and receiving the questions via his colleague who, for his part, was on the phone. All he wanted to do was get the interrogation over with quickly, before my hearing started. He was fishing for a confession; he wanted me to say that I wanted to be a 'martyr', according to their definition of the word – the only meaning they sought and understood. I denied his accusations categorically.

Unlike the other three interrogations I went through, this one was fast-paced. The interrogator demanded that I sign my statement at the end of the interrogation, so I asked to read it first. He refused and told me that the typed lines were my exact words. "You can read the papers after the interrogation is over," he shouted. "If you find something different, you can report me; hurry up! Your hearing is about to start," he shouted in my face. I just wanted it to end. Papers signed.

They took me instantly back to the court, but I was ten minutes late; the judge had already opened the session before I showed up. I entered the hall and looked round for my family. That was my first time seeing them since my arrest; my dad and brother were there, so I smiled at them to let them know I was OK. The judge decided I was mentally stable, according to the doctor's report on my mental condition, which meant I could appear before the court. I was very pleased with that decision as it was what I'd been setting out to achieve. I wasn't surprised; on the contrary, I was confident about it. Although my dad, brother and lawyer seemed disappointed, expressions of happiness and relief were written all over my face, and I felt them deep in my heart as well. That decision did not upset me.

The prosecutors presented new 'evidence' to the judge which consisted of false accusations at which they had arrived based on my answers to the questions during that quick interrogation which took place only minutes before that session. The prosecutors demanded that I remain imprisoned and be further interrogated after I was portrayed as the most dangerous creature on planet Earth. That depiction was merely a figment of their imagination, but they placed it in a well-fitting frame; the image they made up for me was ready to be presented. The judge was told I was a terrorist who wanted to carry out knife and hit-and-run crimes against the Jewish Israelis. Detention time lengthened. That wasn't unexpected, especially after such statements, which were unrelated to what I was accused of, or the type of the questions I was asked during the interrogations. All I did was ask my family to bring me some clothing items to al-Jalameh prison centre.

Nothing took me by surprise any more. I just smiled. I remained silent as there was no point in talking. Yes, I was suffocated by those empty words, but who would believe me if I said that I hardly even used a knife in my daily life. I hated cooking and I hardly ever went to the kitchen, to avoid catching the sight of that tool! If I ever had to use one, I would use a small fruit knife. Who would've believed me if I'd said that even mention of the word 'knife' made me worried, scared and extremely anxious; I endured the feelings of a person with phobia. Israel remained as it was, unchanged no matter what; it surpassed all in arrogance, racism, injustice, oppression and telling lies. By now I had witnessed the best and the worst of humanity; there was nothing left to surprise me any more.

The cell door was opened and, again, I went inside. I was astonished to see a young woman sitting on my blue concrete seat. I could tell she was an Arab because of her hijab, so I greeted her. With a lump in her throat and weeping eyes, she greeted me back. I sat on the other seat and started reading the court protocols to myself. Every time I went before the judge, I would return with a pile of papers where they wrote down more lies, fabrications and imagined things on my behalf. Whenever I read those papers, I would laugh more. If I hadn't been the accused and read such documents, I'd have thought they were meant for the most dangerous criminal in the world.

While I was immersing myself in reading those papers, fully concentrated, the young woman was crying. She didn't stop wailing. Her crying took over my emotions; I couldn't help but approach her; I initiated a conversation by asking her some questions: Why are you crying? Why are you here? She looked at me; her eyes were red and puffy from crying. "I was in Afula and I was shot," she replied. I exclaimed: "You are Israa' Abed!"

I didn't give her a chance to respond, I hurried towards her, hugged and kissed her. I told her: "Thank God for your safety. The most important thing is that you're safe and sound." I could not believe my eyes. Was that a coincidence or some strange fate? I couldn't think of anything else at that moment; I just made her laugh for a bit after all she'd been through. I told her jokingly: "Look, I'm here because I expressed my support for you. I'm here because I shared your picture on my timeline. You're not alone. I'm here because I shared your picture and I was afraid for you." She hugged me tightly, so I patted her shoulder and said: "It's a strange coincidence indeed, yet it's a very beautiful one." She stopped crying when she heard these words and she even laughed.

We had a short conversation about the incident she'd been through and we discussed the moment she was shot. I learned what had really happened. She told me that she had actually carried a knife, but she didn't want to attack anyone. She just wanted to be shot, to be dead because she was desperate. Too frustrated. Suicidal. She told me she had been depressed; she was miserable. All she wanted to do was put an end to that. She didn't even consider harming anyone. Our main lengthy discussion revolved around her health as it was all that mattered under the circumstances.

She was suffering from episodes of excruciating pain. I already knew that she was at the hospital at the time; she was in the ICU after undergoing three operations. She was discharged three days ago, and today was her first day in court. She was bone-weary, and scars from the gunshot wounds were visible on her skin.

She had a serious health condition; she wasn't able to move due to two injuries in her lower back and her waist as well as two more injuries in her abdominal area. She could barely sit down or stand up. Each side of her body was injured, and regardless of how she moved she was still in pain. With all her injuries, and the coldness of the cell, sitting down on a concrete seat was the most tortuous part for her.

I did my best to ease her pain as she was emotionally and physically destroyed. I also asked one of the Nahshon Unit soldiers for help, yet he, initially, brushed me off and was dismissive about her health condition. I didn't give up. I kept trying time after time until I managed to receive two prisoner jackets to provide some warmth after feeling the cold biting into our bodies. That might alleviate her pain.

While she was still suffering from episodes of agonising pain, I was freezing, yet I didn't pay much attention to that. My main concern was Israa's comfort. I folded the first jacket and placed it on the concrete seat to make it less uncomfortable for her to sit down. It was too cold for her wounds. I used the second jacket to cover her and warm her up. Fatigued and in intolerable pain, she put her head on my shoulder and fell asleep for quite some time until a female soldier came; she opened the door and demanded that Israa' step out of the cell to be present at her hearing. She warned her of media representatives and, in a commanding manner, against uttering a word or making any hand gestures even it was a greeting. She barely managed to move; she walked slowly and was limping too. I was even more astounded when I saw that soldier shackling Israa's hands and feet even though she could barely walk.

'How was that injured woman discharged and taken to courts and interrogations without taking her health into consideration?' I wondered. Still, after reflecting on the inhumanity I'd witnessed, I realised that I would never be shocked by anything I saw or experienced any more. It was all permitted here and used to exploit vulnerable and helpless people and to contribute to their misery and pain. Dehumanisation, pitilessness and abuse of the rules. There was no need for me to ask or seek anything about these issues.

Her hearing was lengthy – it took around two hours, during which I waited in anticipation, and I felt more anxious than I did when it was my hearing. She returned to the cell as they decided to lengthen her detention period. Meanwhile, her request to be held under house arrest was still under review.

At 4 o'clock we were taken to the bosta. Luckily, it was the period when detainees and prisoners in court holding cells were distributed among detention centres, prisons and detention camps. Nothing changed about the conditions of the journey in this moving tomb except that, this time, I wasn't alone; there was someone to talk to during those hours. Israa's suffering was vastly worse than mine as a result of her injuries which almost covered her body. The two jackets that we'd managed to obtain managed to insulate us against the cold caused by the AC vents directed towards us – above our heads, to be more exact.

It took the bosta an hour-and-a-half to get started. Suffocating in the airless moving tomb. As the vehicle passed by certain roads, I could identify them; I was familiar with their bypasses and turns. I wanted to be sure of where we were. I stood up and peeped through the tiny holes. Regardless of how difficult that was, I somehow managed to recognise that place. I told Israa' we were in Nazareth and were approaching the entrance of Yafa an-Naseriyye. I noticed immediately how touched she was, the emotions rising on her face. At a loss, she had mixed feelings. "I live in Yafa an-Naseriyye," she began to sob. On tiptoe, I stood once more, attempting to locate our whereabouts more precisely. We were right at the entrance of Jaffa, stopping for traffic lights. The moment she heard my words, she was moved deeply; she looked anxious and terrified. She told me: "My daughter is now at home with her father. I miss her. She scampered away from her seat and tried so hard to stand and see that place through those small holes. I stopped her and told her: "I'm afraid that you might fall or that your wound might get hit. You won't be able to see a thing from here." Touched, she replied: "Help me. I want to see my house; my daughter may be in the playground right now. I want to see it right now, Dareen. I don't know when I'll be able to see my house again." Her words hit home. Her words choked me. Her words overwhelmed my emotions. I helped her put on the two jackets to protect her from the risk of a fall and to prevent further injury.

We were lucky. The bosta was moving slowly due to traffic jams. Busy roads. I sat on the floor, moved downwards slowly, crouching, I asked

Israa' to lean on me, and I supported her. I carried her. A few seconds passed by before she called out her daughter's name: "Leen! Leen!" She did not stop and kept crying until her house was out of her sight. I took her back to her seat and helped her to sit down. Silence enveloped the place for a few moments. She looked at me, smiled and, once again, she drowned in her own tears. I didn't know what to do, but I soon found myself taking her into my arms. I asked her to lay her head on my lap and sleep. I wanted her to get some rest even if it was so little, for the road ahead of us was long and difficult. She placed her head on my leg; I caressed her forehead and cheeks. Her hijab was still on. I did my best to keep the handcuffs, which were locked around my wrists, off her. Suddenly, making her feel safe and comfortable was my main concern. She fell asleep. Ten minutes had passed before the bosta took a sharp turn. I found nothing to grasp onto in order to stay still. I moved. She woke up.

As we were trying to warm each other up, we heard some noise coming from the cage opposite ours: one of the prisoners had thrown up. The foul-smelling vomit made our suffering worse as the cage was closed and had no air holes. To top it off, there came swearing and curses, which then escalated into violence and verbal harassment. Whether that came from the prisoners or the soldiers, it had the same effect: emotional harm. Both were shouting as if taking turns until the moment we arrived at al Jalameh prison centre.

A few minutes past seven. The vehicle stopped as it arrived in the yard. Doors opened; they dropped me off. There was only one female soldier among four other male soldiers of the Nahshon Unit, and according to their rules, one female soldier should accompany the female detainee; if that wasn't the case, then she should accompany one detainee at a time. As a result, Israa' stayed there, but she was guarded. The female soldier took me to the same ward where I used to be; I had to be mentally prepared for strip-searching. However, I decided I would try to ask the warden not to follow through with it as I had been tormented twice in the court holding cells. I had been humiliated in that way numerous times, and every time I found it more emotionally difficult than previously. I would try. I might be able to stop such a humiliating searching process.

The warden held me in the same corner and demanded I take my clothes off. I asked her to believe me. There was no reason for searching me as I had nothing in my possession. I heard the same typical answer: "I can't. These are the rules," she said.

This time I felt even more suffocated and I couldn't hold it in any more; I was deeply affected, so I explained to her my childhood abuse. I also told her how strip-searching affected my mental state. I thought that she might show some sympathy and spare me that process. She seemed a little moved, but I was shocked when she said: "Then just lift your shirt and slide down your pants; I will not touch you. I will just eye you from a distance."

She believed that was an accomplishment on both personal and humanitarian levels in this prison. She also assumed she'd alleviated some of my suffering by her response, but my despair was only made worse. Desperately, I shut my eyes and did what she demanded quickly to avoid noticing her violating the privacy of my body; her eyes had finally finished harassing my naked body. Staring at my body in such a forced manner would also be considered sexual harassment. All the harm that experience brought up would haunt me. Those very few seconds were enough.

The warden opened the huge blue gate for me, I entered the gloomy cell and right before she locked the door I asked for cleaning supplies. The prison cell wasn't in a better state than how it was during the previous times. In addition to all the filth, there were blood spots spattered over its walls. I removed them using water and soap. I scrubbed the walls with a broom brush so as to avoid constant vomit and nausea. I didn't know how long my stay would last. I was thinking non-stop until a wishful thought crossed my mind: bringing Israa' to this cell. That wasn't what happened, though, and I didn't have a clue where she was.

I sat on the bed and tried to go to sleep, but I failed. Severe, unbearable headache. I had to request one tablet of painkillers from the warden. One hour passed before she gave me that yellow 'acamol' pill. I took it and went back to bed; it wasn't something I would normally do, but I started examining that tablet and turning it over and over in my palms. Whenever I tried to swallow it, I would imagine it was a pen, so I retreated. I needed to write and a wave of longing for a pen hit me hard, an unfamiliar feeling that crept inside of me as I held the tablet and attempted to write on the wall. My attempt failed. I put the tablet back in my palm and continued to contemplate it as if I wanted a gush of ink to come out of it.

I felt a little cold, so I zipped my jacket only to take it off again and take out the zipper pull; I attempted to write on the wall using it. It worked! My name, the date and time were the first things I wrote. My hand jotted down a flash prose piece titled 'Feminine Cell Wall Engravings' along with some verses from my poems which I memorised by heart including the accused poem which became the main reason why I was arrested; I wrote random rebellious words and sentences to describe my personality and the circumstances under which I lived.

I was writing as if I had been looking for some language that resembled my dream and embodied the horror I felt; I wanted to pull out my words from silence and announce that they were like windows which look out to the future. The letters inscribed in the wall were like some carved-out pictures in which I kept my trembles, where I decluttered and gathered up my dreams and wishes. I was isolated from everything. Alone. I had no way to communicate with the outside world: no messages, no phone, no books or magazines, no pens for writing, no radio or TV. At that moment I felt that all was said and done, and even if the whole world imprisoned me, stood against me, tightened its fist around my neck to choke me, it would not shut me up. I would still speak up whenever and wherever I was.

I expressed my gratitude to that tablet for giving me such an opportunity; it granted me the idea of using the zipper pull to write. I completely forgot about my headache, so I didn't take it. I put it in my pocket, instead, and I put my magical pen back into its place. I fell asleep.

The next morning, I was led to Moscobiyeh in Nazareth for yet another interrogation. I was placed in a cell next to the admissions office. It was a chilly room, just like the previous one, and despite the fact that it was large, it had no seats. I had to sit on the floor while being hand and leg-cuffed. Every now and then, I banged on the door to remind them I was there; one of them would reply: "The interrogator hasn't arrived yet." At other times, I wouldn't get any response so I tired of knocking and would go back and sit on the floor. The door opened suddenly. A policeman entered the cell while holding a feminine pink perfume bottle. Doors closed. He started spraying me with that perfume and saying: "You're so pretty. Your eyes are beautiful. I will find you a good husband from one of my men. What do you say?" I couldn't hold myself back, I shouted at him and cursed him repeatedly but that still didn't stop or deter him. I realised that shouting wouldn't serve me well; he seemed to be very confident of what he was doing and it seemed it was all pre-planned. My chest was tight and I felt a lump in my throat, so I backed away to be as distant as possible and keep him from touching me. The cell door was closed. Closer and closer, he approached me. He put his left hand on my face and his right hand – in which he was holding the perfume bottle – on my chest. With my shackled hands, I pushed him away and, at the top of my voice, I cursed him. I did not care any more. When I started to hit him, he backed away, left the cell and slammed the door shut. He vanished. Even though it was a difficult situation, I tried to work out what his name was, but his badge was not pinned to his shirt.

After a few minutes, the door was opened again. Someone gave me a sandwich and a water bottle, so I told him about what had happened. "I have been here, sitting still, since the moment you were brought in; I haven't seen any policeman entering the cell. You're lying and making things up. It is not true," he replied. I asked if I could go to the bathroom, so he told me he would let a policewoman know and she would accompany me. Going to the bathroom wasn't my sole and main purpose: I wanted to leave the cell for a few minutes because I might be able to find that harassing policeman. I wanted to respond more effectively to his harassment of me. After half an hour, a policewoman came along with a policeman and led me to the bathroom; the policeman entered the bathroom and inspected it. After that the policewoman told me: "You can go in." I asked her to unshackle my hands. She refused. And, in turn, I refused to go to the bathroom while shackled; the policeman intervened and nodded his head, gesturing that she could unshackle me. She did. I entered the bathroom. She re-cuffed me and took me back to the cell. I didn't achieve my main purpose of that bathroom trip.

That policeman was nowhere to be seen. I was kept in that cell up 'til 4pm without being questioned. When I protested against that and asked for the reason behind the delay, I was told the interrogator couldn't make it, so the interrogation was postponed. I was taken back to al Jalameh prison centre.

Before I entered the cell which I had left earlier, the warden was replaced. I swore that I didn't possess anything and requested that she didn't strip-search me and expose my body. She nodded and said: "I know. My colleague has told me about your situation. I won't search you." I thanked her so much for doing me that favour and her humane response. We smiled at each other for some time before I re-entered the cell.

After that incident, I felt as if my language had deceived me; it could be that something about the nature of those wardens was still unrevealed. I couldn't recall reading about a single incident where wardens treated the prisoners well; they always talk about the worst. That incident occurred, despite the fact that it could be rare, and proved that someone could still be humane even if that person was a warden. Incidents here were just like language which could hide more than the truth it might reveal. Therefore, many people might misunderstand or misjudge one another. In a world filled with mistranslations, it would be difficult to achieve clarity. That being the case, we shouldn't be too strict and stubborn because, in order to live, we need to dive deep inside to get to hidden meanings. Every day resembled the last one in this prison; the only thing that helped me break free from my everyday routine was scribbling on the wall with my zipper pull, my own magical pen!

The warden opened the door, Israa', together with another young woman, came in. I hurried in the direction of Israa' and checked on her; I helped her carry her stuff and sit on one of the beds. I learned that she had spent that period of time in the women's prison in Ramleh (Neve Tirtza[6]).

They both chose to sleep in bottom beds and avoided the top ones so as to keep away from falling off while sleeping; they didn't even consider them because of the difficulty of climbing up and down the ladder. I did the opposite. I had chosen to sleep in the top bed because I knew I couldn't stand staring at metal bed slats; it was much easier for me to look at the concrete ceiling in such an ugly cell.

The second young woman was called Huda. She smoked and used obscene language when she talked to wardens; she was always shouting for no reason. I managed to stand her behaviour for no more than half an hour, then I decided to talk to her about it. I explained Israa's health condition to her, and I asked her to help me ease her pain. I didn't have to put too much effort into it before we reached an agreement to respect one another in that shared cell; we also agreed to accept one another, despite all our differences. She was a 20-year-old young woman; she was kind-hearted even though her behaviour made her seem otherwise.

After a while, I was surprised to see her burst into tears in her bed. I hurried towards her thinking I was the reason why she was crying and falling apart. I thought I'd been too hard on her. I apologised, yet she started unfolding her story and telling me about why she was detained.

I was touched by her story and her suffering. At first glance, I thought she was a 'bird' (an undercover informer to spy on Palestinians in Israeli prisons) who was trying to mislead me, especially as I still had no bill of indictment. I soon realised that my doubts were misplaced; she didn't even ask me why I was there or of what I was accused. I started talking to her, making an effort to ease her pain; the situation soon worsened as Israa' began to cry too.

I filled others up with a strength that I didn't have for myself. I felt as if I was having a breakdown; I felt weak, desperate and frustrated. I had every reason to cry and I desperately needed a good cry, but I still couldn't shed a tear. I envied them for crying; it was a blessing. While I was laughing, I told them: "How about you both sit on the same bed and cry? It would be easier for me than moving from one bed to another." They both responded with a guffaw which filled the whole cell and the dark walls. Within a few hours, without any notice or plan, we became three friends, and it seemed as if we had known each other not for hours, but years. We had a genuine affection for one another; we ate, drank, shared sadness and happiness; we also talked at night and entertained ourselves. If one of us brought something, she'd bear the rest of us in mind. I once told them about one of my funny adventures as a photographer. I was in Nazareth's old market (souk) and I caught sight of an elderly man walking among a group of foreign tourists while wearing the Palestinian traditional costume, a qumbaz (a coat) along with a black keffiyeh (a traditional scarf usually worn by Palestinians). Beautiful and inspiring. I wanted to take a picture of him, so I approached him. After I'd chosen the appropriate angle for that picture, he suddenly raised his crutch and started running towards me. He wanted to hit me with it, so he started chasing me while I was trying to run away from him and explain to him the significance of that picture at the same time. To my surprise, I found out that the tourists themselves were filming me causing that scene. The tables turned. I was the one whose pictures were being taken. Once I wrapped up the story, I heard Israa' and Huda laughing loudly. They laughed continuously about that incident, bringing colour to that depressing place with their laughter.

Israa' went to the bathroom and asked me to help her change bandages which covered her wounds, especially those on her stomach. A stoma bag covered a part of her intestines which poked through as a result of gunshot. The bullets that tore through her body left visible scars; there was no need for questions or any explanation. I didn't ask any questions, so as to spare her feelings and avoid triggering her memory of that event, especially as she started to feel peaceful and safe.

That scene was appalling, it was the first time I'd seen such things. I did my best not to show my emotions. She needed to change that pouch every few hours; that was what she told me. We tried, without success, to put on the new bag that had been given to her from the prison infirmary. The stoma bag didn't match the size of its flange which was stuck onto her stomach. We hurriedly asked the warden and explained the problem to her. I also sought an explanation as to why that injured detainee had to do this herself without the help of a nurse or the prison doctor. She didn't reply. Nothing could explain that except torture and increasing the suffering of the injured detainee. All the warden did was pass on the message to a nurse who took so long to arrive and asked me what the problem was. Meanwhile, Israa' was in the bathroom trying to cover her open wound with toilet paper; her wound was oozing discharge. It wasn't supposed to be exposed to air to avoid contamination or infection. We didn't change the pouch on the bed because the cell was under surveillance, which meant there was no privacy.

I asked the nurse to transfer Israa' to his clinic to assess her health condition and so she could get adequate treatment. He refused point-blank, so I had to hold the old bag that contained her wound drainage and show him the difference between that bag and the new ones. He left and returned within a few minutes; he brought medical tape and told me that it would solve the problem. I went back to help Israa' change the stoma bag and attached it to the flange. I was very worried because I wanted to be precise, yet I didn't want to cause her any pain at the same time. After finishing that task, I thought about what would Israa' would have done if she'd been on her own and how difficult it would have been for her.

I had no idea I could handle such tricky situations and empathise with others. I doubt I had that capability previously. I think my prison experiences had been transformative; they changed me nature well as my lifestyle.

I still had no extra clothes. I would still wash the same clothes I was wearing and put them back on while they were wet. I wasn't alone. Huda had the same problem, but she was new, so her suffering wasn't so bad by comparison. Israa' was more fortunate when it came to this; she was able to bring in some items which her parents gave her when she was at the hospital. Our sizes were different, though. None of her clothes would fit us.

The biggest prize for the three of us was her hairbrush. I realised how precious a hairbrush was the moment I brushed my hair in al-Jalameh. I never thought that I would be deprived of a hairbrush or that one day I would write about its value. My first hairdo in prison helped me discover that gem which I will always remember. I also realised how important my hair was. I wore my hair down, and gleefully, I started combing it. Letting out a laugh, Israa' looked at me and said: "Is this the first time you've ever combed your hair?" Huda overheard her; she laughed too and said: "It's as if you'd found the keys to this cell; you want to leave it and stroll around the place, huh?" Her heartwarming words made me let out a hearty laugh as well. Those moments we spent breaking the monotony were precious. The three of us combed each other's hair while sitting on Israa's bed. I would braid Huda's hair; Israa' would braid mine and then I'd braid Israa's.

One day, Huda told me that she'd been a keen football player; she was yearning to touch a ball and hold it in her hands. Maybe her desire to play with a ball paralleled my desire to write. Israa' was really engaged in that conversation and wished they could play with a ball in the cell. Longing and sorrow took hold of them; one could sense it in their voices. I took off

62

my jacket; I folded it, tied it and fixed it until it was a sphere-like solid object. Then I threw it towards Huda's bed, asking: "What do you think of this ball?" Their faces glowed with excitement. We started playing and tossing the jacket around as if it were a real ball.

9pm

I was pulled towards the interrogation room in Nazareth, and before starting the questioning session I met my new lawyer and learned from him that this interrogation was for another accusation, namely supporting a terrorist cell. Our conversation didn't last more than a few minutes; he was also very surprised by that accusation. He gave me some advice and left after shaking my hand and said: "See you in court tomorrow."

A tiny room which wasn't intended for interrogation sessions, it was the interrogator's private office. I could tell because of the many personal photos which were hung on the walls, pictures with his wife and children. He treated me respectfully; no shouting or pressure was involved. He also asked a policewoman to un-cuff my hands and legs. Afterwards, he explained the accusation levelled against me and the reasons behind it. During our conversation, I came to realise that by 'a terrorist cell' they were referring to nothing but a Palestinian faction whose post I shared and quoted on my Facebook profile, the Islamic Jihad Movement. He said it was a call for an uprising, which was deemed terrorist by the Israeli police and authority.

That news item didn't imply any support to that faction. It was just an ordinary one; there was nothing different about it than the other news. The same phrases would have been used by Israeli media, but the fact that the word 'intifada' (uprising) was mentioned by a Palestinian Arab drew suspicion and was considered terrorist – a crime for which I should be punished severely.

After learning this news, I was certain they wanted to try to pin the allegation on me no matter how and at all costs. They accused me of that crime to cover up for the misunderstanding that started with my arrest. They aimed to expand my case to add more allegations to the bill of indictment to make it worthy enough to be presented to the judge. The

63

interrogation session didn't take long, yet the accusation was serious and could lead to a long prison sentence reaching up to eight years. The interrogator asked: "Do you know anyone from that organisation? Do you support this organisation?" I told him that I only supported Balad and I didn't know anyone from that organisation. Then he asked me: "Then I'm pretty sure you support their work and activity, right?" My only answer was: "No." Sometimes, there are some activities which one can't help but support. Each human being does good deeds as well as bad ones at some point. I only supported the good ones. He followed that by asking: "Which of their work do you support?" He insisted on an answer. I replied: "For instance, when there are demonstrations against the killings of the innocent or children, I do support that, for sure. The death of Mohammad Abu Khdeir as well as Ali Dawabsheh and his family. When that organisation establishes nurseries for the poor, for orphans, I, without a doubt, support such activities because they're charitable and humanitarian." I chose my words carefully while answering him; I tried my best to elaborate on the reason behind posting and quoting that news item as well as my intentions.

After the interrogation was over, he turned off his computer, looked at me and said: "Listen, Dareen, I'll keep this between us, I know for sure that you're innocent. I'm not content with the fact that I have just questioned you. I had to do it. Be sure that I wrote each and every word you said exactly. Word for word. This is all I can do." I looked at him and said: "You simply could have refused to interrogate me. Why did you do that?" He remained silent. He opened the door; we left the room and headed to the yard. I asked him to call one of my family members and ask someone to bring me some clothes. I explained to him that I hadn't been able to get changed ever since I got arrested. He agreed without question. Very unexpected. I was used to starting long discussions even over the slightest things. I gave him the number; and he actually dialled it. My brother arrived within ten minutes and we were allowed to hug and give each other a handshake.

My brother gave me a bag of clothing items, yet the interrogator said I wouldn't be allowed to keep it; I was only allowed to get changed there. I took the items I needed and he went with me to the bathroom entrance and waited for me outside. I gave my brother the outfit I was wearing; he

64

said goodbye and left. I asked him to bring them to al-Jalameh. Only then did I realise they had been trying to do so, but the administration refused every time; the request would be postponed for no reason. Despite this, I asked my brother to give it another try that night.

I was buoyed by the humanity displayed by the interrogator as well as his politeness and respect in contrast to the rest of the interrogators I'd come across after my arrest. I thanked him sincerely. I showed my appreciation for giving me the chance to get changed, although it was one of my rights as a detainee or prisoner. Those rights had been denied for Palestinians under that racist authority; the only way to gain such rights was by using unexpected tactics.

The policewoman re-cuffed me and I was taken back to al-Jalameh, to the same cell where I left Israa' and Huda. Within a couple of hours, the warden brought in a black bag of clothes. I was exhilarated. My struggle with clothes was finally over. At last, I could take a shower and get changed. I checked that bag only to realise that all the elastic was removed. I gave Huda and Isra all they needed from what my family had sent me.

Despite the seriousness of our situation and how bad and depressing it was getting, I would burst out with some funny lines to comfort myself, Israa' and Huda, in trying to adapt to those dire circumstances. I was trying to survive.

My gut instinct told me they were about to leave this place and their arrest would be over. I didn't say so, though, as I didn't want them to get their hopes up. They would be shattered, devastated if that didn't happen. In the morning, I hugged them goodbye before going to court. They, for their part, wished for my release.

I carried my clothes bag, which almost didn't made it to my cell, I wanted to take it with me yet the female soldier refused. She claimed it should remain there and it wasn't allowed in court. She said it would be well kept and, wherever I went, it would be sent back to me. My name was written on a yellow piece of paper which she took from the warden's desk. Yellow paper stuck on the black bag and left in a small storeroom, I stood there watching each of those steps. Strip-searched and re-cuffed. Off we went.

CHAPTER 11

November 2, 2015
3.30pm

Accused and leg-cuffed, I was standing in a wooden cage. A female soldier and male soldiers were standing on either side, watching me, silencing and paralysing me. I was forbidden from uttering a word or even giving my family members a handshake. There, facing me, the judge sat and initiated conversations and discussions with my lawyers and the prosecutors. Then the prosecution announced the completion of the interrogation process. While their conversation revolved around me, I looked around and watched those in attendance. Sign language pervaded the courtroom – head and eye gestures as well as smiles.

Crowded courtroom, almost full. Familiar and unfamiliar faces surrounded me; some had shown up to attend my court hearing while others had nothing to do with my case. Some were there to show their support, some relatives; my mum; my dad; my aunt, Hayat; my maternal cousin, Bilal; my brother, Saher; my uncles, Mansour and Muwafaq along with a group of friends and supporters. They are all anticipating the ruling. Convicted.

They read aloud my charges:

Publishing my poem 'Resist, my people, resist them';
Posting a photo of the injured, Israa' Abed, while lying on the ground;
Posting a picture which had "I'm the next martyr" caption;
Posting a news item regarding an uprising which was originally posted by a Palestinian faction.

Based on that, the lawyer predicted a seven-year sentence awaited me. My eyes were glued to my mum's face which showed every bit of sadness. I look at my dad's face – tears, grief and pain filled his eyes. Rage, fear, worry, uncertainty. What was yet to come? And yet I smiled at everyone in the courtroom as though what had been going on, inside the walls of the room of lies, was not my concern and had nothing to do with me.

Suddenly, I call out: "Yemma, Yemma, have you picked the olives yet? Do you need a hand?" The female soldier tried her best to shut me up, yet she failed. Nothing could stop me. A laugh, everyone has laughed; that laugh made the keyboard's clicking sounds seem quiet and the judge's as well as the prosecutor's voices fade into the background. This was what I wanted. I wanted everyone to laugh so I could conclude this court hearing on my own terms.

The above list recaps two accusations against me: an incitement to violence and terrorism due to publishing a poem and two photos as well as supporting a terrorist organisation by quoting one of the Palestinian factions and posting it on my Facebook account. Consequently, the judge decided to lengthen my imprisonment period until the court's legal processes were finalised.

I wasn't surprised either by that charge sheet or the decision to extend my detention period. My intuition told me so; I trusted my gut. I told myself: 'Is this a charge sheet or a certificate of honour?' especially as one of the items on that list was a poem. I was on cloud nine the moment I realised how forceful my poem was; my words were powerful enough to scare a whole nation. It was listed on both the charge sheet and the protocols. Israel vs. Dareen Tatour.

Back to al-Jalameh and put in a cell. Alone. It looked very similar to the rest of the cells in which I'd stayed; only it was smaller. There were two beds and a TV. First and foremost, I asked for my bag of clothes; the warden couldn't find it. I was on the verge of losing my mind. My rage over such negligence and the drawn-out discussions we had led us nowhere. I had lost the clothes which I'd endeavoured to obtain. I asked her for alternative clothes to make up for the loss. After a long wait and much struggle, she came back carrying one shirt and two underwear items.

I tried to turn on the TV but it didn't work. I asked about it only to learn that it could only be turned on by wardens in the warden's office, so I asked her to turn it on. She rejected my request saying: "You are also forbidden from watching TV. Those are the rules."

Funny response. I replied: "Don't blame the rules, it's not the rules. It's the joy our torture brings you." I didn't give her the chance to respond. I let her think over what I said. I moved away from the door and sat on the bed. I took out my magical pen from its shelter, the jacket – my companion. I didn't keep that jacket to warm myself up but rather to be able to keep my secret pen and scribble on walls. On one of the walls, I wrote a new poem titled 'A Poet Behind Bars'.

The next morning, at around 6am, I was taken out from my cell. I asked: "Where to?" to which they replied: "To Sharon Prison[7]." Searched twice. Hand and leg-cuffed. I was led out of the building to a yard packed with bosta vehicles, policemen and K-9 dogs. I was carrying a small black bag where I kept the very few objects that I got to keep from that prison. One of the policemen approached me along with his K-9. The K-9 started barking at me at times, or near me at others. It stood tall on its hind legs and seemed to be about to attack me with its claws. Once the soldier uttered a word or made a certain gesture, the K-9 would completely stop barking and jumping and would start sniffing at my feet. The K-9 would be rewarded for that with a chunk of meat. The soldier would tell his K-9: "You're such a wonderful dog! What was that smell? Of course, it must be the odour of terrorism. Hey, dog! Your being here is very beneficial, but her and the people of her kind are useless, they can only incite killing. Keep sniffing at her. You will definitely find something. Arab trash. She's a filthy Arab. 'Ikhs' (what a shame!) Disgusting! How could we allow her in the car?"

Every time the K-9 was able to intimidate or offend me, the soldier would reward it with some food to encourage it to keep going as if it had been doing a good job. I am friendly to animals by nature; when I'm approached or touched by one, I don't normally feel frightened. I didn't feel the same way about that dog, though. I was horrified when it barked; I jumped backwards involuntarily. I just wanted to keep my distance, but I fell down because my legs were shackled. Luckily, I wasn't hurt. As I was collecting myself, three more soldiers came in my direction; they moved closer and closer until I was surrounded by them and their dogs. The four dogs started barking at me and another group from the Nahshon Unit joined them. They mocked me, they laughed loudly. They also made some remarks; the soldier who was holding the dog that caused me to fall said: "You're horrified by this dog and you wish to be a martyr!" Again, he rewarded his dog with an extra piece of food. He started petting him and saying: "Good dog! You did exactly what you had to do."

Another soldier added: "You want to kill Jews? You subversive! You terrorist! It's about time you knew what real fear was all about. You will finally get what it means to say something against the Jews and Israel."

The third soldier with a dog demanded that I put my black bag on the ground so the dog would check it before we boarded the bosta. I told him: "I could show you what I have in this bag myself," yet he rejected the idea and told me: "No, the dog is going to examine it. Not you. Open the bag and put it down on the ground. The dog knows what to do."

I opened the bag and dropped it on the ground. The dog began to sniff at the clothes and walked all over them; it smudged them with its paws. After the five-minute inspection was over, the soldier demanded that I pick that bag up, but I refused. "I don't need it any more," I told him, to which he replied: "That's better. We don't need any more trash in our vehicle. You and people like you are more than enough."

That dog didn't frighten me any more despite the fact that its barking increased and the distance between us grew less as the dog was incited by the soldier. I didn't react. I only smiled; behind that smile was a mixture of contradictory emotions. After one hour of waiting passed in that yard while surrounded by the constant barking of K-9's, the female soldier held my cuffs, pulled me and demanded that I enter onto the bosta vehicle.

The bosta looked different this time; it was similar to those public transport buses. My cuffs held me down; my steps were restricted and I barely made it to the bus. I was accompanied by one of Nahshon Unit's female soldiers. Two male recruits followed her to provide assistance in guarding me. The dog and the recruit who held his leash were there as well.

And suddenly all I could see was a group of rectangular black cages. It didn't seem like a bus any more. The cage door was opened; the K-9 went in to inspect every angle of the seat. Obviously that was why the fourth soldier was there. The female soldier demanded that I sit down inside the cage then they slammed the door shut; its sound echoed everywhere. The loud bang would be forever stuck in my ears.

There was a metal seat for two, yet it was a narrow cage. A surveillance camera was hung on the ceiling; it was a windowless and unventilated cage. I had been cuffed inside this tiny cage for about two hours before the bus started moving away from al-Jalameh. The fact that it was a different bus didn't change anything about the hideousness of such a journey. I had to endure the same conditions. In fact, it was even more brutal this time because of its narrowness, not to mention the design of the 50 cm long and 80 cm high seat; I had to be seated in a 90-degree upright sitting position. Unlike this seat, those of the Nashshon members had fabric seat covers which looked pretty comfortable. They sat next to big windows which served as lookouts. They could travel at ease and in comfort.

This tortuous journey inside this cold metal cage took four more hours. I noticed that the bus stopped three times in different areas. I couldn't locate or recognise just exactly where. I heard chains rattle and bang against the bus flooring as the detainees were treading, so I guessed that those were either detention centres or other prisons. Through one of the cage door holes, which resembled those of holding cell as well as cell door holes, one of the soldiers passed me a sausage-stuffed baguette. I couldn't eat it because I was vegetarian. I was thirsty yet they ignored my request to have a bottle of water. I wasn't able to use the bathroom either.

The cage door was finally opened; a female soldier demanded that I get off the bus. I wasn't alone, there were numerous prisoners who got off from several vehicles in the same area. They were small groups of people guarded by some soldiers and K-9s. I was the only woman amongst that crowd which consisted of Palestinian detainees except three who were convicted of 'criminal' offences. I was able to detect those three by how they were dressed. Palestinian detainees mainly wore a brown uniform; some hardly ever wore street clothes. However, the rest wore an orange uniform. The two groups were later separated and had different destinations.

I entered an eerie building where I saw some silver square-shaped, 3x3, wire-fenced metal cages. Numerous detainees were shoved into the same cage; they were all for men except one – it was intended for women. It was filthy, sewage water was flooding in, so that my feet sank with every step I took inside the place. I tried to identify it; after a struggle and lots of eavesdropping I learned it was called Mibar el-Ramla, a place that was used as a station to receive the detainees before they were either transferred to prisons or court (a temporary detention facility). Hell on Earth.

I stayed in that cage for over five hours without food or water. To make matters worse, I couldn't go to the bathroom because it was a unisex shared bathroom with a half-height door. Besides, there was a soldier to guard the bathroom; he would make fun of the person using the toilet with obscene language or by laughing with his colleagues. I decided to keep myself away from that torment, so I didn't use that bathroom for long hours. I even stopped drinking water, despite being extremely thirsty, so as not to feel the urge to go to the bathroom. I couldn't go through yet more sexual and verbal harassment. I'd rather suffer physically than emotionally: that experience would mean accumulating more painful memories. Those soldiers lacked feeling and morals. I envied the detainees because they didn't know any Hebrew; they couldn't fathom the viciousness of those words and sentences uttered by the soldiers. Deep down, I felt the need to unmask the bitter truth, yet I was frightened for them. These soldiers tried to provoke us by all means. They used power games; our torture was their biggest thrilling victory. After thinking on the consequences, I chose to remain silent. My helplessness pierced my heart. I couldn't do anything to stop their torture of my people. Now, I was just one of them; I was just a detainee.

5pm

I was transferred to a small bosta, but right before I boarded one of the soldiers read my file thoroughly, contemplating each page and what was written in there. Then he let the K-9 into the cage and checked the seat. The bosta set off. Ten minutes after the inspection, slamming the door shut and locking it, the soldier reopened the cage and let the dog in one more time. He told me: "The dog left you a present."

He gave it certain commands after which the K-9 urinated on the seat opposite mine. When the deed was done, he petted the dog and gave him a treat. He let him out of the cage. Slammed the door shut and locked it.

The tiny moving tomb started to stink. I couldn't stand it. My body trembled, I vomited, and I had a severe throbbing pain in my head. That was the soldier's purpose after reading my papers, and he achieved it. He must have come across the fact that I suffered from osmophobia and that I was allergic to odours. He used my weakness against me; he took advantage of my case to humiliate me. I asked for help yet the only response I got was: "Why are you complaining about the smell? Do you think you smell better? You smell like trash. No, even worse! That smell won't harm you." I tried to seek another soldier's help and got a one-word response: "Sheket.[8]"

An hour had passed since we started that journey, then we arrived at Sharon Prison. More than twelve hours of pain and exhaustion to complete my transfer from al-Jalameh to Sharon. No food. No water. No bathroom. That journey would normally take two hours maximum.

CHAPTER 12

6.30pm

I couldn't stand straight any more; my body was worn out. I had a severe headache. I walked along with one of the female soldiers, and we were followed by three others in a long hallway and through many electric gates. I was about to black out any moment. My headache turned into crippling dizziness which affected both my consciousness and vision. Taking one breath every now and then restored some of my resilience. 'This nightmare must end,' I reminded myself. I still had hope. I was in a yard surrounded by metal door cells, which were no doubt intended for prisoners, and ordinary wooden door rooms for the prison employees. I was delivered to a police officer by one of the Nahshon Unit's soldiers; he went through my papers and confirmed my identity. The metal door was opened, I was un-cuffed. Into another cell. Door shut noisily with a bang.

A very dirty, stinky tiny prison cell with an unwashed toilet. It seemed like it hadn't been cleaned for quite some time. It didn't take me more than a few minutes to start throwing up in that bathroom. I felt as if I were letting out all of the poison which had been overwhelming my body since I was arrested. A very dim cell, there was no light around except for some rays barely making their way from the yard to the cell through the door hole. There were no seats, the walls were covered with rough concrete. I couldn't sit down or even lean on one of the walls. I had no choice but to sit on the floor and rest my head on my knees for two hours in spite of my persistent attempts to call out one of the wardens. No response. Then, suddenly, a warden came, opened the door and shackled my hands and feet and led me to an office where one of the officers sat at his desk. His questions indicated that it was the admissions office. After some time the warden returned and took me to the doctor's room for a quick check-up and recorded some data in my file. At around 8.30 pm, I ended up in ward 2: Palestinian women political prisoners (as they are called in Geneva Conventions). Now, I was in the hands of a new warden. The former warden un-cuffed me while the second led me to the bathroom, used a

73

hand-held metal detector to search me the strip-searched me. She made me stand by her side. Waves of sounds hit my eardrums. My ears picked up some lines: "Girls! A new political prisoner has just arrived"; "We have a new guest in this ward."

The warden opened the metal door and ordered me to go in. Then she called out "Lina!" and went straight back to her office after I was delivered to Lina.

Lina al-Jarbouni was a political prisoner. I'd read a lot about her and was acquainted with her case through pictures and online news. I was well aware of her struggle and steadfastness behind the bars of that prison. We stood facing each other; I was right in front of her, silent, astonished and filled with emotion. She extended her hand, so I gave her a handshake. She asked me to remain calm and go along with her for a quick chat in her room.

I felt as if I was in front of an icon of resilience and determination, a unique painting with daring colours. Suffice it to say she had spent 15 years in that prison. I respected and appreciated her; I recognised her great sacrifice. I remembered at once all the suffering I had gone through during such a short period of detention and imprisonment. I realised that my experience was as nothing compared to hers. I was nervous and I didn't know how to explain this sudden feeling to her, so I remained silent and waited for her to talk.

I walked along with her in a hallway with rooms and cells on each side. Numerous people were there; all eyes were glued to me. Everyone was watching out of curiosity, they wanted to know who the new arrival was. Their greetings kept on coming as well.

She wanted to introduce herself, so I told her she was well known, so she didn't have to. She began to talk about the prison and explain some rules. She told me how things operated there and explained the general rules that should be followed by political prisoners.

In this ward there were specific rules as well as general ones. The general rules related to Prison Service included the head count as well as inspection. The women political prisoners, though, had one spokesperson regardless of their affiliations; the spokesperson who would mediate between the political prisoners and the administration was Lina. Direct communication with the administration was forbidden. In each room, there was a 'Shawish' (a cell boss) who would communicate our needs to Lina who, in turn, delivered the message to the administration.

I was exhausted. I didn't fully comprehend the rules and why they were there in the first place. I didn't ask about anything. She could tell I was fatigued, so she wrapped up our chat by saying: "I will elaborate on our lifestyle here first thing in the morning."

I asked: "Will I share your cell and sleep there?" to which she replied: "I'm afraid that my cell is already full, you will sleep in cell number 7." She asked the warden to open the door for me and asked my cell-mates to take good care of me. She left.

Too crammed. Too crowded. It was a 15m² square-shaped cell, where there was barely enough room for the inmates. One half-opened yet fenced window. Neither air nor sunlight penetrated the room. There were six bunk-beds, a grey old TV in addition to eight metal cabinets and a tiny white sink, and a small rectangular mirror was hung on one of the walls. There was also a white plastic wall mounted clothes hanger where four towels were hung, and on one of the cabinets there was an electric kettle and an electric stove.

The bathroom was very narrow. There was a water pipe hung up high without a shower faucet. There was a toilet which was placed right next to the pipe in an uncovered entrance, and which the prisoners later covered with a yellow curtain.

I was the sixth political prisoner. After I greeted them, they introduced themselves, one woman at a time. They greeted me warmly, politely and courteously. By the time I got there, they had already prepared a dinner for me which was fancy compared to what I used to have back in al-Jalameh, at least.

A square-shaped white table was filled with all sorts of food: vegetable soup, rice, Mulukhiya (cooked Jew's Mallow), a piece of chicken and bread, yogurt and a bottle of grape juice. It was a pleasing shock for me because I'd almost forgot that type of food existed. Another liquid to drink other than water – I'd almost forgot about that. I couldn't see that I would be able to see such food throughout my stay. I thanked them for their generosity; I asked them to excuse me if I only ate a little. I was too exhausted to eat and that throbbing headache crept into my body and took over my senses. I begged their pardon and asked where my bed was. They pointed to the only bed left. It had a pillow and a blanket. Fortunately, it was a top bed and that was what I preferred. I walked up the bunk bed stairs. I slept until 5am. Count Time.

At 10.30am all the doors were opened. *Fawra*[9], or Yard Time. That was the name that the political prisoners gave to recreation time. The process began to clean the cells. I suggested that I help clean up the cell along with my cell-mates, but my suggestion was refused; I was still a 'new guest'. We would take turns; mine would be soon.

Yard Time was a period determined by the administration when the prisoners were allowed to go to the yard for recreation and let their eyes enjoy the sight of sunshine. I left the cell and took a trip around the prison to learn more about the ward and the regulations. Besides, I wanted to get to know the women political prisoners. I then met with Lina in a room called 'al-saf' ('the class') which was a hall intended for meetings and gatherings. The fact that there was a small library opposite that hall filled my soul with happiness. There were a number of books, and in the far left corner was Lina's own office, which consisted of one small table. She would follow up her own matters as well as those of the other prisoners from there. Behind her 'desk' was a wooden cabinet. In the opposite corner, there were two shared mini fridges: a refrigerator, a freezer, and another small table on which there was a bag of bread.

During my meeting with Lina, we discussed many issues, especially my case. We also talk about the conditions outside and the changes that Arab countries had undergone. Moreover, we discussed their economic and political states. One of the things that intrigued me the most was her question: "What is Facebook? I've been in prison for fifteen years. When I was imprisoned that 'invention' didn't exist."

I tried to tell her about the developments outside the prison that she would eventually find herself up against, but it wasn't easy to describe everything. Living in the prison for a long time, during which the world outside had undergone a technological revolution, would certainly make any freed prisoner feel like an alien visiting Earth for the first time. They would have to re-learn how to live. By contrast, anyone who had witnessed the technological advances who suddenly entered the prison would feel as if they were living in ancient times; they would lack all forms of globalisation and development.

She, for her part, elaborated on matters concerning the prison, including the terminology and rules which were common among the female detainees. She offered me some clothes and other essentials, such as a towel, a toothbrush and a loofah sponge. I asked her for a pen and a notebook; she gave me two: a small brown-covered one and a big white-covered one. She also gave me two pens: a blue ink and a black ink one. She gave me all I asked for.

My second station was, of course, the library (bookcase). It was a small one with a limited number of books; it contained a hundred to a hundred-and-twenty books. They were classified according to their subjects. I went through them and found some books on religion while very few were historical books. There were dictionaries of Hebrew-Arabic, and vice versa, as well as an English-Arabic dictionary. Other books included those on embroidery, cooking, handcrafts and so forth. The rest of the books, however, were Arabic literary works, two of which were poetry collections: Ahlam Mostighanemi's 'Alayka Al Lahfa' ('For You is the Yearning') and the other written by Dr. Ibrahim Abdullah and titled 'Al-Arood Bayna Al Asala Wal Hadatha' ('Prosody: Between Tradition and Modernity'). I asked Lina's permission to borrow them. I took them to the cell.

And then I went out to the yard. It was a square yard with a wired fenced ceiling through which the sky's endless horizon seemed nothing but a square. The ground was painted red. Looking out the fence was eye-straining; my eyesight was restricted. It was a reminder for every one of us that we were in prison; our memories would be jogged even when we strived to forget about it. We were in prison. Despite that, I gazed at the sky. It was the first time I'd seen a square-shaped sky. A square. That was how it seemed to me while looking at it through the wire-fenced ceiling. I kept looking at the strange-looking sky hoping that a bird would fly over it, but things didn't go the way I hoped. I was shocked to see a scarecrow hanging on the right side of the ceiling's window; it was hung there by the Prison Service to keep birds away. Observing the red flooring was like stepping back to my school years. I thought back to the times when my teachers marked my wrong answers with red lines and circles; I recalled how my grades would be written in red. Use of that that colour alarmed me, even if I got a good grade.

I sat on a plastic seat in the yard and kept staring at the red ground which extended beneath my feet. I lost my train of thought at once and started having flashbacks. I thought back to the day when I was in second grade. I was a shy, well-mannered, smart and hardworking girl. My teacher asked me what I wanted to become when I grew up, to which I answered: "I want to write." I didn't understand the words I uttered at the time.

I don't recall how much of the second semester passed before the day my teacher gave me my Arabic dictation notebook. It feels like yesterday. When I got full marks three times in a row, my teacher rewarded me with two stickers: a red one which I stuck on my forehead and a green one which I stuck in my notebook. She asked my classmates to give me a big round of applause.

The sound of the students' applause was echoing in my head as I held my notebook firmly on my way home. My cousin saw me. Golden hair. Two braided pigtails. He stopped me and I told him that I got ten out of ten on my spelling test. He said: "Come along! I will get you a present." Off to the shop.

He held my hand tight and pulled me away from my house until we arrived at an abandoned room close to his house. He let me in and shut the door. He lit up a small flashlight which he carried with him. He took the backpack off my shoulders and slowly started to take off my clothes. One piece at a time. I was waiting. I wasn't aware of what was going on, so I cried and screamed: "I'm scared! I want my mum!" That didn't stop him. The first thing he took off were my pants. I panicked and stepped back. I whispered: "I want my mum."

He answered me coldly. My child self didn't comprehend that coldness, but I fully understand it right there and then, standing in that red-floored yard and in that prison. The room wasn't large but I kept backing away, trying to escape until I reached a corner. My pants were still half down, stuck between my legs, and I was still holding my notebook. He came closer and kneeled. His big hands were all over my small body after he took all my clothes off. I was sobbing but he was stone-cold like a wolf preying on a ewe lamb. "Don't you worry. Let's play a little then we'll go home."

He didn't leave a single part of my body untouched. While he was 'playing', I was losing myself in a world of fear, so I lost track of time and I didn't realise how much that brutal play continued. After he satisfied his animal instincts, he started to piece together what he had already broken. My notebook fell out of my hand.

I held onto my notebooks and pens tighter than ever. Now I was in this prison surrounded by many restrictions. I was only seven when my childhood was stabbed for the first time; I was unaware of it all. I was a child.

He composed himself. Clothes back on. Backpack on my shoulders. Dictation notebook in my hand. He held a knife against my tongue; with his eyes wide open, he stared at my face and said: "Don't you dare tell anyone about this or else! I'll cut your tongue and kill you."

He opened the door and looked around; he explored the place carefully. He held me in his arms and started tickling me as if nothing had happened.

That memory sent shivers down my spine. I quickly looked at the prisoners around me then up at the chained sky. I talked to myself and screamed: "I'm not that kid any more!" yet I kept those screams to myself. I stopped my memories from bleeding as if applying a tourniquet to my bleeding soul. I went back inside to explore the place further.

Four washing lines made from strings as well as two plastic ones were strung up on the right side of the yard. On the left side, there was a small room which was divided into two sections: the first was designed for a washer and a dryer while the second was a mini kitchen. There was another room right next to that one but separated from it by a wall; it was designed for the administration.

The more I mused on the colour of the blue metal doors in front of me, the more I remembered the chained sky scene which could be viewed from the yard. The strange part was that I had never experienced such feelings before arriving at this prison despite the fact that I had seen the same colours during my first stage of imprisonment, whether in al Jalameh or other cells. My emotions seemed to be completely different.

Yard time ended at 1pm; doors closed again and we all went back to our cells. I was deeply attached to my bed because it seemed to be my own property in this cell. I didn't have to share my bed with anybody, as opposed to everything else. Even our breathing was shared; everyone could hear the intake of breath and breathing out of the other cell-mates. I also breathed in my fellow prisoners' particles. The 'barsh[10]' served as an office, a seat, a table; it was where I read, sat, wrote and slept. I sometimes even ate and drank while sitting on it.

Waiting became an obligation in this prison: everything was timed; every move counted. One couldn't do anything without the involvement of the rest; it all depended on them. Our freedom was confined by a smothering metal door. We moved within a very limited space; each one of us used her bed as her own space to maintain the rhythm of her life: sleeping, sitting, reading, writing, sewing and embroidering.

Everything in this prison was about waiting, even using the toilet; I had to wait my turn for that. Turns had to be agreed on by all the cellmates.

The ward was just like a small village which represented the Palestinian society with all its social spectrums, blocs, organisations, traditions and accents. Despite all the differences and social tendencies, it functioned as a whole. The cells could be seen as the houses in this small village; the political prisoners were family.

We performed our prayers in congregation and we prepared and had all three meals collectively. We would take turns to do cleaning, de-cluttering and organisational tasks.

On a tiny empty spot between the cabinets and the beds, a piece of paper was hung; it was a weekly schedule which divided tasks and duties between the cellmates. One of my cellmates took it down and added my name to the list, and after consulting the rest, we agreed that this day would be my turn to clean up the cell. My turn would be on Thursdays. The paper was pinned up.

At 2.30pm the doors open again. It was our second yard period in the afternoon; it lasted until 5pm. During this time, many seminars, social gatherings and recreational activities took place.

5.30pm

All the rituals performed by the political prisoners suddenly came to a stop. The first one turned off the TV; the second one left the bathroom in a rush; the third one put away the canvas she was embroidering; the fourth one closed the Qur'an while the last one held her transistor radio and moved about while tuning it in until she heard some noises coming out of it. She didn't change the channel, though, 'Sawt Al Asra Broadcast' ('the voice of detainees') and left the radio in the corner where the signal was detected; she turned it all the way up. Everyone went back to their beds, including her. I was about to ask about what was happening but one of them made a silence gesture; she put her hand over her mouth. I didn't finish my question. I sat and watched what was happening.

6.05pm

The presenter's introduction started with Abu Arab's 'Hadi ya Bahar Hadi' ('Slow Down, Oh Sea, Slow Down') melodies in the background; then he announced the start of his programme: 'Ala Janah el-Teir' ('on the wings of a bird'). I learned that it was a programme to receive messages from the political prisoners' parents. Things became less ambiguous as I learned why the political prisoners showed so much interest. I listened intently to that broadcast, assuming it was an interactional news programme which addressed the political prisoners' concerns and cases, discussed their issues and presented their news with their parents. Everything was crystal-clear with the first call. My pain increased as I saw one of my cellmates crying as she heard the voice of her dad telling her: "At this moment, we are picking olives. I'm standing right under your favourite tree which you once fell off and broke your arm. Do you remember that day, love?" He paused and then continued: "Hello, daughter. How are you, daughter? I miss you, daughter. I miss the way the word 'dad' came out of your mouth." He stopped for a few seconds; she replied through tears: "I'm okay, daddy. I miss you too. I miss you so much, daddy." He let her know that he has sent her some money and some clothes with another woman political prisoner's parents because her family visits had been denied – the Israeli authorities refused to grant them a permit for security reasons. He said: "I wonder if you have received them." She was still weeping when she answered: "Thank you, daddy. Yes, I have."

He was communicating with her through that broadcast; he would ask her a question and pause for a few seconds as if he were giving her time to answer. He was talking to her as if they had a phone call; he was waiting for his daughter's voice to come through but knowing all too well that it was not happening. The call was over. She hugged her pillow and started sobbing. One call at a time, the broadcast lasted for an hour-and-a-half straight without any pauses or commercial breaks. My heart ached and my feelings were mixed. I had no idea where to get patience and endurance when all I witnessed was suffering and misery. Yet again I was shocked by the reality. No matter how much they talked and wrote about the struggle of political prisoners, nobody would ever truly understand it. Whoever lived outside those bars would never be able to fathom the depth of their feelings unless they experienced it first hand. As time passed, I learned that many political prisoners, both men and women, resorted to that programme as a way of contacting their parents to hear their voices. That was the 'phone' they were allowed to use inside the prison; the phone of this era, the era of injustice and oppression. A one-way speaker; the sound came from one direction. The other part could do nothing but listen. It never eased the longing; rather, it intensified their feelings of pain and helplessness.

A political prisoner could only contact their family merely by listening to the radio. If I had not lived through this experience, I would never have believed such things happen these days.

The whole world grew insignificant compared to this pain. This vexed question had grown within me: 'Why this brutality? Why do the Palestinian people have to endure such cruelty?' The voices I heard on the radio tore me up inside time after time, yet I was still the same resilient woman despite the deadly feelings taking over me. Around my cellmates, I kept my pride intact and maintained my appearance of steadfastness, but I secretly grieved and got lost in a harsh, loud, obsessive, strange and mad world. I lived with the rest of my cellmates and with every passing day I grew. However, I didn't grow physically like a baby would. I grew sadder and more wounded.

Day after day passed, I was still in ward 2 in Sharon Prison and given complete freedom to explore it, immerse myself as I wished and learn about its rules bit by bit. No discussions regarding parties or factions took place. We didn't bring up our accusations; we didn't have the right to ask one another as to why we were arrested or discuss the details concerning our cases except with Lina. It was only a matter of time before I found out that such rules could easily be broken. Secrets could easily be revealed in prison.

I would wait for late-night hours and the calm that pervaded throughout the cell and the entire ward after the detainees went to bed. I would live inside my head; I would write and read and I would let my imagination break free of all the chains, locks and doors. I let it run wild. On the floor, back against the huge blue door, I would sit so as to make the best out of the tiny spot of light which shone in from the wardens' room and travelled through the door holes. My journey with words as well as the joy of discovering the true meanings of freedom among all the chains would begin. That was the right time to write poetry and read with love and a mindfulness I had never experienced before.

In no time, I was able to gain the women political prisoners' love and respect. Moreover, I was able to bond with them in less than a week. Since I was fluent in Hebrew, I started teaching it to them. I also organised creative writing workshops. In the evening, right after the second Yard Time, we would sit in a circle inside the cell and I would read some of my poems and flash prose. I would be on top of the world when one of them read aloud what she had written down about her feelings and emotions.

The 19-year-old Shorouk and I became close friends. We started talking, discussing matters, laughing, crying and feeling joyful. Shorouk was a bookworm. Every day she would come to the cell where I was and with a beautiful smile on her face she'd say: "Dareen, Dareen, have you written something new? Please read it out to me, please. I would love to hear you reading."

During Yard Time, I would start reciting the poetry I'd composed; she would be so moved. She would always express that by smiling or, spontaneously, clapping for me. Sometimes, she would say a word or two:

"So beautiful," "Amazing," while sometimes I could tell by her tears. At the same time, I told her: "Shorouk, write. Write down everything you feel or experience."

The next day, she rushed towards me, exhilarated, and in her hand she was holding a pen and a notebook. She told me: "Dareen, I wrote something and I would love to know what you think about it. I wrote something and I want to read it to you."

Indescribable happiness surged inside me; I hadn't expected her to actually write or to take my words seriously. I read what she'd written. To me, her writing, despite its simplicity and spontaneity, was wonderful. She simply talked about what she had been feeling. Later, we sat down, talked and corrected her grammatical errors. Her first piece emerged from the darkness of the prison. It overflowed with creativity, feelings and questions. She had never written anything before; it had never even crossed her mind, yet she did. On that day, she recited another flash prose piece about her pain feelings in prison, her injury and occupation. From that day on, Shorouk wrote a lot.

Shorouk loved drawing as well, even though she didn't really master it. Whenever she drew something, I would laugh hard. What bothered her most were gossiping and noise, but what made her happiest was eating Loacker wafer. Whenever I ate a piece, she would run in my direction carrying another. She would force-feed me. I would tell her that I didn't like it but she would reply jokingly: "This wafer is the taste of life in this prison. You'll be missing out on a big part of the meaning of life in this prison." Then we let out a laugh. And whenever I told her I was vegetarian, she would laugh even harder and tell me in her Palestinian Jerusalemite accent: "I wish I could understand what being vegetarian means. How's that working out for you here in this prison? As if we had so many options."

Shorouk loved doing impressions and acting as well. A settler shot her in the area between her shoulder and chest. It happened when she slapped him with her bag so he would leave her alone and not take off her hijab. She was arrested and was waiting for a verdict; she could be sentenced to sixteen years in prison. One day, I asked Shorouk if I could see the injured area and she, right away, uncovered it and placed my hand on the scar that bullet left after it went through her body. At the moment I touched her

84

shoulder I wished I could take away all her pain, along with the painful memories, and offer her everything she loved instead. Together, we read Ghassan Kanafani's 'Men in the Sun' and discussed its plot.

Shorouk was vibrant and skilled; she could write, challenge, live, be hopeful, she had faith and morals. Shorouk had it all, knowledge and creativity.

One should bear it all in prison yet there were some detainees who were injured as a result of open fire; their wounds covered various parts of their bodies and they were left without any medical follow-up or in need of treatment. It was beyond intolerable. I had that experience with Israa' in al-Jalameh. Having to witness it repeatedly stoked my anxiety. It was hard to live with the suffering and moaning of others while being unable to do anything but express the pain you felt using some words of solace. They, on the other hand, would live in pain inside and out.

One day I had some olives for breakfast and I was about to throw the seeds away. One of my cell-mates told me not to. "We don't throw olive seeds away, we keep them in this box," she said.

At that moment I realised that everything inside the prison was utilised; the ward was turned into some recycling plant. Things were born from nothing in this prison despite the simplicity and scarcity of tools: empty boxes were turned into storage boxes or presents for family and friends after being covered them with embroidery canvas; lids were turned into 'scissors' or 'knives' since both were prohibited in cells; seeds of fruits and olives were turned into beads to make necklaces, prayer beads (rosaries) or bracelets into which names were carved after washing, drying and filing both sides until a hole was made using a concrete edge. The concrete edge was at the bathroom door. In fact, it was the only area that was not tiled. As for nylon strings, they were taken out from potato bags. And when it was cold, plastic bottles were filled with hot water; caps weren't replaced until the bottles shrink. Then, women political prisoners placed the bottles inside their beds to get some warmth: the administration banned the use of heaters in cells. Being surrounded by these walls and staying among these political prisoners made me grasp the proverb: "Necessity is mother of invention."

CHAPTER 13

Once or twice a week I had to endure the exact same journey in the bosta, back and forth. Never-ending, pointless hearings, three of which I chose not to attend so I wouldn't have to go through those hours of torture. I signed some prisoner service consent paperwork. The papers stated that I willingly requested absenting myself from those hearings.

Wednesday, November 4, 2015
4am

I woke up to the sound of the warden calling out my name. She ordered me to get ready, and when I asked her for the reason she told me I had to attend a hearing immediately after the count was carried out.

An unscheduled hearing. I had no clue what the reason for that hearing would be. The document I had signed confirmed that my next hearing was to be held the week afterwards. I got ready, anyway. I waited until Lina woke up so she could enquire about what was going on and make sure of the unscheduled hearing. I also asked her to check whether I was able to absent myself from the hearing and sign a consent form. I wanted to save myself from being racked with pain in that bosta.

When Lina returned, she told me I would have to attend that hearing because the list of indictment would be announced; my attendance was required by law. I learned as well that the hearing would be held the next day. I would be taken to 'Mivar[11]' al-Jalameh and would be brought back to Sharon Prison on Sunday.

I left with the warden who turned me over to the Nahshon Unit after conducting a strip-search and shackling my hands and feet. Into the bosta. My journey began at around 6am. The bosta stopped at different stations, and three hours later we finally reached our destination where I stared into the eyes of death while I was still alive for four more hours. I was taken back to the bosta. By 8pm, I had lived seven hours in that moving tomb. Making a stop at four prisons before I reached my station where I was led into yet another bosta. I was at some prison; the shift of the unit responsible for my transfer was finished. I didn't receive any water or food throughout that journey; neither did I ask for anything, so I wouldn't need to use the bathroom. In fact, during the bosta journey, a bathroom trip would be out of the question.

Many stops. Longest journey to date. Every time I asked what time we would arrive at Sharon prison, all I got back was silence or an angry "sheket". After hours of this agonising journey that left me dead-tired, I was finally able to locate the area. I saw a sign next to where the bosta made a stop. I was in the far north of the country. We were in Qiryat Shemona settlement which was established after the destruction and depopulation of the Palestinian village, Al-Khalisa, in 1948. I was clueless as to why I was there instead of being dropped off at al-Jalameh.

It was almost 1am. The day was over and a new day had just begun. I was still in that tomb. Another shift was rotated; another bosta with another group in that unfamiliar place. I listened attentively to the discussion taking place between the two groups of the unit. They'd forgotten to drop me off at al-Jalameh. Forgotten! That was good enough reason for them to giggle. Hurting another human being was merely a joke that made their faces light up. The bosta started moving again after taking on a detainee. Two hours later, it stopped. We were at Jalbou' Prison. It was almost 5am. I was still in the bosta. They were somewhere getting rest and drinking coffee. They returned and said there would be no need for them to take me back to al-Jalameh and they would drop me off at Nazareth District courthouse itself. My hearing was at 9am. I didn't know how I could handle such news when I felt as if I was one step away from death. With my cuffs, I banged on the sides of the vehicle. They said, carelessly: "We're setting off soon." They put two more political prisoners in there. Off we went.

Thursday
7am

I arrived at Nazareth district courthouse; they dropped me off there and led me into the building. The soldier who was pulling me towards the building and her colleagues were told there were no available cells. They weren't able to put me in the cells where prisoners in criminal cases stayed. I was a 'security prisoner,' after all. They didn't know where to put me, so they led me outside the building. I asked: "What happened? Was the hearing adjourned? Are you taking me back to al-Jalameh?" The female soldier replied: "No, you will have to wait in the bosta until your hearing begins."

I yelled in her face: "What you are doing is illegal. I've been left inside the vehicle for an entire day." She didn't budge. Cage opened again. Into the bosta which was parked in a garage. Doors closed. No AC, nor air. No lights inside or outside the vehicle. No ventilation; I was suffocating. Ulcer pains were growing. A coughing fit. It was more than I could take; my body had been tortured enough. I screamed, but all my screams were unheard. Every half an hour, a soldier would check in on me. They would stand right next to me and ask: "Is everything okay?" I would answer: "Absolutely not. I'm suffocating. I need some air." They would open the door for a few minutes and say: "Here's some air. Breathe. You can breathe now," and would bang the door shut.

As usual, my hearing was late. Another five-hour wait until I was led there. As I entered the courtroom, my lawyer asked me: "Why do you look so pale?" In brief, I summed up what had happened. My lawyer wanted to tell the judge about it all, yet she stopped him, saying: "This hearing is intended for announcing the indictment list only. If there is another different or additional complaint, a special hearing should be requested. Anyway, I will let the Nahshon Unit know. They'll take care of it."

It was a ten-minute hearing during which the indictment list was read out loud. It was over. I was pulled back to the bosta, to my very special holding cell. Despite the fact that I wasn't given any food or water until that very moment, I had the urge to go to the bathroom. Not a single piece of food or drop of water had entered my body for two whole days. I called out and asked them to allow me to go to the bathroom. Nobody came. My very simple request and one of my basic rights as a human being was simply ignored. I tried to hold on a little longer until my last ounce of energy. I was just too weak, it got the best of me. I wetted myself.

The bosta set off for al-Jalameh at around 6pm. When we got there, the soldiers noticed my wet pants and started laughing at me. They hurled sarcastic words: "trash", "disgusting", "you deserve this" and "filthy". My eyes had had of defeats. The soldiers looked at me as if they were victorious. I, the one who didn't know how to put on a big smile to retaliate, was struck to hear myself singing at the top of my lungs:

In the Ansar Detention Camp	Gather the detainees
When the sun rises	It will promise the revolutionaries
You imprisoned the heroes' bodies	But failed to imprison their souls
Their souls as great as a mountain	For we can bear those wounds
The sun of liberty is within us	Who could lock it up?
The prison of an enemy	Can't shroud those suns
What could those prisons do?	When the dawn is summoning us
The prison of the enemy can't	Shroud our homelands
We're crossing to Palestine	And we remain devout to it

The way they looked and laughed at me turned to astonishment. The recruit then led me to the ward; I was handed over to the warden, yet I kept singing. Strip-searched and mocked. She enjoyed the same hobby of humiliating me as much as her comrades did – "disgusting", "stinky", "I have to search you," she said repeatedly.

I didn't tire of repeating that song until I was put back in the grey cell. Only then I stopped singing. I instantly washed my clothes and put them back on while they were still drenched. I spent the rest of the night vomiting and coughing.

I stayed in the cell until Sunday morning. I was taken on another deadly, gruelling trip back to Sharon Prison. A hellish road trip. That was one of the worst parts of being imprisoned: it was nothing but a method of humiliation used by the Prison Service to crush the patience and endurance of a detainee. The journeys seemed to be part of the punishment.

As soon as I arrived at the prison and entered ward 2, I hurried towards Lina and hugged her for quite some time; I hugged all the pain away. She was surprised and asked me why I did so, yet I didn't respond. I entered my cell to find my cell-mates had already prepared my dinner. We greeted and hugged one another. I hopped into bed and fell asleep at last.

One morning, while I was with a Nahshon Unit soldier waiting for the registration officer in the prison yard to record my departure time, I came to the entrance of the yard only to see a group of soldiers circling a child, one of the brave young detainees, who I estimated, based on his facial features and overall physical appearance, to be around twelve years of age. He was shackled with a number of chains: two handcuffs, two leg-cuffs and a chain connecting those hand and leg-cuffs through a loop in the middle. His left forearm arm was wrapped with white bandage which indicated a recent injury. The boy seemed to be weighed down by the chains. He could barely walk. Four or five steps. Pause. Take a break. Catch a breath. Repeat. However, the soldiers forced him to move forward at a quicker pace. They shouted at him using some heavily accented Arabic words which translated as: "Come on boy! Move! Faster!"

He drew nearer and nearer to where I was standing. He was only a few steps away from me when he tripped over the chains, lost balance and fell. He started crying. My body, reactively and involuntary, moved in his direction so as to help him get up from that terrible fall. The soldier held my cuffs and stopped me: "Let me help him stand up; he needs help to stand back up. Look at him, he's an injured shackled child," I told her. "He is a 'subversive' and he deserves what is happening to him. You have nothing to do with him," she replied.

For the first time since my arrest I felt oppressed. I felt oppressed enough that I actually considered acting on it by beating the recruit up. I almost did. I regained my self-control. I have no idea how I managed to gather myself and I suppressed the anger that was burning inside after seeing a child in such a condition. I have always had a weakness for children; I can't stand by and watch them suffer. At that moment, I was nothing but a helpless political prisoner. I couldn't achieve that duty of humanity. He was lying on the ground right before my eyes. I couldn't find a way to offer my help. Words were all I had. Loudly, I encouraged him with some uplifting phrases. Mental support. I hoped he'd be able to overcome that ordeal. "Stand up! You're stronger than they are. Come on, stand up! You will be just fine," I reacted out of emotion.

He looked right at me. His innocent expressions and teary eyes were smiling at me. Then he expressed his gratitude with a "thank you."

He managed to stand back up after a long struggle. Soldiers immediately started shouting at him: "Yalla walad! Lazim nroukh min hon! Yalla imshi bsura'a, makhabeel (a Hebrew word for subversive) which would translate as "Come on, boy! We have to leave this place! Walk faster, you subversive." After this he began to move away from my eyeshot. Still, his shadows haunted me, no matter where I went.

Alone in this dark trench, I groped my way. I was trying to learn how to be blind among the sighted, or maybe sighted among the blind. I failed in both attempts. I had even started to ask the world around me questions as if I were asking myself. I pleaded with my own conscience as if I were pleading with the whole existence. All human languages were inadequate to express the pain I witnessed in this spot. I felt as if I had reached the peak of human tragedy, as if I were on some mountain-top where the loudest waterfalls, scariest summits and darkest caves are.

I arrived at the courthouse and returned with nothing but the image of that boy stuck in my mind. Late at night, I re-entered Sharon Prison: ward 2, prison cell 7. The deep sea within me was raging and I got carried away. I started to ask myself whether I would taste more intense humiliation or that greater humiliation would feast on me.

CHAPTER 14

Two weeks passed by since I first arrived at Sharon Prison; I was used to its harsh environment. I prepared a daily schedule to benefit myself and my cell-mates and make the most of our time. And just like the rest of the political prisoners, I became a part of that ward.

Monday
9am

Lina showed up at the cell door and announced the names of the female political prisoners who had family visits. Surprisingly, my name was on the list. However, three of my cell-mates didn't get the chance to have visits, for security reasons, according to the prison administration. For that reason, I tried not to get too excited about my family visit. We congratulated one another as if it had been some celebration. Those whose visits were denied couldn't hide their feelings – their facial expressions said so much. It was yet another tale of a new struggle and grief. This was the day I came on a new type of art: it was the political prisoners' art of burying their pain and resorting to imagination. They would live in the hope that family visit permits would be granted by the administration. Those emotions were too painful; I felt as if there had been a dagger stuck in me. That art had to be mastered by each one of us.

The Yard Time turned into a wedding-like scene: it was filled with laughter, delight and the political prisoners' spontaneous ululation and hails. On hearing the news of their family visits, each one of those women political prisoners picked out her best outfit and scarf. Many exchanged clothing items, they mixed and matched colours to get the perfect look. Some wore lipstick and eye kajal to look charming, elegant and composed for their families. Those who were denied visits glanced at each other, cried, or comforted themselves by praying, reading the Qur'an.

Up until that morning, I had been looking forward to my family visit, yet my perspective changed as I watched those three political prisoners. My heart went out to them. Neither silence nor speech would suffice. I started my journey of introspection. Reality and memories began to get blurred bit by bit. I needed some silence to make sense of my deep-rooted pain and to live in the present moment while trying to reconcile myself to what was going on. Only then, I thought, might I be able to put it into words.

12pm

The political prisoners lined up behind Lina, who was accompanied by a warden, right in front of the wardens' room. There were two more wardens to help complete the task. One by one, we were allowed into the room. It was my turn. I entered the wardens' room then into the bathroom; I had to cross the checkpoint which meant that I had to be searched with a security wand then be strip-searched. Right after that, I was shackled by the warden. Every one of the political prisoners had to go through the same process.

We had to walk in long hallways and narrow corridors which resembled prison cells as they were surrounded by high walls on each side. Some had ceilings. Between one hallway and the other, there was a gate where we had to wait for a few minutes until it was opened. It took me 15 minutes to reach a small building. During that journey, I peeked at the wide-open sky and the blueness of it that I missed so much. Once we reached the building our wrists were unshackled. With shackled ankles, we entered the parloir (prison visiting room). The officer standing at the door announced the beginning of the visit.

From where I was standing, the room looked rectangular. It was hallway-like with huge aluminum-framed glass windows on the side; each of the blue aluminum frames (glass partitions) represented a booth designated for one woman political prisoner to meet her family. Leg-cuffed, I sat on a plastic chair right in front of a glass window with a narrow stool. A very old black telephone with a beige base was hung on one side of the window. From the opposite direction, families rushed in, scanning the room and looking for their daughters. Each wanted to sit in front of their daughter, yet they would greet whoever they passed. In came my brother. I waved at him, he saw me and sat facing me.

I picked up the telephone in my booth and made a gesture so he would pick up his too. The audio quality was awful, it wasn't clear at all. It cracked and broke up, so I tried the other speaker. It was still bad yet a bit better than the previous one. I was certain that all of the phone calls were censored and recorded, so I jokingly smiled and told him: "It's like we are holding a phone call for real. We're talking but we don't know who is listening." My brother just smiled at me and nodded. I asked him how he was treated when he came to visit me, so he told me that they bombarded him with questions, very personal ones, about me. He also told me about all the scenes of humiliation he had witnessed prisoners' families had to go through because of the prison administration. It was unbearably painful for him to witness such humiliation of women, especially at the prison entrance. He, too, had to wait for more than two-and-a-half hours in an open yard where there were no seats or even a ceiling that would protect those families from heat, rain or hail. I asked him if he was treated differently compared to those who had come all the way from the West Bank, yet he said: "We're all Palestinians. I had to go through the same exact process. Whatever they had to go though, I also did." We mainly talked about family matters, the prison, how I spent my time, life among other inmates. From time to time, I would wander, pause and observe the rest of the political prisoners.

"Dareen, this is my daughter. The one whose picture I showed you. Come here. You can meet her in the flesh," the woman political prisoner who sat next to me called. I looked at her seven-year-old daughter's face. I waved and smiled at her and I blew her a kiss from behind the glass, and she did likewise. Looking around me, I glanced at families and women political prisoners, one at a time. I could recognise one political prisoner's family from a poetry reading evening I'd attended, where I'd taken photographs of them. Those pictured were saved on my computer, the one which was confiscated by the police. I hugged that political prisoner and in that moment I realised who she was. Her parents recognised me instantly. I grabbed the phone and talked to them. They were astonished that their daughter and I were together behind that glass; they said: "You're also here, in prison?" I returned to my visiting booth, just next to the political prisoner who was talking to her daughter and mother. Her husband's visits were denied by the prison administration on security grounds. Her daughter started to cry her heart out. Still weeping bitterly, she screamed repeatedly: "I want my mum!" She went towards the officer in charge of the visits and pleaded with him to grant her a few moments to hug her mum. He brushed her off. The glass was sound-proof, but I heard her cries through the phone that my brother held. Her cries pierced my soul; I wept along with her as well as her mother. I wept in silence.

I watched another political prisoner talking to her mother through the telephone while being separated by the glass partition; they could only see each other. Untouchables. No hugs. No kisses. My eyes lingered on that scene which captured my mind and heart. Deprived of family visits since her arrest, that woman placed her hands on the cold glass window; they longed for a touch. They kissed each other but were separated by that glass window. In that booth and from behind that glass window, everything had a different taste to it: meeting, yearning, kissing. Two forces attracted each other but in opposite directions.

Forty-five minutes passed. The whistle was blown announcing the end of visiting time. They said goodbye to one another. Wrists re-shackled. Led outside that soul-draining booth. I vividly imagined a love epic of lovers travelling to a wishful place: an open window through which they might get a kiss, a touch or a hug.

Yearning was the political prisoner's worst enemy; their oppressor which drained them of their steadfastness. In spite of this, those political prisoners' capability to hide their pain remained, along with their determination and resilience. It's true that I endured pitched battles with this bitter enemy of mine since I had my heart set on writing with my pen more than meeting my family. Longing for different things didn't really matter since it all led to the same result in the end – silencing our agony and attempting to paralyse our thoughts while walking patiently along the prison corridors.

It had been two months since I was arrested and one month since I joined the political prisoners in Sharon Prison. I became a vital part of the prison. My relationship with the political prisoners there grew stronger as we bonded more with each passing day. Their trust, amity and respect increased and became our motto. During Yard Time, we had many political and social discussions; we also discussed what the society deemed as taboos. Initially, I struggled with criticism and rejection even from the educated and the cultured ones. That did not hinder me, though. I kept discussing those ideas time after time to the extent that the vast majority of them became more open to and accepting of my mindset. I did everything within my power to contribute to their advancement.

Each day, they'd ask me about what I had written recently. One of them would ask me to write a letter to her son for her, so she could send it to him through the Red Crescent representative. Another would ask me to write a love poem to express her yearning for her fiancé after telling me about their love story. I would respond to their request without hesitation; my emotions and theirs became one. I would write for them as if I had been writing about myself and giving voice to my own emotions. With time, I supervised creative writing workshops which were satisfying and, above all, successful. I struggled when I realised there were some women I couldn't come in terms with by giving advice or by lending a hand. I came to realise that some of their reactions should not be interrupted, including crying, collapsing or having suicidal thoughts. Some psychosocial mindsets struck me as peculiar. Sometimes, some of the inmates' outlooks seemed illogical, anomalous and beyond belief. At first, I assumed they were pretending, diminishing, falling down or exaggerating, yet I remained silent and accepted the drastic differences of opinion and perspectives. As a matter of fact, I enjoyed watching and observing them in various circumstances. They shaped a whole new culture of steadfastness and resistance in this prison which I would never experience myself.

After adapting to this lifestyle, I marvelled at my ability to smile, sacrifice, tolerate, ignore, embrace, empathise and comprehend. I was surprised that I was a brand new person. Things went on unchanged in prison: routines, emotions, scenes and incidents. An endless cycle. The only change was the number of inmates, which was on the rise. Crowded cells. No more empty beds. Mattresses were placed on the floor to accommodate the rest of the political prisoners which reached up to forty-three while the capacity was thirty-eight. Five more were either at some hospital or detainee centre and they had to be brought together with political prisoners.

It wasn't Yard Time yet. Doors opened at once. Lina asked us to go to the 'classroom' where she broke the news of the latest Prison Service's decision to transfer some of us to Damoun Prison due to overcrowding and the rise in the rate of Palestinian women's detention and imprisonment. The Prison Service administration and the Israel Securities Authority had decided to re-open Damoun Prison after having shut it right after 'Wafa al-Ahrar' agreement, which was signed in exchange of the release of the soldier 'Shalit'. The agreement stipulated separating unsentenced detainees from sentenced ones. Lina announced that the transfer would take place the next morning; transfer would be done in two installments.

Startled by the news, it dawned on me how everything was temporary, especially in prison. I had flashbacks of the things to which I'd grown accustomed, such as the relationships which I had assumed would last throughout my arrest period but were about to change. I realised that nothing is permanent and seeking stability in prison is impossible. I also learned that I needed to practise embracing the impermanence of places and people as well as the things I had learned at any given moment.

I recalled at once a well-known saying by Moshe Dayan which I'd read in a book on the history of Palestinian political prisoners: "Exhaust prisoners by ceaseless transfer." He was the one who devised that abusive transfer policy. Political prisoners' sense of stability in prison would turn into a motivation for creativity and innovation. Stability would lay a good base for setting up a mini society from which light could emerge amid the darkness of prison. Ensuring our constant drain and burnout was the core of the policy deployed in Israeli prisons against political prisoners; that state would completely use us up, mentally and emotionally, leading to constant anxiety. Persistent transfer was the means to that end. Stability was deemed dangerous, according to the Israeli prison convention: it must be ended straightaway. The most effective tool to achieve that would be unscheduled and unforeseen transference.

After unfolding a paper, Lina read the first installment list of names; mine was at the top of the list. She gave us enough time to answer all the questions we had. I was one of those political prisoners who had so many simple yet detailed questions. I don't know why I asked so many questions; it was the curiosity which took over my emotions and thoughts.

A few moments later, I was silent, so Lina asked: "Who would like to take on the tasks of a spokesperson of the detainees in Damoun Prison?" No response. She asked me: "Dareen, would you like to be in charge of this responsibility?"

Despite the fact that I was utterly surprised by that suggestion, as I was new and inexperienced, I couldn't refuse. I said: "If everybody approves, I will have absolutely no problem with that." The ultimate surprise was when they all agreed; none of them objected.

CHAPTER 15

That Monday was supposed to be a family visit day, yet it turned into a day of sorrow and parting. The warden distributed black duffle bags in which we packed our possessions, including pillows and blankets, in a sombre atmosphere. We said goodbye to one another and parted ways; it was tough and harsh especially for those who grew on one another and became best friends after spending months living together. The transfer took place before Yard Time; the administration refused to open the cell doors to allows us to hug and say goodbye. From behind the blue doors and through the tiny windows, it was our last goodbye. Some of them sobbed for leaving their best friends behind while others refused to look, as saying goodbye was too painful for them. Instead, they covered themselves and buried their heads in their pillows while hurting and drowning in tears.

We left the ward. Shackled. The 'first installment' was how the Prison Service referred to us. Hand and leg-cuffed, we walked along carrying our big heavy bags. We were walking towards the unknown, which we were to experience in the corridors of a new prison.

A three-hour, arduous journey on the bosta. Luckily enough, it was a non-stop transfer from Sharon Prison to Damoun Prison[12] in Haifa. We were all in the same boat. Together, we went through the same struggle and details in that Ford vehicle; it had the exact same interior design and measurements. The significant difference between the Ford bosta and the previous ones was that the window holes were a bit larger – they were large enough for us to be able to look outside and see the road ahead.

Every now and then, I would look outside the window holes, read the signs and let the political prisoners who shared the same cage with me know where we were. I would tell them the names of the cities we were passing through. It was as if I had been in some history or geography class. Eagerly, they would look outside the window, and with every name I uttered they would ask me bitterly: "Are we going to see the Wall? Are we going to cross a checkpoint? Are we going to stop at a crossing?" and they would give rueful laughs. I didn't reply to those questions since they already knew the answers. They simply used those rhetorical questions as a compass-point to the origin of the historical injustice we'd experienced and its tragic proportions.

That continued until we reached Haifa borders where Mount Carmel and the sea were in view. I told them all that they could see the sea from there. I was overwhelmed when I realised a yet more appalling tragedy which left its mark on me: right at that moment, inside the cage and through those holes, was their first time of seeing the sea. Ever. I saw their eyes sparkling with eagerness. I could sense their emotions. I could feel the desperate longing in their hearts. That hurtful truth hadn't dawned on me until that moment, although I already knew of it. With my chains, I banged on the cage walls and loudly told the others to look outside the window and contemplate the sea view.

A whole generation of Palestinians didn't know what a home was and what borders were without the Separation Wall. That generation wasn't aware of what it would be like for streets to exist without checkpoints or how moving from one city to another wouldn't require passing through a border. A whole generation didn't know what the sea looked like despite reading about it in geography books which state that Palestine is surrounded by the shores of the Mediterranean Sea, the Red Sea and the Dead Sea; the books also mentioned that the Lake of Tabariyyah is located in Palestine.

The vehicle stopped and the cage door was opened. One political prisoner at a time, we disembarked while carrying our bags. One of the officers opened a cell door adjacent to the vehicle's parking slot. After the recruit unshackled our wrists and ankles, we went in. Door closed.

It was an abandoned, very old cell; it seemed like it hadn't been used for a long time. It was very dirty as well. The bathroom consisted of nothing but a hole in the ground; it was in one of the corners. I walked around and explored each inch of that cell. It was divided into two more cells. There, I noticed a red information sign hung on one the walls. It was written in Hebrew and it translated as "The building is under restoration. Shut down in 2010."

It had been two hours, and there we were, in the very same cell. Close to the blue door, I stood still and watched the outside world go by through the tiny fenced window. Two wardens arrived. One of them tried to unlock the door, yet it didn't work, so the second one gave it a try. She, too, failed. The lock hadn't been used in ages. It was obvious. The two wardens called on a male warden to lend a hand; he came and tried to unlock it. At first, the lock eluded him, but within a few minutes of constant pulling and pressing, he managed to get it unlocked. It took them fifteen minutes to unlock the door. In order to avoid facing the same problem in the future, the male warden sprayed it with some substance.

I took on translating from Hebrew into Arabic to help the political prisoners understand; each warden would call for one of them and demand that she accompany her to another cell. They would bring their bags along with them. It was time for strip-searching and inventorying. The list of items would later be given to the Prison Administration.

In a small cell, the warden started to strip-search me following the usual pattern. Later on, she demanded that I open my bag and remove every item. Meanwhile, she took out a pen and a piece of paper from her pocket. She listed my possessions. She piled up the similar clothing items together and classified them; she counted them and jotted the number down: shirts, pants, pens, notebooks, underwear items, pairs of socks, the pillow, the blanket and my watch.

The process wasn't any different from the inventory of goods in stock conducted before presenting them to tax authorities at the end of a fiscal year. Inventorying my possessions didn't take longer than fifteen minutes. It was the fastest compared to the five other political prisoners since I carried nothing but some clothing items which Lina gave me when I was at Sharon Prison. Four consecutive hours of inventorying. Whoever completed that step would go back to the cell and wait for the rest.

And then it was time for our information to be recorded so as to officially finalise our transfer process from Sharon to Damoun Prison. Afterwards, we walked through an entrance where we had to step through a body scanner after which we had to go to another building. One by one, we were required to enter a room and talk to a prison officer. There was a consensus that we didn't want to meet him individually in his office. The administration, though, insisted on holding those face-to-face individual conversations. The political prisoners asked me to discuss this issue with the officer on their behalf. After a lengthy discussion, I managed to find a solution to end the conflict. After I proposed my solution to them and got their approval, I proposed it to the officer. I suggested that I go in with each political prisoner and witness the discussion. Rejected. And, in return, we also rejected carrying out any further discussion or yielding to them. We were strong-willed. Our determination eventually prevailed even after we had a long wait which lasted for more than one hour. While we were waiting for the administration's response, we agreed to keep our answers abbreviated to cut the conversation short. Besides, we agreed not to discuss any personal details or any information regarding this group. We agreed on an eye gesture as a warning against answering a question. I alerted them to the presence of an officer from Sharon Prison in that room together with two more from Damoun; I told them what his name was as well.

Although I had never aspired to lead a group, i.e. to be in control of the 'steering wheel' of the group, there I was accepting that task, playing and enjoying the role of a leader under the conditions imposed on me, forcing my lifestyle and emotions to change. That role motivated me to put in more efforts and sacrifice for the sake of helping the others; offering the political prisoners' services and alleviating the suffering that came with their imprisonment. I hadn't expected to succeed in that task; I surprised myself by being capable of accomplishing it from the outset. I passed that humble first test.

We were asked to move forward in the direction of the second, and last, station so as to reach the new ward, the one intended for us. Two female wardens took the lead. We walked behind them but were followed by two more male wardens. We walked in a narrow corridor which was between prison administration offices on one side and a number of blue gates on the other. After pressing a button, the gates opened automatically. We were dragging our bags behind us with our hands and chains with our feet until one political prisoner became exhausted and stopped. She was carrying two over-packed bags, so she couldn't bear it any more, especially with those shackles and the weight of the two bags she was carrying along. Besides, the corridor was too narrow and tough to walk down. I helped her to pull one of her bags. Surprisingly enough, one of the two male wardens came closer and carried the other one. We thanked him for his gesture. We moved ahead.

The blue gate opened when it almost struck 11pm. We walked through that gate until we reached a large, high-walled yard with concrete flooring. Above us there was the sky. Free, unchained and unfenced. It was bitterly cold there. After taking a few steps, I noticed an open light-brown wooden door through which I could see a man wearing a military uniform sitting at his wooden desk. Up ahead, two blue cell doors caught my eye. And right before me there was a white window through which I could see the head of a male warden whose eyes were on us. In the centre of the yard, there was a small square building with three concrete stairs and a white aluminum door next to which there was a brand new white fridge; it was still wrapped.

A few minutes passed, the wardens unshackled us. The man left his room and came towards us. He stopped at his room's entrance. "I am this ward's administrator. This is your new ward in this prison," he confidently and proudly announced.

Lowering his tone of voice, he told us what his full name was. The sound of his voice suggested how proud of his rank he was; he seemed to be proud of his rank more than he was of his own name. He began explaining a list of rules and clarifying some primary points as we were "new inmates" in the ward. He drew a distinction between what was allowed and what was prohibited, stressing that Sharon Prison was different from Damoun. He started asking some questions of each detainee; he was anticipating some specific answers to his questions. They simply pointed to me and explained that I would be the mediator and their spokesperson. He didn't look convinced but didn't really get into it. "We'll discuss this later," he said then demanded that I go into his office to put our heads together and figure out how tidying and cleaning up the rooms should take place as well as how female political prisoners were to be distributed.

I went along with him and had a long conversation on many topics concerning us, the political prisoners. At the top of the list was providing the basic requirements in our cell, including an electric stove and kettle. He rejected my request and, as usual, his excuse was "orders" which prohibited granting such a request. He said that getting those items would require the approval of the Prison Administrator; the process would be lengthy too. I was scared that if I accepted what he said, then I would never be able to get the items in, so I didn't take no for an answer. I insisted on my request:

"We won't get into our cells unless we have those items which are of great importance to us," I said sternly. He picked up the phone and explained the matter. After his phone call was over, he said: "The administrator approved your request to bring in those items but only if that would be at your own expense." I answered: "No problem. I have enough money to cover those expenses in my personal canteen account. I will buy the same items for the two cells and will pay for them."

He didn't expect my response or the instant solution I'd offered. My suggestion was bad news; his face said it all. He pressed some keys on his keyboard searching for my name and he wrote down the number of my canteen account. "While you're cleaning and tidying the cells up, I will be getting you the stuff you need," he said. I added sugar, tea and coffee to the list. Through a walkie-talkie, he ordered the warden to provide us with the necessary cleaning supplies. He demanded that another male warden bring six mattresses as well as a number of blankets. I left and told the political prisoners about what we had discussed and agreed on.

Night colours took over. Darkness fell and overshadowed the yard. From the top plates, spotlight rays gleamed and spread over the yard. Light poured into it from all directions. On a narrow edge sat three political prisoners while two more were standing close to them. Eyes gazed up at the sky. At first sight, they seemed like they had been watching some action movie in the cinema. Slowly, I approached them. I was trying to put a finger on it. What were they watching at those moments? What caught their attention? Closer and closer, I approached them until I stood right beside them. I looked up in the same direction only to find out who the protagonist was: the moon.

None of us had even caught a glimpse of moonlight since her arrest. The longest period of arrest was a year and nine months, and the least was two months – that was mine.

Captivating and magical. Waxing crescent. And behold. I contemplated its tiniest details and I sensed its glowing halo. It looked more beautiful than ever; it seemed like I saw it for the first time and discovered its existence in this universe. It was different scenery indeed. The moon didn't resemble the one I observed the night before my arrest as I was taking pictures of it. I wished I had my camera to capture that moment for others to see. Then the outside world would see the real moon through the eyes of the political prisoners and how it made them feel.

In front of us, we saw two male wardens carrying our mattresses. They interrupted us while we were watching that one-of-a-kind movie. The female warden followed them and gave us our cleaning supplies. We probably would not get another chance to be out in the yard at that hour and enjoy watching the moon. Yard Time ended at five in the afternoon. Each in her own way said goodbye to the moon and went about our other chores in the prison after I told them what the conversation between the officer and I revolved around. They were completely satisfied with my position.

We began to divide the cleaning chores. At that time, that ward turned into our own new and sole refuge in that gloomy prison. The first cell was small and contained four double-storey metal bunk beds; they were painted light brown. In one of the cell's corners, there were a sink and a square shaped ceramic piece so as to place kitchen utensils as well as eight new metal wall mounted cabinets. A modern TV was hung on one of the walls. There was a toilet; it had a metal door which could be fully closed. The second cell was almost identical except that it was larger and contained nine two-storey bunk beds. All in all, the ward would accommodate twenty-six people.

Shower rooms were shared as they were built outside the ward in a building in the yard: that was the square-shaped building at the centre of the yard. There were four shower faucets; the area was divided into squares where each was intended for one faucet. Curtains separated each square from the other. The showering system wasn't the same as in Sharon Prison. In Damoun Prison it took place during Yard Time specifically.

Our days in that new prison were passing by. With the increase in the rate of women's arrests, the second installment of the political prisoner transfer from Sharon Prison as well as bringing detainees from detention centres or hospitals into the Damoun Prison, the ward was full. We were twenty-three political prisoners in total; in the small cell, there were seven, so the eighth bed wasn't occupied. We used it as a shelf on which we placed the things which we bought from the canteen. Similarly, there was one empty bed which was used for the same purpose in the other cell, as there were seventeen inmates.

Same rituals. Ward 16 in Damoun Prison wasn't different from ward 2 in Sharon Prison; the details and rules were the same. Our suffering didn't change at all, either. Being occupied with arranging the female political prisoners' matters and following up with the administration on requirements took a lot of my time during the daytime. I would spend my night-time in solitude with my pen, papers and poetry. One day, while I was sitting on my bed and embroidering a piece of cloth, which I obtained from Lina along with some threads, the prison administrator suddenly opened the cell door. He said he was on a routine inspection tour. I put away everything I held in my hands to see what was about to happen. He looked instantly at the embroidery piece and yelled: "What is it that you're doing?" to which I replied: "I'm just embroidering." Shocked, he asked: "What is that? What is it that I'm looking at?"

Smiling as I noticed his reaction and anxious facial expressions, I held the piece of cloth, and indifferent to his screams, I pointed to it and said: "This is the map of Palestine embroidered with the colours of the Palestinian flag, while this is an olive tree." "This is incitement against the state of Israel! This is a threat to its security!" he thundered.

As he said those words, I couldn't help but laugh. I looked around at my cell-mates who exchanged sardonic looks and laughed to themselves. He demanded that I bring along that piece of cloth and go with him to hold a disciplinary hearing in his office so as to record my violation and 'punish' me for breaking the prison rules.

I went along with him but couldn't keep from laughing and smiling. Into his office we went. He sat on his chair while I sat facing him. He began to talk: "This time, I will only give you a verbal reprimand and take away that piece of cloth from you. The flag of Palestine is an incitement against the country's security. You are not allowed to draw it in any manner." As I was laughing, I asked sarcastically: "What about the olive tree?"

He seemed perplexed. No answer. He walked a couple of steps and took out a pair of scissors from his cabinet. Back to his seat. Embroidery cloth cut. The olive tree was separated from the map of Palestine. He kept the piece with the embroidered map of Palestine using the colours of the

106

Palestinian flag. Hearing was over. I left his room and went back to the cell. My cell-mates were waiting impatiently for me to know what had happened. As soon as I stepped foot into the cell, I held the cut piece of embroidered cloth up high and showed it to them. They all broke out in laughter; it could never be put into words. Their laughter probably echoed all over the prison and in every corner there. Had there been a laughter measurement scale, ours would have been the strongest in human history.

CHAPTER 16

Tuesday, December 22
6pm

I was about to climb down my bed to fetch something from my wardrobe. The corner of my top bed formed an angle with another, so it was impossible to use the bed ladder to climb up or down. Time and time again, I filed complaints about it to the administration so as to find a solution. They would tell me that switching ladder sides wouldn't be easy and it would be time-consuming as it required dismantling the built-in bunk beds. The solution I suggested was less complicated than what the administration made us believe it to be; my suggestion was simpler than the difficulties and impossible scenarios they had told us about. I pitched an idea: bring a new ladder and fix it on the opposite side of the bunk bed; nothing else would be required. The ward's administrator couldn't bear the idea of my outsmarting him or my ability to offer solutions. It showed on his face as he was responding furiously to my clear-cut solution, saying: "I took note of your complaint. We'll solve the problem when the time is appropriate." Two weeks had gone by and I kept following up on the process, yet every time I received the same response: "Your complaint is still in process. The problem will be solved soon." In fact, it would only take them ten minutes to fix the new ladder to the bunk bed.

The problem remained unresolved, so I had to use a circular plastic table to help me reach my bed or descend from it. It was just like climbing a trunk-less tree. Then came the moment my right-foot toes touched the table, I slipped, lost my balance and tumbled down the table. I felt shooting pains in every inch of my body. Splintered ankle. I couldn't move at all. Shocked and worried, my cell-mates gathered around me; two of them helped me stand up and sit on the closest bed.

My foot hurt so badly; I felt as if it had been detached from the rest of my body. A spot on my ankle turned dark blue. My toes turned blue too. And in a split second my foot had swollen up like a balloon. With every breath I took, and with every passing minute, bit by bit, it got bigger and bigger. At every moment, I imagined that it would blow up; the pain was extreme. All the symptoms indicated that I had a broken ankle.

Through the vision panel, one of my cell-mates called the warden. When she arrived, my cell-mate talked to her in Hebrew and told her that I had to be taken to hospital to receive the necessary treatment. The warden, in turn, told her she would tell the ward's administrator immediately, the doctor as well as the nurse. After ten minutes, the warden returned; she said she had let them know and they would come to assess the situation and do what was necessary.

It took two-and-a-half hours for the door to be opened, at last. Four people came in: two officers, a nurse and a female warden. "What happened?" one of the officers asked me, so I explained the accident to him in detail. "Are you sure you haven't been beaten up by one of your cell-mates?" I was about to explode. How silly! I had just explained to him what had happened and from where I fell. The pain was getting worse and I had no energy to discuss or even listen to his nonsense. I simply told him: "I told you that I fell down." The second officer asked the paramedic: "How bad is her case?" The nurse approached me and looked at my foot before he said: "There's nothing to worry about. It's not serious. I will bring some medication from the prison infirmary." Enraged, I told him: "My leg is broken. I can feel it. What kind of medication are you talking about? I need to go to be hospitalised and get an x-ray."

He took another look at my leg and said: "Twitch your toes." I replied: "I can't even place my finger on my foot and you're asking me to move the toes of my injured foot! I can't do that. I'm in so much pain!" He said: "Don't worry. I'll get you the necessary treatment." They conducted the Count and left the cell.

Another hour passed. Distressed, I was still waiting around for the nurse's magical solution that would heal the intensifying pains of my broken foot. He came and gave me his advice and instructions through the vision panel after he handed his proposed medical treatment for my foot over to one of my cell-mates, and said: "Place it on your foot. You'll be just fine by tomorrow morning." My cell-mate handed over that magical treatment the paramedic had talked. At that moment, it was in my own

109

hands. A rectangular blue ice mould and a painkiller, a white Voltaren tablet.

Five political prisoners were in need of medical follow-up care as they were wounded after being shot. I was the sixth on the list, yet one thing was different about my case: it was urgent. I would only get my treatment by being hospitalised, getting an x-ray, and a cast for my fracture.

Any move I made would cause me intolerable aches and pains and would increase my suffering. That was a rough night. I couldn't stretch out my leg in front of me while I was lying on bed; I couldn't even put my foot on the floor. Whatever came into contact with it would intensify the pain. I did my utmost to elevate it and fix it up in the air with both my hands; the searing pains tore me up inside. It was 1am. All my cell-mates were fast asleep. Too silent. It was terribly cold outside which heightened my suffering. Utter silence. I could hear nothing but my echoing aches and pains. The warden walked by the cell door. She shone her flashlight on me and said: "Why aren't you asleep yet?"

It was the same warden, and she knew what had occurred all too well. In spite of this, I answered her question so that she would stop talking and my cell-mates wouldn't be disturbed. "Extreme pain is keeping me from falling asleep," I said. "Do as the paramedic told you and you will fall asleep," she said back. With dismay, I shook my head. A few seconds later she left and she wasn't in sight until the Count was conducted at dawn.

Despite the fact that my cell-mates did their best to help me out, I wasn't able to stand up as I was expected to during the Count. I could barely balance myself on one leg while standing right next to my bed. The officer asked me why I didn't do so, and again I explained to him what I had been through; I reiterated my urgent need to get hospitalised and receive the necessary treatment. He replied sternly: "The paramedic said that there would be no need for that. End of discussion. Only he or the doctor is responsible for medical follow-ups."

Humanity is not for sale; it's not a material possession, yet it's similar to a currency, available for all. Some have lost it while others haven't put it to good use. Human communities, consequently, are chaotic: wars, disasters and injustice have become the prevailing language of the century. In spite of human poverty, humanity is still of value regardless of whether it is kept in a safe or scattered underneath our feet like dust and soil.

Oh how I wished that only one member of the administration would find such treasure, especially at those very moments and lend me a hand to save me from the cruel pain and take me to some hospital to receive the treatment I needed to heal the fracture.

Pleasure lasts but a moment, pain lasts a lifetime. That saying finally clicked. Only then, when I was in pain but couldn't find a cure. I didn't cry or scream; I suffered in silence and wished I was dead. The cries of my soul became louder than ever. What were those voices that were toying with me? Deep inside there is nothing but a large stage; I could hear Shakespeare dictating to each of his plays' protagonists their own roles. To me, everything had turned into a scene out of Hamlet. It was happening right before my eyes with all its tragic conflicts – evil, hate, malice, betrayal and inhumanity. Groaning, I recalled the scene where death was described, and I lived every detail of it. I could feel the noise of that scene and thought to myself: 'Did Hamlet go through the same experience as I did so that now that his emotions resonate with me? Or did I only just discover the real pain of humans during these moments? Or was my perception of everything around me influenced by my pains and aches? I didn't want freedom – I wanted a treatment. I only wanted something to wash all that pain away. Death would be more merciful than fighting my pains.'

Wednesday
12pm

Seventeen hours, full of suffering, had passed but to no purpose. All my appeals and cries of pain were unheard. The administration took no action; none of them wanted my agony to end. The women political prisoners were getting ready for the family visits. I was told that I, too, had a family visit and I would be taken to the prison medical centre for a doctor's visit. I felt a little happy to learn that I would be transferred to the prison clinic, yet the news of having a visit was accompanied by burning pains shooting up my leg; they took over my emotions and numbed all my other sensations.

Warden shifts rotated; the shift warden demanded that I move to the doctor's room with her. I stressed the fact that I couldn't move my leg; I couldn't even put it down on the ground. She believed me without having to enter into further discussion. She asked me if I could walk on one leg while leaning on her shoulder, so I replied: "Let's give it a try." I was required to hop. One hop was enough for me to feel the pain shooting through my leg; it was as if my leg was broken into tiny little pieces with every move I made while I was hopping. The warden could tell I was in great pain, and as soon as she realised that she took no further steps. She stopped and helped me sit down, kindly and quietly. I asked her whether there was an available stretcher, yet she said that there was none. At that moment, she spoke quickly to another warden over her walkie-talkie and asked her to dash into the ward so as to lend a hand. Within a few minutes, the second warden arrived. With one warden on each side, I simply leaned on their shoulders. And just like the stretcher, they used their hands to help me move, slowly, one step at a time. They endeavoured to move me. The route leading to the doctor's room was long and difficult. I apologised to them and extended my thanks for their help along the way.

Those two wardens were one of a kind; they were that gem in the prison on which I had bet. That gem still existed despite the gravity of the tragedy. They both created a beautiful picture which showed the true meaning of being human. Not only that, they renewed whatever hope there was left in me: humanity wasn't non-existent in the face of it all.

They helped me to sit down on a seat in the clinic. A police officer then joined them. The doctor came in and stared at my foot, which was swollen and had turned black and blue. The doctor had a talk with the officer and the two wardens in a foreign language. It might have been Russian. He wrote a doctor's note which stated the need to transfer me urgently to a hospital. "Come to the visitors' room. We'll head off immediately to hospital," the officer told me. And so the doctor gave me two walking sticks to help me move around. I entered the room with my walking sticks in which my parents had been waiting for me in front of the window. I had to tell them about what had happened. I kept it short. I couldn't endure the pain for forty-five more minutes; I preferred to go to the hospital rather than follow through with the visit. And that was what actually happened.

Supported by two walking sticks and guarded by five soldiers as well as one female soldier of the unit responsible for transferring political prisoners, I boarded the bosta. One of the soldiers took away my walking sticks after I sat down. While in the cage, the female soldier approached me, hand-cuffed me and was about to leg-cuff me. "How will you place those metal chains around an injured leg?" I shouted.

She left without answering my question, consulting her colleagues and getting their approval. She left my injured leg unshackled yet tied the other one to the chair, then banged and locked the cage door as she left.

A broken leg and two shackled hands. A moving tomb and an increasing pain with every move, stop and turn the vehicle made. The misery I had to go through before doubled up with my broken leg. There were no words for the pain, especially when it hit the metal sides of the cage. Luckily, the journey of suffering lasted for only twenty minutes. Whatever patience I had was exhausted, yet, at the same time, I felt happy as I was drawing closer to some end to my pain.

The vehicle stopped and the cage door was opened. The female warden brought me a wheelchair. She demanded that I sit in it while shackled after descending the vehicle. I refused. Hands freed. With the help of the two walking sticks, I managed to descend the vehicle and sit in the wheelchair. Hands shackled. She also re-shackled my left leg and connected the chain with the wheelchair. They started negotiating who was to push the wheelchair in which I was sitting. Each would give the task to another. A few minutes into the discussion, they finally agreed that the female soldier would push it; she had to take on that task. We entered the emergency room in Bnai Zion medical centre.

Sandwiched. Two soldiers walked behind me while two others walked in front of me. The female soldier pushed my wheelchair. Everyone else watched that scene of humiliation. Laughing, gloating faces and sad, sympathising ones. I saw both.

My leg was x-rayed. The orthopaedic doctor examined the results; he found out that my ankle was broken. I was transferred to the nurses' station. The doctor asked me to sit on the bed. That was when the warden un-cuffed me. I moved towards the bed and barely managed to sit on it. The orthopedic doctor as well as his assistance, who was responsible for

113

applying the cast, came close to me. He looked at his computer screen where my x-rays were displayed and then looked back at me. He said to the female soldier: "Re-cuff her. I have to apply the cast on her leg." It just dawned on her that she had forgotten to put my hand-cuffs back on my wrists. I deduced that the doctor was afraid to come closer to treat me without my being hand-cuffed. And so, up to my knees, he placed a cast. Back to the bosta. Re-shackled. Attempts to shackle my legs failed because of the leg cast. The female soldier didn't give up on the idea, so she shackled my left leg and connected the other end to one of the wheelchair edges. Inside the cage, and with the leg cast on, I was chained.

I could not move without those walking sticks. I came into the ward. I rejoined my cell-mates, yet in a new reality, different from the one in which I lived before. The ward's administrator didn't allow me to bring my walking sticks into the cell. I insisted. As a matter of fact, the doctor recommended that I didn't bear my weight on my broken ankle at all at this stage as it would make the fracture worse despite the leg cast. After the discussion, he let me have them inside the cell, yet warned me threateningly: "Never let anyone write anything on the cast. Doing so would be deemed as incitement, a security violation and breach of the prison rules." In spite of the pain I'd undergone, my heart was filled with laughter when I heard his words.

My cell-mates gathered around me and wished me a speedy recovery. We began working on a new project of helping and sharing. Whenever I was in need of their help to accomplish a task, they would spoil me with their generosity and sacrifices to ensure my comfort and to ease the pain caused by the cast.

Sunday, January 3, 2016

In the afternoon the administration let me know that I had a visit. It wasn't the arranged family or lawyer visiting day, so I was taken by surprise. I asked the ward's administrator who the visitor was but he didn't give me an answer. He simply demanded that I move along.

With slow steps as I walked holding walking sticks, I was taken past the usual lawyers' visiting room, and the way we were taking didn't lead to the family visiting room. That was until we arrived at the entrance of one of the rooms which belonged to the administration. I peeked in the room. To my surprise, the visitor was Deputy Speaker of the Knesset, Haneen Zoabi. Despite the fact it was unexpected and exceptional, it was the right timing. I was allowed, for the first time since my arrest, to meet someone who wasn't behind bars as I was and who I got to shake hands with and hug. No barriers. No timing. In a regular room.

I felt confident and at peace; being supported by decision-makers and leadership at that stage would raise the cause I bore on my shoulders. We discussed my health status as well as a few topics related to social matters. Most of all, we discussed my case, the course of interrogation and imprisonment. We talked about the poem which was also accused of incitement and terrorism alongside the other accusations against me. Additionally, we conferred about how the police's strategy: they would arrest a person first and then begin their hunt for whatever accusation they could find to frame them. It was exactly what happened to me.

She gave me a hug that was loaded with feelings of warmth, amity and pain, and I sat facing her. I could only move using the two walking sticks. I looked into her eyes and at her face and saw the pain hidden behind them, as if the pain I felt in my left leg made its way and reached her. She directed her gaze towards my broken leg and saw my bluish freezing and pained toes. She bent forward and brushed her fingers against my toes; her palms embraced them, sensed their coldness and tried to warm them up. Suddenly she removed the scarf which covered her shoulders and covered my toes with it. Then she headed to talk to the ward's administrator and told him: "How can you leave her in such a condition! Her leg is freezing."

That was the first time I'd ever met the Deputy Speaker of the Knesset, Haneen Zoabi, one on one; all the previous times she was either behind podiums or delivering public speeches. What an exceptional meeting it was. How fruitful and valuable our discussions were. It was a lot different from the previous official meetings. It was personal, spontaneous and filled with feeling which left a permanent mark on me. I felt as if I had been getting to know a new Haneen, someone different from the one I had already known for all those years. Her visit confirmed that I was not fighting alone for freedom of speech; it was a battle and the fate of many of my people, especially for the '48 Palestinians.

Our meeting came to an end and it was filled with laughter, hope and positivity; I said goodbye and returned to the ward. My heart was charged with energy, just in time. My resolve, determination and my commitment to what was right were boosted despite all the hardships and suffering that I and the other political prisoners had undergone. Haneen, her words, embrace, compassion, gentleness, sweetness, humbleness, spontaneity and humanity filled my heart with hope and vitality.

Ninety-six days had passed since I was imprisoned. As if I had been through a mystery-coated journey. It was a journey of humiliation, disrespect and, ultimately, cruelty. In the company of my fellow women political prisoners, however, we turned that also into an enriching and beneficial experience; we made the best of it. Its bitter memories, the harrowing experiences and embarrassing situations had also taught us some life lessons which would always be lie deep in our hearts and minds.

Life in prison could not be considered as life in the first place. It had nothing to do with everyday life, yet we, as political prisoners, convinced ourselves that we would live it to the fullest regardless of the bitterness. We live it as if it were normal. In prison, we felt happy, sang, danced, cried, had celebrations, said goodbye, felt sad, held discussions; we disagreed and fought. We sensed all those feelings which anyone would in their ordinary life. In reality, though, all of those emotions were connected to one shared feeling, which resulted from injustice and occupation. In this very prison, we had one wish in common which connected us: attaining freedom in a free homeland.

This deprivation of the political detainees – denied the enjoyment of our hobbies, including art, sports, sports, drawing, reading and education in prison – made us dedicate all of our time to politics. It was enough to have a few political prisoners with various political backgrounds to assimilate the rest into this culture and strive to raise political awareness among every single one of us. Those who entered the prison with no political background would leave with it after they'd served their sentences; they would become politicised and partisan.

How funny was the policy of the Israeli Prisons administration towards Palestinian political prisoners. To think for an instant that their policy of repression might actually prevent the proliferation of political ideas! Didn't they realise that preventing marital relations, books, drawing tools, musical instruments as well as education in prison would automatically and eventually turn prisoners into grade-A political ones?

The trust which grew stronger between the political prisoners and me, with the passage of time, gave me a chance to get to know them on social, psychological as well as political levels. Each one of them hid a story within her which encapsulated yet another aspect of the misery of a Palestinian woman under the occupation in all its shapes and forms, including the prison where they ended up. I heard many stories about numerous experiences and each had nothing to do with the other in terms of the conditions, causes and consequences.

I was hurt deeply to learn that some of them chose the occupier's prison and constraints as an escape from the constraints imposed by society and the injustice of its traditions. The catastrophe became even greater when a girl or a woman ran away from social injustice, her family or violence towards another prison, yet a tougher and a more complex one. They would do that intentionally but at the same time because they were forced to do so. One prison was exchanged for yet another, as she believed initially that the Israeli occupation prisons would protect her or that they would be more merciful than the prison of society, its traditions and domination, only then to be shocked by the painful reality of being victim of an environment which lacked the appropriate frameworks for solving the social and psychological problems she'd been suffering from all along. There would be no women's societies or associations to address her problems, and if she managed to find one she would still suffer from male domination there. Male figures would be in control of decisions and would pose a threat to her life and stability. From the yoke of the society and traditions to the yoke of the land's occupier. Same result. Women remained the victim of imprisonment. Societies which were supposed to be the producer of life, safety and dignity, became a source of humiliation, hurt and violence. This was all as a consequence of occupying Palestine. Violence, force and male domination were the allies of settler colonialism.

The occupation's violence wasn't merely geopolitical against our homeland but, with time, it developed into a psychological, physical and social one that was inflicted on women.

As for the country, the authorities and the officials who were required to protect women and their rights, and provide safety from such a danger and threat, were often the primary guardians of transgression and violation. A female was transformed into a bet and an effective tool of political pressure during any internal or external conflicts managed by the Israeli occupation government and its policy. Under such harsh social circumstances and violence, as well as imprisonment and detention, the question that echoed ceaselessly was which one encompassed the other? Especially as the concept of violence which most of the women political prisoners expressed, included, from my perspective, an act of domination which had left them with deep emotional scars and affected their mindsets and emotional processing (defence mechanisms). This would interfere with and impede the public or private social and political courses of their lives.

Any social practice which aimed to restrict the freedom of Palestinian women, intimidating them or attacking their dignity or individuality by social, familial or political pressures, was an immediate cause of the Israeli occupation, and it served the existence of the occupation and its racist, colonisation policies. It's true that cultured, educated sections of society were well aware of this reality and they showed amazing ingenuity in diagnosing its psychological impact as well as pointing out the consequences of the occupation and its deeds. Despite that, they lacked the ability to confront any of it by developing effective and viable remedies to the status quo. In prison, and for women political prisoners, discussing psychological or social issues would be deemed abusive to struggle and resistance, odd or something they would describe as shameful or religiously forbidden.

Women constitute half the society. Therefore, depriving the society of their capacity or potential squandered the opportunity for liberation, and that was what Israel was seeking so as to entirely destroy Palestinian society and gain complete control over Palestine: the land and its people. As long as Palestinian women were under social, cultural, familial and political occupations, our homeland, Palestine, would remain under Israeli military

118

occupation. True liberation, national independence, advancement would not be achieved until Palestinian women were liberated from social oppression and made them equal to men in terms of rights and decision-making in varied familial, social and political fields. The Israeli political strategy was based on a good understanding of Palestinian women's liberation as the only way to achieve freedom, and thus it spared no effort in preventing Palestinian women from gaining their economic, social, political and cultural liberation. Aside from that, Israel supported and deployed the theory of women's oppression by the Palestinian society itself, so as to continue the Israeli occupation. If women were taken over, oppressed, enslaved, absented from social, political and intellectual awareness; if they were paralysed emotionally, expressively and intellectually, all aspects of life and reasons to hold onto our homeland, its soil, air and water would end up paralysed as well, since women in Palestine were the weakest link. Those women were the ones who bore the consequences of the occupation's crimes, and they, additionally, were the first to be affected by its diverse forms of violence.

I had many discussions with the rest of the women political prisoners to seek their support for this theory, as well as their contribution to change their stereotypical ideas towards liberation and resistance, and to find ways to achieve victory for themselves before anybody else, whether during their prison term or after they had served it. It was paramount to me. My mind was restless, I worried and couldn't seem to think about anything else but that. I can't say that I succeeded, but I was able to influence some of those political prisoners whose perception of many things, including struggle, resistance, the quest for liberation, getting out of trouble and facing problems without being ashamed of expressing emotions, instinctual and sexual needs regardless of the circumstances as they were not shameful or religiously forbidden: they were part of our human nature and an inherent right for us all.

I said goodbye to the political prisoners in the morning before I headed for my hearing. The warden accompanied me so as to conduct a strip-search. Physical and naked search. Afterwards, we moved towards the x-ray 'baggage' scanner. I had nothing but the two crutches, yet the warden responsible for monitoring the machine demanded that even my crutches be checked and that I walk through the x-ray body scanner. I did try to walk but I couldn't move without my crutches. My leg was still too weak to put pressure on. Attempting to convince him to give up on that idea, I said: "The warden has just strip-searched me." "I have no other choice. You will have to do it. How do I know you aren't hiding something underneath the cast?" he insisted. As I was looking at him in despair, the other warden intervened. "Let's get it over with," she demanded. "What do you want me to do? Crawl?" I replied. "You don't really have to do that. You can hop," she said. That argument smothered me. I couldn't comprehend such humiliation. I wanted to put an end to it immediately. In excruciating pain, I took some slow-going steps. I was afraid it would cause more complications. I hopped. Every time I hopped, the sharp pain intensified. I was moaning and groaning with pain when I heard them laugh sarcastically. While she was laughing at the top of her lungs, she remarked: "And now you have a leg similar to Lionel Messi's." Loud giggles filled the place, louder than ever. Still hopping, I didn't turn to look behind me until I went through the body scanner and got my crutches back. Those moments filled me with deep repugnance and loathing like never before; I felt as though I was in dire need for revenge.

During my court hearing, the judge ruled that I be placed under house arrest under severe restrictive conditions and circumstances, in particular being under a guardian's supervision 24/7, and being away from my house, environment, place of residence and family. I had to wear a house arrest tag which monitored and detected every move I made. I wasn't allowed to have access to the internet in the apartment where I had to stay. Besides, I had to pay a 6,000 shekel bail and sign 20,000 shekel bailouts.

The judge's final deliberation on such tough conditions was based on the prosecution report, as my poem and I were accused of posing a threat to the Jewish public and the conditions would act as a deterrent to harm any Jew, incitement to violence or spreading terrorism. Just like that, the prosecution office and the judge accepted that I be sent away to Kiryat Ono, the Jewish town located at the heart of Tel-Aviv, as I posed a threat to the state's security and the safety of the Israeli public.

The courtroom was packed with people who wanted to champion my cause, including intellectuals, media figures, activists, some of my immediate family members and three of my relatives, deputy speakers of the Knesset representing the National Democratic Alliance (Balad) as well as the chairman of Higher Arab Monitoring Committee, Mohammad Barakeh. They were all exhilarated when I was released to that exile and under those restrictive, strict conditions.

Out of the courtroom. Back to the holding cell. The company responsible for my electronic tag didn't allow my release instantly so I was to be transferred to al-Jalameh Prison immediately in spite of the judge's decision which stated that I was to be released from my cell but remain under house arrest. After that, a Nashon Unit female soldier strip-searched me and I was taken back to the bosta. I remained there for two hours, my hands were shackled, my leg was broken and had a cast on while the other was tied to a seat on a two-hour journey. I bottled it all up and buried my pain. I arrived at al-Jalameh and entered it while leaning on the two crutches I'd got at al-Damoun Prison. The warden in charge searched me. Again. Then she got me into one of the cells there with which I was already rather well acquainted and familiar.

Late at night, the warden opened the vision panel and shone the lantern on my face while uttering the words: "Get ready, you'll be released from cell into house arrest. We have already let your parents know and they're on their way to pick you up. This is what the judge has ruled. At midnight, you'll have to be in Kiryat Ono where you will serve your house arrest." The paperwork relating to my release was handed in to me and they demanded that I sign it so that I committed to my attendance at the upcoming hearing and my confinement to my house until the hours mentioned. One of the papers stated that I had the right to pay the doctor one follow-up visit. And sign, I did. The gates were opened wide. Leaning on my two crutches, I headed out, plodding towards the gate until they stopped me. I was told I wasn't allowed to leave while keeping the crutches with me. I explained how difficult it would be for me to walk without being supported by them. I asked that I keep them just until my family arrived, and, immediately, I would give them back. They refused. "You have to let go of them and leave them right here," was their only reply. I suggested that somebody accompany me outside and take my crutches once my parents arrived. Without any justification or obvious reasons, that request was rejected as well. I negotiated no more. I realised that what they had been seeking all along was to torture me until my very last moment at that place.

The weight-bearing was difficult for me – I could barely walk. The cast hindered my movement and when my foot touched the floor, terrible pain shot through my leg. I crawled; I had no other way of moving towards my parents' car. Slowly, I pulled and dragged my body along outside. My brother noticed me as I was getting closer and he ran towards me. We hugged one another, he carried me and took me to the parking lot. My dad and maternal cousin were there; they, too, were waiting for me. I hugged them yearningly. I arrived home and hugged every single family member I had, one person at a time until I finally managed to enter my room. I went in and closed the door. I hugged and kissed my cats, Cady and Simba. For five minutes, I lay on my bed while I checked every corner of my room.

Gathered to see me, the room was filled with guests and well-wishers, friends and relatives. They were all there just to see me before I was released yet again into a new and faraway prison. I barely managed to eat a bite of my Mujadara plate which my mum had brought me before the electronic monitoring company contacted my brother demanding that he hurry up, saying: "If you don't arrive right on time, we will take her back to prison tonight." "You have just released her from al-Jalameh at 10pm. How do you expect me to arrive at Kiryat Ono by 12am? Could you give her more time so as fetch her personal belongings from the house? We'll set off right after she does," my brother replied. For once, my brother's stubbornness worked, so they set another date, tomorrow at 3.30am. In spite of the tough time I had moving around due to the cast, I greeted each and every guest we had over, fetched some things from my room, including: my debut poetry collection which was brought out in 2010, The

Last Invasion, as well as all of Fadwa Tuqan's and Nazikal-Malaika's poetry collections, and some poetry collections by Mahmoud Darwish and Aboul-Qacem Echebbi. I brought along some pencils and notebooks for writing, my work backpack which I used to wear for work before I got arrested. Everything I left was untouched: the last two books I'd read. One of the books was written by Ghassan Kanafani while the other was by Ibrahim Nasrallah. Besides, I had my unpublished book titled Galilee's Canary Songs; it was expected to be published at the end of December, 2015. There was also a novel which I was working on titled An Appointment with the Whales, which discussed my childhood. I had a journal and some drafts. I had my workplace keys along with the keys of my new electric car which I'd bought just three months prior to my arrest.

From my room, I also collected some clothing items, my blanket, two pillows, my headphones, my radio, my turntable record player, the phonograph records of Fairouz, Abu Arab, Julia Butrus and Mayada Bseliss, Mohamed Mounir. I also had some tape recordings of my close friend singing as well as a picture I'd taken of us, my guitar, perfume, toothbrush, hair comb, body lotion and shampoo bottles and a teddy bear which I had received for my last birthday from my friend. I left.

CHAPTER 17

When I arrived at my new 'prison' with my brother and his fiancée, it was 3am. It was an apartment which they rented so as to meet the requirements of my house arrest and which was approved by the state prosecutor's office in Tel-Aviv in order to limit the threats my poems and writings posed to the state's security and the Jewish public. Those were their accusations my defence lawyer went along with, as to get me out of the actual prison was the priority, at all costs. My brother and his fiancée made some slight changes to their lifestyle to carry out the court's ruling. They rotated shifts: one would leave while the other would stay to supervise me. I was strictly prohibited from being left alone or unaccompanied, even for a few moments, as though I had been an infant.

After a few minutes of entering the apartment with my broken leg, four soldiers wearing prison service uniform and two others wearing police uniform knocked on the door and came into the apartment. They fixed the monitor on my left leg. It was a plastic electronic ring connected to a bigger device which looked like a phone, and then they connected the phone line to it.

One of them asked me to walk within the limits of the place until I reached every corner. They wanted to determine the space within which I was allowed to move. They finished setting the device up and tracking all my movements. They left. I, for my part, began to map out my new prison so as to help me face everything that was waiting for me in this exile and this lonely, strange place.

The moment they left, I grabbed a plastic bag and covered my leg cast with it and took a shower. At last, I was taking a shower with clean water: it had been so long. In prison, I would take showers with yellowish water. I submerged myself in soap and let the shower water pour over me for over half an hour. I imagined the tap I would stand under to shower while I was in prison, and then I thought of the women political prisoners who had no clean water to shower. I applied body lotion then put on ointment to treat my blisters as my skin was covered with them, not to mention the mosquito and bedbug bites I'd endured throughout my detention and imprisonment.

I recalled the time when I asked for proper treatment only for the warden to laugh it off sarcastically, tell me it was nothing but scabies and they had no cure for such blisters; laughing, she left me there. I put on my pyjamas and threw myself down on the bed. I still couldn't believe I was sleeping on a clean, thick, comfy mattress which had nice, sweet-smelling bed sheets instead of that smell of dampness. I looked at the walls surrounding me and remembered the cockroaches and bedbugs on the walls of the prison cell where I'd been kept. Sometimes, with my hands, I traced the wounds which the cuffs had left on my wrists and feet. The noises of the door being knocked on, the chains and the nightmares I had stopped me falling asleep, so I put my headphones on and listened to my friend's songs. It wasn't easy for me to fall into deep sleep. My thoughts took me back to many places and instants I experienced in prison, and yet again, sometimes, these thoughts still haunted me here in my new prison. How was I to adapt? Finally, my friend's beautiful voice won the battle against those discordant voices in my memory. Her voice comforted me. I fell asleep and granted my body and mind calmness and serenity.

Three months had passed and I was still exiled. I'd been living with my own thoughts. I couldn't get accustomed to my brother and his fiancée; they didn't grow on me as we had extremely different lifestyles. Writing and reading were my only refuge and that was how I let my time go by; I was banned from leaving the house. No yard, no balcony, no fresh air, no sky, sun or people, no internet, no sophisticated electronic devices and not even an ordinary phone to stay in touch with my loved ones. I had nothing but some books, notebooks, pens. A TV, a radio and some music. I had a small window overlooking buildings which ached and burdened my eyes. Suffocating and melancholic, I would look outside and immediately close the window to return to my precious and delighting treasures.

I made up my mind: I wanted to be steadfast, that was my choice despite everything. I accepted the current situation and began to create things out of nothing. Life, the land and its people were dear to me and so was writing; I wouldn't accept any compromise of it. Confined and exiled in this house, I needed to meet people, despite my love of writing and reading. I needed to feel like I was part of human existence even if I had to do that within these mute walls. Interacting and socialising with people, no matter how limited, would have been of great help to me as it would stimulate me to write and interact emotionally which, in turn, would inspire me deeper when I wrote.

Indescribable happiness. As my case crossed all borders and turned into a matter of public opinion, many supporters visited me during this predicament. It all took place after the political activist, Yoav Haifawi[13], wrote about it for the first time in his blog 'Haifa al Hurra' which translated as 'Free Haifa'. It was hushed or censored as he brought it to light. It became the hottest topic and word was circulated and spread widely.

The media took interest in my case and showed support. Many arrived to pay visits and discuss my struggle, the case behind this home confinement/exile, the extent of Palestinians' right of self-expression and Israel's lie of democracy. The accusations filed against me in my list of charges and my arrest proved the Israeli Authority's democracy was limited to one category only: it could be said that it was limited to Jews. There were many visitors: authors, poets, artists, activists, intellectuals, Arabs and Jews. Visits from all fields and spheres/communities: social, political, media, artistic and intellectual, to which I wholly belonged, in addition to the Deputy Speaker of the Knesset, Haneen Zoabi, and a group of youths from Balad who would occasionally visit me to alleviate – even if a little – the difficulties of this prison/exile.

Yoav Haifawi, Iris Bar and Ofra Yashua-Lyth[14] followed up on my case the most; they would always pay me visits. It wasn't some temporary friendship: we bonded and our friendship grew stronger. Their visits were my only respite, especially as my family ceased their visits over this period of time. I barely felt alive when I was with them. The two 'wardens and guardians', my brother and his fiancée, started to play the roles of actual wardens and guardians. Clamping down on me, they would ensure that their tasks were performed perfectly. To top it all off, the conditions of the prosecutor's office and the court weren't enough for them – they added their own. They wouldn't put any of my friends' or family's calls through to me; they rejected any visits for personal reasons, reasons which didn't represent my mindset or conventions. It's true that they were suffering too, because they were restrained in this prison, yet they overcomplicated things. They added yet another type of imprisonment to the home confinement. Did they make my living with them impossible or did I make theirs impossible? I couldn't tell any more. With the house arrest and all the conditions imposed on me, the mystery of it got deeper. Our differences started to become more noticeable and with those restraints, prohibition and suffocation, the disparity was growing. I had run out of every ounce of patience. I couldn't bear to be under their control even when it came to my simplest personal matters, yet I bottled it all up and stayed steadfast.

I tried everything within my power to respect their privacy as an engaged couple, especially when they were spending quality time together. I close my room's door, put my headphones on and listened to music. I didn't allow myself to eavesdrop on their conversations. I managed to endure it all except the interference with my visits; those was non-negotiable. Still, I was hard on myself and made lots of compromises even when it came to that matter. I convinced them falsely that I was the guest and they were the owners, so they had the right to do whatever they wanted, even if it was torturing me. I was nothing but a prisoner and all I had to do was accept and tolerate it all.

And again my visits were denied; those visits were my only breather, and they were the only source for me of a sense of belonging to the human race. Through those visits I got the opportunity to practise my most basic rights: to talk to someone about the restrictions imposed on me. I am a very sociable person: I enjoy socialising. I love people and I like empathising and exchanging thoughts and feelings with them. Even when I was in prison, a social life had existed and I was engaged in it with the rest of the political prisoners. Being with these unique, modern wardens hindered me from practising the most basic human right of meeting others. Having people coming over to this place was the only feasible thing, given the restrictions imposed on my movements and being forbidden from leaving the house.

From the very beginning, I knew the road ahead was bumpy; I knew that leaving the prison to home confinement wouldn't be that simple, yet it never occurred to me that what would made things worse would be people of my own flesh and blood. Those who were closest to me. And although I had never pictured myself living in a social prison, what I had truly been living in was harsher: family prison.

I wept. In fact, it was the first time I'd wept since my arrest. My overall health deteriorated; I lost so much weight and became skinny. I vomited whatever I ate despite the fact that I barely put any food into my mouth. I spent most of my time in the bathroom to eject everything that suffocated me: injustice, suffering, the tragedy I had been undergoing, the memories which strangled me as well as the injustice and cruelty of fate. I saw nothing but ghosts. I lived all alone. My shadows faded. I started talking to the walls, the music, my notebooks and books. I began to read the poems I wrote out loud. I read my books aloud too, so I wouldn't forget the sound of my voice or how to make sense of the sounds a human would utter. I started hunting any source of sound and listened to it to the extent that the sounds of flipping through papers or book pages acquired some new significance. My right to converse with others was forfeited, so I decided to seek refuge in music: it relieved the pain of my soul. Through poetry and music, I stepped into the world of the unknown and I set on for my journey of discovery. It felt as if music and poetry had been twins born from the prison's womb and from the slavery of wounds. They both set me free. It was the first time for me to find out that the deeper I sensed the notes, the deeper I felt this life and acquired a greater level of understanding. I would discover emotions within me I never knew existed every time I listened to music. Despite all the chains surrounding me, music granted me moments of freedom I had never had the chance to experience. At all.

I got the feeling that my brother and his fiancée were humiliating me intentionally and that they weren't any different from the wardens of the prisons I'd been transferred to and from before I was on their watch. In spite of these soul-wounding emotions, I expelled and constrained those thoughts and made excuses for my brother and his fiancée. Learning to adapt, control my emotions and accept living with all types of people while I was in prison might have helped me. I was content and satisfied by nature with what I had.

This home confinement turned into solitary confinement where I had to live all those painful details. I started pretending to be sleepy, knowing all too well that I wouldn't be able to fall asleep. I was lost and hurt living in loneliness. I felt hollow. I was in need of someone who would empathise, someone who would understand my feelings. Above all else, I was in need of human beings. A paradise without people isn't worth living in. Paradise. What about being in prison without anyone around?

After a while I was able to obtain an old non-smart phone and a SIM card. My dad sent it to me after consulting my lawyer. Through it, I was able to make calls with those who I truly missed and loved. Maybe that would ease some of my pain, even if the calls only lasted for a few minutes. Talking over the phone couldn't replace my need to meet people in the flesh. I called my mum and dad first. After that, I called my friend and my photography-buddy, Sameera, who I'd influenced to take up photography. I told her about how much I longed to touch my camera and go out to spend hours taking photos. At the end of the call, she promised she would visit me soon. I finally called my friend, the singer whose songs accompanied me throughout my detention period and whose voice was my escape from the voices of my nightmares; she sounded astonished when she heard my voice. "Dareen? Is that you?" she exclaimed. "Yes, it is me, Dareen," I cheered, rushing towards my stereo, and I turned it up. "Your voice has accompanied me at every moment of my arrest. I just want you to know that you have always been on my mind in spite of all the distance and the spaces which have kept us apart. Never stop singing. Keep spreading this voice." She said: "Dareen… I love you so much and I am so happy for you, but I'm sorry. Forgive me. I can't speak to you any more. We cannot keep in touch. Never call me again. I don't want our friendship to go on any longer." Her words crushed me as though they were some heavy mountain; I couldn't breathe. I threw myself on my bed and to the floor, I threw my phone. Our eight-year old friendship echoed loudly in my head. I looked at our pictures which I had taken from my room. I wanted to tear them all to pieces, but I couldn't. I loved her still but I was shocked. I wept. A lot. I cried and cried and cried. I buried myself under my blanket and stayed there for three days; not a drop of water or a bite of food entered my mouth. I couldn't even get up.

I became weak. I started seeking salvation no matter how much that would cost me. However, I didn't give up on writing or poetry. I would frequently ask myself where my lifeline and my God's mercy were all this time. I would wonder what I could have done to deserve such a punishment from this life which had done me wrong all along, and it never ceased to. A million questions raced in my mind, yet none had an answer.

There was but one witness to the details of my suffering during home confinement in the apartment which I shared with my brother and his fiancée. She was the only one I could meet in the face of the siege imposed on me, whether by them or by the Israeli authorities. It took this witness many lengthy discussions until she came to an agreement with my brother; she would visit me on Fridays or Saturdays on a weekly basis and that would be when his fiancée was not home. She was Ofra Yeshua-Lyth who then became like a mother, a sister and a friend to me. Her presence made up for the absence of the whole world. She even volunteered to give me lifts to court for my hearings and to pick me up. Of course, my brother would accompany us as well.

April 16, 2016

My birthday. For the first time ever, I spent that day alone with my suffering. I used to go out with four friends. Very close ones. We would escape to the embrace of nature and celebrate it together. Other times, I would go out with no-one and nothing but my camera. I would spend my day taking pictures in Akko (Acre) and around the sea. On this day, I couldn't do any of those things I always cherished. My friends would not be with me. Going out was impossible. I held a paper and a pencil. I tried to write. I couldn't let out my feelings and jot them out on paper. My fingers, suddenly, started moving along with the pencil and doodling. Those doodles turned into a drawing which expressed my feelings during those moments of loneliness and loss. I was surprised when I drew. If I hadn't held the drawing between my hands I would never have believed that I was the one who drew it.

I had loved drawing since I was seven years old. I would always draw a picture of a jailed girl surrounded by countless squares and rectangles. I would write my name in a square as if I had been besieged by something I couldn't name. It was probably my fear of the harassments I had been experiencing and from which I had been suffering at the time. I also remembered that, on one of my drawing quizzes, my art teacher once asked me to draw a picture which would represent the winter season; my drawing was very similar to the one I was holding at the moment, but with childish characteristics. When she saw it and contemplated its details, she told me, heartlessly: "This is not a drawing. This is mere foolishness."

Then she held the paper and tore it up. Her high-pitched scream terrified me. She slapped me on my face so hard that it hurt and made me cry. Another paper. She asked me to draw again. I don't recall what happened afterwards; I don't remember if I drew something else or not. All I can remember is that art classes and that teacher scared me from that point forward. The seven-year-old me didn't enjoy having boxes of coloured pencils any more and detested drawing. Around the same time, I could remember that my dad hit me with a metal belt while my mum hit me with a wooden stick because I got a low grade. Before they hit me, they locked me up in a room and didn't allow me to leave. It was the second term of that school year. The words my mum uttered as she was hitting me are still stuck in my head: "Even at drawing, you're no good." And ever since then, I don't recall holding coloured pencils or drawing something. Until this day. I don't know how my ability to draw re-emerged on this day: the day when I experienced sensations of loss, deprivation and hurt.

On this day and with that drawing, I felt as if I had been reborn with a new passion for challenge. I broke free from the memories that burdened my heart; they stung me over and over and poisoned me with pain. On this day, I discovered my ability to express myself not only through writing but through drawing. I'd found a new friend that gave me a sense of freedom, the freedom I'd striven for in the midst of loneliness of arrest and exile. Drawing had turned into a positive tool to vent my anger, worry and pain. With time, I started drawing in various ways and the techniques and tools became more professional: a pencil, coloured pencils, pastel, oil paint; I even started using acrylic paint.

6pm

My face was too pale: it was as white as a sheet. Excruciating pain tore me up inside. A headache. Unbearable, searing pains made my body ache all over. I trembled. Fever, dizziness and nausea. Feeble. Ceaseless vomiting. I had to go to a hospital to get treatment. I couldn't because first I had to call the Israeli Prison Service and the security company to let me out of the house so that the monitor wouldn't record that I violated the terms and conditions of the home confinement.

With the help of my brother and his fiancée, we managed to call them and explain my condition in detail. Their only blunt answer was that I wasn't allowed to go, by car, to a hospital to receive treatment, and if I was really in need to be hospitalised, then I should call an ambulance. We disagreed. We made it clear that we had our own car, so we didn't need to pay any ambulance emergency charges. We had a discussion with the office which lasted for an hour; my pain was growing more intense. Then they had a different reply; they suggested we make a house call and if the doctor said there was a need for me to be hospitalised, then they would approve. We had no other option; we accepted that offer as my health was declining. I needed treatment.

It took the female doctor three hours to arrive at our place. She checked my blood glucose levels as well as my blood pressure to find out they were too low. She took my temperature only to find out that it was high. Later, she asked me about my symptoms, so I told her about my cramping stomach and how painful it is. She immediately wrote a report in which she expressed the urgent need for me to be transferred to a hospital for treatment and tests.

We called the prison administration office and told them that we had the doctor's note and permit since my case was an emergency, so they asked us to send a fax. We had no fax machine at home! My brother suggested sending a picture via WhatsApp. They rejected his suggestion. After thirty more minutes of debating, they allowed me to leave under one condition – we fax the document once we arrived at the hospital along with another paper from the hospital which stated the time of my arrival and, similarly, another which stated the time of my discharge once I left the hospital. A police car was already waiting for us near the entrance as we left the rented apartment, and at the moment we set off another car followed. When we arrived at the hospital, a few policemen were waiting for us there as well. They followed us wherever we went. Suddenly, I had to use the bathroom, yet in order not to be accused of breaking the conditions of my arrest, my brother's fiancée came into the bathroom with me and waited for me at the door.

I spent the whole night at the hospital and I received the appropriate treatment for my case. I faxed the required documents.

May 13, 2016

Five months had passed since I was first put under house arrest. With the judge's ratification, the Prosecutors' Office approved an easing of the conditions of my house arrest. I was granted six hours per week to spend outside the house for recreation, yet I had to spend those six hours in the company of one of the guardians on Thursdays, Fridays and Saturdays from 5 to 7 pm.

House arrest was still a complex matter, just like my case was. Its conditions and system were tough. In fact, it served the Israeli authorities and the Prison Service well in breaking Palestinians down and killing their inner determination. Both of them worked toward the same goal – the suffering and punishment of both the accused and their family. This was an evident model of collective punishment policy not only through detention or imprisonment, but also by exerting financial and psychological pressure. That would also result in affecting family relations in general. I was trying cautiously to prevent the Israeli authorities from achieving those aims. The circumstances under which I lived would often frustrate and weaken me. My emotions might be affected by any change in my mental wellbeing. Admitting that I had been suffering wasn't a weakness: it was the fragility of 'human coal' before turning into glowing diamonds under the pressure of suffering.

I was worn out, my nerves cracked and my health deteriorated. My mental health was worse than ever. There were times when I regretted accepting house arrest instead of staying in prison. I wept and cried alone so many times despite the fact that I hadn't weakened or shed a single tear throughout my stay in prison. So many times, it would occur to me that I should return to prison to reduce my suffering. Loneliness and disappointment in those around me were soul-crushing, yet I buried it all

133

inside and decided to keep going. As always, writing was my only remedy; it cured my brokenness.

Nobody could understand the difficulty of being under house arrest except for those who experienced it first hand. Many people regarded it as if it was normal, as I would serve it while I was with my family, but the question then would be: What family were they referring to in such an exile? It was a punishment far more difficult than being in actual prison. It was merely arbitrary and politically discriminating; it aimed at extending the period of the punishment and my sentence.

Under house confinement, I felt like a bird which, after being let out of a metal cage, was allowed to stay only on one tree covered with a glass dome through which one could see a large garden and an open horizon, and once the bird attempted to soar it crashed into the glass surrounding the tree. Only then would the bird realise that nothing changed but the shape of the cage.

Throughout this time, word spread of my case; it exceeded the limits of time and space in which I lived. And so, my poem, which was accused of incitement, crossed the boundaries of this prison. It, in addition to some of my other poems from my collection, The Last Invasion, which came out in 2010, was translated into various languages and proliferated. The more I suffered in my prison, the more poetry poured out. That alone was enough to maintain my resolve and to resist the difficult circumstances I had to endure. I was paying the price of my relationship with poetry, writing and defending their existence in my life. It was all worth it. They had been the essence of my life.

True, the Israeli authorities could imprison my body in a prison jam-packed with chains, but they couldn't imprison my soul, the soul of a poet. They couldn't imprison my ideas and poems. I was imprisoned in body yet my poems and thoughts were at liberty, and I broke my silence. My poems and ideas echoed not only locally but globally. The tighter the chains, the freer I feel. Free more than ever. Oh, how happy that freedom made me feel!

Vigils in solidarity and many protests were staged against my arrest in front of the Israeli authorities inside and outside the region. The most prominent ones were in Jaffa, Haifa, New York and Washington, during

134

which my poems were read aloud after being translated into many languages including Hebrew and English.

With all of these sensations and the news which Ofra and Yoav brought me, I started to adapt to the situation, although negatively, striving my utmost to convince myself that the house was where I was supposed to be rather than prison. I tried my best to convince myself I would soon be able to leave and break free from all restrictions after serving my sentence, and that I would carry on with my life to realise my dreams about writing, poetry, photography and education. And in order to do so and succeed, I had to suffer; realising my dreams, then, would have a magical taste to it which I would forever enjoy. I had to endure this tragedy and overcome it as true creativity broke out from the depths of suffering and pain. That was what life had taught me in those times and throughout the hardships I'd had to face since I was seven.

After writing, it was this solidarity – which I only had the chance to hear about and which I hadn't witnessed or lived first hand – that motivated me to continue on the path of struggle and resistance; by myself and for myself, I chose this path.

As for the support for my case by various political parties in the Arab society, it was significantly related to the cadres, the youth and the leaders of Balad, particularly the Deputy Speakers of the Knesset, Haneen Zoabi and Basel Ghattas, who followed up closely on my case developments. They would always call and check up on me; moreover, they would always attend my ongoing hearings. So did some of Abnaa el-Balad activists as well as Mohammad Barakeh, chairman of the Higher Arab Monitoring Committee, and a few of the Democratic Front Liberation of Palestine activists. Additionally, the Deputy of the Joint Arab List, Yousef Jabareen, called me twice – unlike the rest of the members of the Joint Arab List, whom I didn't hear from, although they would deliver rousing speeches preaching the support of the Palestinian cause and political prisoners.

Ninety-six days of imprisonment were enough to turn my life around. I spent six more months under house arrest and in exile in Tel Aviv, during which I learned what cruelty, loneliness, separation and challenge were all about.

It had been six months since I last met my family members or my close friend Sameera Jamaa't, who I'd seen only once and waited for passionately.

CHAPTER 18

My hearings continued. At this stage, the prosecution witnesses took the stand. Those witnesses consisted of my interrogators as well as the officer who translated my poem into Hebrew. Surprisingly, they also called my youngest brother, Ahmad, and my close friend, Sameera, to testify against me since they were on my Facebook friends list, in addition to another friend of mine who organised a poetry reading on the anniversary of the Kafr Qasim massacre to which he invited me and asked me to recite my poems. It wasn't long before the testimonies turned into some comedy stage-play. Every person who attended my hearing and the prosecutor's interrogation of the other witnesses laughed along.

I hadn't met him until the moment the prosecutor called him to take the stand: he was the 'translator.' He'd served at Nazareth police station for thirty years and he seemed afraid and confused as he answered the prosecutor's questions. He looked uncertain of himself but then admitted it was his first time he'd ever translated a poem from Arabic into Hebrew and he wasn't a translator in the first place. He admitted he was chosen just because he loved the Arabic language and had learned it throughout his school years. He added that now he could point out some mistakes he'd made while translating the poem and they were an oversight. An entire line of my poem, he continued, was omitted inadvertently. He'd misspelled a word. Other words were either unintended misspellings or typos. He found some words confusing and couldn't get their meaning, so he transcribed those in Hebrew. Was he actually translating my poem or typing some WhatsApp message while he was chatting with his friends? I asked myself that question many times. At that moment I laughed at what I saw before my very eyes and the words I heard.

Hearings where prosecution witnesses testified were over, and my lawyer finally submitted a request for me to serve the rest of my court-ordered confinement in my own house which was located in Reineh. The support for my case extended to two-hundred-and-fifty public figures – including authors, well-known poets, artists and cultural figures, some of whom had been awarded the Pulitzer Prize – who published an open letter which demanded my release. Among the signatories were Naom Chomsky, Naomi Klein, Dave Eggers, Alice Walker, Kathryn Schulz, Richard Falk, Jacqueline Woodson, Claudia Rankine, Kim Johnson, and activists and supporters. There were seven thousand signatures from all over the country and around the globe.

The letter signed by these public figures and that massive support filled my heart with hope; it was certainly effective. Shortly after that, and after the hearing which was intended for prosecution witnesses, on July 26, 2016, my lawyer's request was approved by the court. From Kiryat Ono to Rineh, I got permission to move back to my place to serve the rest of my sentence at home, as I had had enough and couldn't cope any longer. I decided not to go back to the exile in Tel Aviv, at all costs, even if that meant going back to prison. In fact, that was what happened. I had to stay one night at al-Jalameh despite the fact my request was approved. The hearing reached an end at around 4pm, and the judge ordered another for 9am the next day. After my family members were made my new custodians, I signed all the papers and was bailed out. The issuing of some paperwork by the security company, which provided the electronic monitoring device services, was delayed. Part of it was the lawyer's dereliction. We couldn't complete the process by the due date set by the judge, so I had to return to prison until all the paperwork was sent.

I spent that dramatic night at al-Jalameh together with another political prisoner from Sharon Prison: she had to spend the night there waiting for her hearing which was to be held the next day.

Time went by fast. It was an exciting night and it was full of emotions, words, conversations and discussions. We talked all through the night about everything related to prison and its conditions. We also discussed some general news about the rest of the women political prisoners, as well as her case and mine. I said goodbye to her in the morning and, after the warden had searched me, the bosta transferred me to Damoun Prison. I thought I was heading to the courthouse, but that wasn't the case, apparently. I was surprised as I arrived at al-Damoun Prison. When I enquired about it, I was told my hearing had been cancelled. The files weren't ready. Worse, the administration of the al-Damoun Prison refused to let me into the women political prisoners' ward. They did not have the slightest idea what to do about it. Deep within me, I'd wanted that to happen; I wanted to get into that ward so as to check in on my fellow political prisoners, yet since I had an indictment list I was not allowed to remain in al-Jalamah, either – by law, I was not deemed detained. For an entire hour, I waited in a small cell until I was taken to the office of the officer responsible for receiving women and men political prisoners. He could identify me in no time; he remembered who I was. As he was going through my paperwork he asked: "Why are you here? Why did they bring you here?" and right after that, he asked the warden to un-cuff me. He made me sign a paper which stated that I was to be released. He continued: "You are released. Keeping you here, in prison, is prohibited. Do you have money to get back home? Do you have a phone on you? Call your parents, let them pick you up." I smiled and remarked: "A phone? How would that be possible? I was in al-Jalameh. Since when do you allow detainees to keep their phones?" He took my brother's phone number which was the only number I had memorised by heart, called him and told him that I was released and they could come to pick me up. He opened the prison's main gate and asked me to wait for my parents outside.

I left and stood by the prison's entrance gazing at all of my frustrations. Up ahead of me, I noticed a K-9 dog cage which belonged to the Prison Administration. Only then did I realise where all those barking noises came from that my fellow women political prisoners and I would hear while we were in our cells. My gaze shifted and I looked into the distance. I saw a sign that read 'wedding hall', so I instantly worked out how that music, from a distance, made its way to our ears while we remained in our cells. On the horizon, I saw the Carmel Mountains replete with green trees. It had always been known that it was there, somewhere around us, but none had ever had the chance to actually see it. My electronic monitor was still shackled to my ankle. What a silly system! They said I was dangerous and threatening. They put me under house arrest and never let me have a moment to myself unsupervised, and now they released me out of the blue and there I am, walking down the streets all by myself. I walked anxiously back and forth near the gate wondering what was behind such an act. Some sort of a wicked trap to pull me down.

My dad and brother arrived and I got into the car. We set off towards the house. When we arrived, not only did my brother receive a call from the electronic monitoring company, he also received another from the Prison Administration Services. Caprice. Although they had decided to get the second monitor, which was in Kiryat Ono, they'd changed their minds abruptly and insisted that I travel back there and take that device home to Reineh where I would have to serve the rest of my house confinement. Later they sent a representative to program and activate it, restrict my movements and limit my permitted area to within the confines of the house. My internet access was disabled and the electronic monitor was connected to that company's system. Once again, I was not allowed to step outside the permitted area. I could pick a lemon from the tree in our garden no more. I was released after all my paperwork had been submitted. Same restrictive conditions yet a different place.

At last, I was in my room reunited with my cats, Caddy and Simba, and with my family. Finally. After all this suffering and patience, I could now meet others and have guests over. I could talk to people freely. I could finally exercise my most basic right under this arrest. I could live and share feelings with people; I could talk to them without restriction.

For many reasons, I reached a dead-end yet again with my defence laywer. I couldn't overlook his pile of mistakes any more. His greatest, which caused my patience wear thin then snap, was when the hearing in which I had to testify and had long awaited was adjourned for months to come. I couldn't bear such a silly mistake; it cost me three more months of house arrest. Only then did I make up my mind; I decided to hire a new lawyer.

My journey searching for a new lawyer began. This time, I insisted on finding a female lawyer; a female defence lawyer would be my only choice this time. After consulting closely with many, and the help Ofra as well as my brother had offered, I was able to reach out to the lawyer Gaby Lasky[15] who specialised in human rights and freedom of speech. I talked to her and showed her all my case's paperwork. She was persuaded; she decided to take my case. I didn't allow anyone to interfere this time, despite the opposition of my family, including my dad, who was still hung up on my previous lawyer.

In August, as since I was not allowed to leave the house, my new lawyer, Gaby Lasky, came over to my house together with Ofra and another lawyer who worked with her in the office. That was the first time I gained an opportunity to converse with a private lawyer about my case. At 11am, they arrived, yet on that day I was extremely sick. Every time I wanted to go to the doctor's clinic, which was close to my house, the Prison Administration and the electronic monitoring company would make a big deal out of it and made it sound impossible. They would always order that I have a private doctor who would make house calls, but I had no job, no income. I didn't want to burden my family with the expenses; that would have cost me a fortune. I would rather suffer and struggle with my sickness.

"You look so pale. What happened to you?" Gaby said after she first saw my face, so I told her all about the harsh circumstances of my arrest. I told her about the humiliation I faced to receive approval to go to the clinic. I apologised to my guests a number of times before I left the meeting only to rush to the bathroom and vomit; it was unfortunate that we met on the day I was in such a difficult state of health, so our meeting went on like that until the clock struck 4pm. Gaby asked to listen to me talking to her directly about my case so she could understand the story of my arrest and all the goings-on. The paperwork which she had acquired from the court, the police or the public prosecution, was not sufficient for her. Up to that moment I had replaced two lawyers. Gaby was the third lawyer and chosen by myself. The first handled my case for three weeks only, while the second took it up for eight months. Both of them had barely met up with me for an hour. I would run into them either in court or meet up them before an interrogation. Gaby was the only one who asked to listen to me, to my first-hand account of my arrest story. That request was enough to give me some peace of mind. I knew right then I was in safe hands.

I'd finally found a woman to defend me who shared my convictions. At last. A woman who would make a good fit to represent me and offer proposals based on the principle of freedom; I was a female poet and I had every right to write freely with no limits or restrictions, just like any other artist – without discrimination, be it racial or national. Finally, I'd come upon someone who would comprehend the significance of my dreams and ideas, someone who would cherish and defend them in courts without any patriarchal authority or domination. At that very moment, I felt was truly set free from patriarchy: it was not intervening in my case any longer. I started exploring a new meaning for freedom, a meaning I had long missed.

It has been a year since I was arrested; an entire year had passed with its aches, pains, forced exile and my resistance to it all. I was still under arrest and suffering from harsh conditions at home. The hearings at the magistrates' court of Nazareth was not over just yet. Voices were raised to demand my release and on this occasion one-hundred-and-seventy people, including authors, scholars, poets and intellectuals, signed a petition in Hebrew demanding my release and that the charges against me be dropped. They included Tal Nitzan, David Grossman, Sami Michael, Ariel Hirschfeld, Michal Ben-Naftali, A.B. Yehoshua and Agi Mishol, to mention but a few. Haaretz published that petition on visual and written media in both Hebrew and English. They published an editorial on behalf of their staff demanding my release.

PEN International adopted my cause and took it as a symbol of how writers and artists were prosecuted and the policy of gagging them and suppressing their freedom of speech. They held a conference in Galicia which was attended by hundreds of representatives from numerous of its centres all over the world. During that conference, and on the International Translation Day, September 30, my poem 'A Poet Behind Bars' was translated into eleven languages. I received many awards from various organisations and societies which supported art, creativity and poetry, including PEN International, the poet Carl Scharnberg's institution located in Denmark, and the local Naba'a Society.

Jewish Voice of Peace (JVP) as well as Adalah NY's activists set up an online solidarity campaign on social media platforms calling for my release. There were over one-and-a-half million tweets; it went viral. The campaign was also acted on with various activities, such as protests, poetry readings and letters sent to my post office box.

Roti Hiller, Ofra Lyth and Bilha Golan started a fundraiser. They called for support from activists and free people all over the world. They were able to collect the money I needed to cover the lawyer's expenses and to help me and my family's financial burdens brought on by the case. We'd been spending money non-stop since the day of my arrest so as to stand up to the unjust judiciary system. I couldn't go to work, so I couldn't make any financial contribution. All of the above had affected my soul and scarred me.

My case was an inspiration to many writers, poets and artists who specialised in multiple fields to express their own art too. I became a voice, a scream which influenced many of the free people out there as well as militants and revolutionaries around the globe to achieve freedom. I was a scream let out in the face of the racist, dictatorial Israeli policy – a policy that would suppress freedom of speech, poetry and art.

Those many events and incidents hugely impacted my life, especially during that period of time. It was ironic and painful. I received great and full support from the Jewish and Western communities through literature, art and media. I also received financial as well as personal support. By contrast, I received hardly anything similar or even close to that support from Arab countries. Only a few people showed their concern and took the initiative. As for Arab organisations and official societies, only two offered their support. It was mediocre and very disappointing. The General Union for Palestinian Writers had published one of my poems alongside a statement of solidarity and a Karmel Union Writers and Poets delegation expressed their support. They vanished after that.

The only source of support and motivation for me to keep up with my writing was from Jewish and international organisations and I was determined to keep practising this form of art, no matter what. Deep down, I was certain I was not alone in that battle; there must have been thousands of people fighting alongside me for the sake of victory. They believed I was innocent and they would offer support. That was the most beautiful bit of truth which eased the pain of my confinement. It was not over.

Wednesday, September 14, 2016

I started yet another day of my confinement, as usual, with my morning rituals in my bedroom: reading and writing. I left my room because I wanted to take a shower and while I was out, my cat, Simba, went missing. I looked for him everywhere and in every corner of the house, but I found

143

no trace of him. I was extremely worried about him and then I was certain he'd left the house, which wasn't something he would normally do, but he didn't come back. And then came the electronic monitor. It shackled my ankle and restricted my freedom to move around inside the house as I pleased. I couldn't even leave the house to search for my cat and get him back. All I could do was move from one window to another and call his name out; he might, I thought, hear my voice and find his way back. An hour, two and three passed but he was nowhere to be found. Helplessness crept in and made me curse this arrest a thousand times as I tried to think of what I could do. No matter what, I wanted to make sure he was okay, to the point where I called the Prison Service Office, as well as another one which was responsible for the electronic monitor and told them about what had happened. I hoped they would grant me a few minutes to leave the house to look for him. Cold and cruel. They didn't budge. They did nothing about my worries about my cat. The employee who picked up the phone ridiculed my request. She let out a sarcastic laugh. I ended that call. It was pointless. How did I expect them to understand being sympathetic or humane? They were some creatures who worked at that office and who hadn't allowed me to leave the house and get hospitalised when I was screaming with pain. What mercy would be shown by those who tamper with people's fates? I felt as if my call had been a decision I made at a moment of foolishness. There is an Arabic saying which goes: "Those who are in desperate need foolishly rush in." I couldn't put up with his absence any more; my patience ran out and my anxiety level was out the roof. I shouted and called his name at the top of my lungs and in every direction, time after time. I checked every direction and let my eyes linger. I started guessing where he might have been hiding; I would look around and call out his name.

I entrusted the mission to my mum and brother; they looked for him in various parts of the neighbourhood. In vain. As time passed, I didn't hold out much hope any more of his return. It was the first time he'd left the house. Ever. I had nagging worries about him and was haunted by the idea he might have been in an accident. It took over my mind and heart. Every time my helplessness increased as a result of the restrictions, my worries increased terribly too. I called a vet and asked him about the place where cats might hide when they disappear and how far they could wander away from home. I also sought his advice on what to do in such cases to get the cat back. The solutions and advice he offered had one perquisite in common: being free of restrictions and shackles. I didn't give up. I thought over the solutions and the instructions the vet proposed. I followed them step by step in spirit, but my brother did that in body as he could move freely. I kept calling out to my cat through the window. I gave my brother the bells I typically used to play with the two cats to entertain them. From one narrow ally to another, my brother moved and I, alternating windows, called out to Simba. A six-hour debilitating search finally led my brother to him; he was scared and isolated at the entrance of a house in our neighbourhood.

Simba was back in my arms. I kissed and hugged him. I examined every part of his body to make sure he wasn't hurt. His beautiful, pure white hair was dirtied; his eyes were filled with fear. That was all that had happened. I instantly let him into my bedroom. I cleaned him, played with him and petted him. And then I gave him a piece of 'la vache quit rit' cheese, his favourite, to ease his worry and fear. He would feel safe again.

With all of those incidents and with the ongoing supportive events, on November 15, 2016, a month-and-a-half after transferring my case to my new lawyer, Gaby Lasky, my case was back on track. She submitted a request to loosen the conditions of my home confinement. She succeeded. First pleading. She defended me successfully and made removal of my ankle monitor possible. I could also leave the house for work any time between 11am and 5pm. I still had to be accompanied by a guardian and I wasn't allowed to use the internet at all. I was granted two more hours to go wherever I wanted, yet again I had to be under my guardian's supervision.

I couldn't make the best out of that bargain and I couldn't get back to work. It was impossible to meet the requirements. No guardian would be able to remain with me at my workplace. Well, so, at that point, the removal of my ankle monitor after all of this time was the most significant event to me; it alleviated so much stress. It freed me from some of the restrictions of my home confinement, one of which was be the feeling of something hung on my body. It had been with me all the time. It spied on every breath, sensation, feeling, movement and word. The electronic monitor haunted me just like that ghost of rape. It was raping me; in what way wouldn't that be considered rape? It raped every single moment of my days. The sensation of having that weird device whenever and wherever I was and having it against my will were enough. It always reminded me of the rape and harassments I was subjected to as a child.

My imprisonment hadn't changed. I couldn't go to work or leave the house except on very rare occasions during the two hours I was granted to go shopping for my essentials from a close shop in my town. Accompanied by one of my guardians. Always. Where could I go within a two-hour timespan in the first place? What about the traffic jams in the streets of my town and the towns around it?

The more I held onto writing, the longer my sentence was going to be. The more I was hurt, the more I would pour my heart out on paper. I didn't know that I had to pay that high price for defending my right to write. Prison did not break my pen, nor did it hush my voice. It's true I could not publish any of my writing, but even that obstacle turned into a bigger motivation to express myself. I was certain I would publish everything I had written in this prison. I would spread the word and it would echo through the ages and have a high value.

My soul didn't lose its spark. The burning fires of my rebelliousness were not put out despite all the strictures, restrictions, nervousness and stress, as well as the fear of the unknown lying in store for me.

My nerves were on edge; nothing could put out the burning fire except my pen. It would absorb all the lava of my anger. With my pen, I would restore the balance of my thoughts and resilience. My pen. My words. Those were the most loyal of everything and everyone that surrounded me.

What hurt me the most was having high hopes for many friends who continuously let me down. Body flaws could be covered even with a little piece of cloth, but friendships would be tested in difficult situations, and once exposed nothing would ever make up for them. A broken friendship cannot be mended. Oh how many flaws were exposed during this period, even among those I once considered the closest, the most loyal and honest. When I was imprisoned and exiled in Tel Aviv, I came up with some excuses for them when they didn't check up on me, especially given the

146

circumstances under which I lived. Now it had been five months since I was first confined to the house in Rineh and, after aimlessly waiting around for them, they still didn't call or visit. They didn't spare any time for me, not even five minutes. The wait was painful. I couldn't think of any other excuse for them. With my arrest I had the chance to discover my true friendships and become aware of the fake ones. It was as if I had put them in some sieve which I could call 'difficult times'; three of them were left on the list of friends I kept in my heart. Salt and sugar do not differ in colour; they're both white. Their difference lies in their taste. The tongue of my imprisoned self got to taste it all, experiences with all kinds of people, until realising the difference between who was worth it and who was not. It was a chance I seized to filter my memory and dust off the worn-out ones which were beyond repair.

November 17, 2016

My hearing turned into a strange conflict among women which I hadn't ever witnessed up close. After my defence lawyer joined in, it became an 'equation' which only involved female elements: the accused, the defence attorney, the prosecutor and the judge. That scene perplexed me. A woman against another. I was pained to see a woman, my counterpart, exercise psychological, emotional and financial stress so she would, eventually, gain promotion or attain a higher position at the prosecution office. I laughed the most when the prosecutor paid lip service to the principles of rights during some of my hearings. I have no clue what rights she was talking about. I was deciphering the nonsense of a woman oppressing another. Paying close attention to the fact that she was only doing what her institution dictated – that institution which stripped Palestinian women, even ones who had Israeli nationality, of the rights their counterparts enjoyed, including the right to free speech which had always been the most salient in women's struggles throughout history. I didn't blame her position, but I was puzzled. I knew she was only obeying the institution she served and for which she worked. She was doing her job by her obedience and her intransigent stance towards me. She deemed me a big threat to 'the country' and its security, with my poetry, and that poem, in particular. She believed her compliance with the institution's policy was out of the righteousness and virtue of the existentialist discourse: to be or not to be. That was what she was taught.

I finally stood behind the courtroom podium after my hearing had been adjourned several times for various made-up excuses, the latest of which was the lack of a Hebrew-Arabic interpreter, but I insisted on using my mother tongue, Arabic, to testify. My oral testimony hearing began. The judge, my defence attorney, the spectators as well as the plaintiff's attorney were all in front of me. Everyone was all eyes and ears.

In front of everyone, I confessed I was the one who posted the poem, the picture, and reposted that news item. I was as fully convinced as my lawyer that I must stand behind that podium and defend my right to freedom of speech. I must not fear anything.

The plaintiff posed an endless sequence of questions; my answers went through a mixture of reactions. Within a few hours, I experienced emotions that a woman might hardly go through in a lifetime. I felt happy, angry and sad, then I laughed and felt nervous. I drank water to recharge and soothe my dry throat due to the many questions I had to answer.

Four hours of my being under the spotlight; I was there as a witness and an accused at the same time. Sometimes, I was even transformed into an interpreter when the court's interpreter failed to render some words and phrases properly. I intervened immediately and put an end to that joke. The judge didn't know any Arabic and what the interpreter said was to be taken down by the court reporter and transformed into an official certified transcript. That was enough to make my task more difficult. I had no way out; I had to answer her questions. I practised the hobby I'd picked up during detention: controlling my impulsive reactions and emotions.

With every question I was asked by that prosecutor, she implied that the hearing was coming to an end, yet it would go on instead. When my hearing lasted until 8pm, there was no time to proceed any further; my case was adjourned. The judge scheduled the next hearing for December 24. She prohibited the circulation of any details regarding the case's course and developments. She ruled that I was utterly forbidden from discussing any of the details with anyone. At the prosecutor's request, she denied me the copy of the written protocol: it wasn't negotiable.

A week passed and it was the scheduled hearing date. Again, I stood behind the podium and the prosecutor bombarded me with questions. Time was up. The prosecutor was not done with her questions. Another hearing was scheduled to proceed with the interrogation. The next hearing would take place a month later: January 26, 2017. Conditions repeated: forbidden to discuss or circulate any details regarding the hearing.

I occupied myself with writing, and during my wait under this arrest I found refuge with my pen, papers and books. I tried to inhale the meaning of freedom with those who visited me, whether they were supporters or friends, with discussions, dialogues and talks. As a result of this confinement, I became more attached to my poetry, writings and books. They were my only concern as well as the racing thoughts I had about the case, its course and my testimony. It was time for my third hearing. I was done; I gave my testimony before the judge, and it took me hours to do so. Finally, the prosecutor ran out of questions, like a well running dry. That scene was over. Moving on to the next: defence witnesses' testimonies. The judge set the date: March 19, 2017 and time: 11.30 am.

March 19 was finally there. After a three-hour wait and enduring the delay of the judge in opening the hearing, it finally began. I had no idea who the witnesses that my defence attorney had chosen were; I knew nothing about that testimony until the moment it was given. All I knew was that a History of Hebrew Literature researcher would attend the hearing in addition to a specialised translator who would translate the poem. Those were the moments when I learned who the two of the witnesses were: Prof. Nissim Calderon, a researcher in the Hebrew poetry, a lecturer at Tel Aviv University and an editor in a literary magazine which specialised in poetry, and Yonatan Mendel, a specialised Arabic into Hebrew translator and vice versa.

Prof. Calderon took the stand, introduced himself and swore to tell nothing but the truth. The prosecutor, as she would normally do, bombarded him with questions.

She was talking about my relationship with poetry and discussing with the professor whether I was a poet or not. For a few moments, that discussion made me wander, and it took me back in time. With my mind wandering off, I went back in time to the moment when I didn't think twice

149

about ending an affectionate relationship, which lasted for two years, for the sake of poetry and its significance in my life. I recalled everything that happened on that day.

I had not been in a true affectionate relationship except that one; I experienced it with all my heart and soul. It was the last and almost the only experience I had with so-called love. It all happened four years before my arrest. A relationship just like any other woman would experience in her life: a beautiful, fun, exhilarating and an intensely emotional experience. Then it ended in an unexpected way, with much surprise and strangeness. Taking the initiative to end a strong relationship cold turkey and cut all ties was even more surprising as it was characterised by deep, passionate love, mutual agreement, respect and faithfulness. Strangely enough, the existence of writing and poetry in my life were on the alert for it.

Late at night, I was about to start writing a new poem, and then I got a call from him. I picked up the phone but explained that I was swamped with work. I simply asked him to call me back some other time. There was nothing important for us to discuss, it was just an ordinary phone call. I had already told him that, during my writing moments, I was engrossed and no-one could distract me. He also knew that writing and poetry had always been at the top my list; everything else would follow, including him. "Oh, now, your poem is more important than I am?" he asked to which I replied, unhesitatingly: "Yes. I have to finish writing my poem and then we can talk as we please. My heart and mind are both preoccupied with the poem I'm in the process of writing."

After that night, I didn't hear from him despite my several attempts to call him. I realised he was upset. I completely understood his position although it was nothing new or strange; poetry came first. We had already agreed on everything I mentioned during our last conversation. For two whole days, he vanished, then he answered my calls and we met. I was surprised when he said, as if it has command or order: "We are getting married soon. If you want this relationship to continue, you will have to quit composing poetry. Once we are married, you will no longer write any poetry. It's either me or poetry. Make up your mind. Now."

His last words on my relationship with poetry were shocking. I had never imagined, not for a second, that I would face someone who would make me stand at this crossroads: choosing between keeping poetry as part of my life or completely giving it up. That topic was non-negotiable. It was settled since the first poem I'd ever written; writing, in my life, was a destiny, not a mere choice. I am a poet by nature. This is who I am. I was born to be a writer, regardless of anyone's opinion. No power could separate me from poetry, even if it were the power of an affectionate relationship or a love story. I asked him: "Is this your final word on the matter?" to which he replied: "Yes." Right away and without thinking twice about it, I took off the ring he'd once given me as a symbol of our relationship. I gave it back to him and said: "I choose poetry, for sure."

We haven't seen each other again ever since. Hearing that sentence from him was enough for me to decide to part ways and end it. What drew the line between us was how he dared to make me choose between him and poetry, as well as his attempts to put me under the pressure of his certainty of my love for him; he was sure I was a sensitive and a very emotional person. He thought my feelings towards him would turn me into who he wanted me to be, but he wasn't aware of the fact that my feelings for poetry were the strongest. I ended it all; I didn't say goodbye. I left. I didn't cry or even feel sad for leaving him. Instead, I laughed and felt happier as I was set free from the prison that he waiting for me. Deep inside at that moment, I sensed the victory of poetry's will against everything that surrounded me. More and more, I held onto writing and this fate. My laughter and victory on that day were similar to my laughter at those moments when I heard the loud-mouthed prosecutor's discussion about my relationship with poetry, and her claim that I wasn't a poet in the first place. Pause. I put these memories on hold and, with a big smile on my face, returned to the present moment: the atmosphere of the hearing.

What was the definition of a poet? What was the definition of a poem? Was I a poet? That was the only concern the prosecutor had. All of her questions revolved around the same idea, as if she'd been itching to formulate an exclusive theory defining poetry and poets, some theory that would fit her beliefs and thoughts so she could scratch that itch. With her questions, she laid down her own principles of poetry and applied them. Based on that, she concluded that I wasn't a poet. I wasn't a poet in spite of the fact that I'd written poetry using all the well-known rhythmic structures of the Arabic language since I was a child! Poetry analysis, atmosphere, imagery – both complex and simple – figurative language and rhetoric: I employed them all. The fact that I brought out my first poetry collection in 2010, containing numerous diverse poems, didn't really matter to her.

Had I known what her claims would be, I'd have brought in all the poems I had written, published or not, and explained to her about their structure and prosody, which took me many years to learn and master. I would have analysed each poem I'd written, its metre, circles, original parts and conventional ones. Had I known she would dare do this, I would have presented my convicted poem and analysed each poetic foot and circle verse by verse and line by line. I would have explained circle derivations, the 'hashu' (tautology, or, literally, the filling), the 'arūḍ' and 'ḍarb' (the forepart and the rear), not to mention the purpose that each served.

From her perspective, I was not a poet. If I was considered one, then the whole hearing in which she pleaded against me would be a joke and an insult for her and those she represented in this country which claimed to be democratic. In democratic governance, and under democratic rule, a poet wouldn't be brought to court, be imprisoned and arrested under the accusation of composing a poem. She didn't want me to be called a poet by any means; she didn't want my poem to be called so. The professor stood up and clarified that my poem would be classified under the Palestinian national, political style and that thousands of poems adopted the same style. He also explained that the poet was the only authorised person to determine the genre of their poem. My poem, he added, had verses, lines, a metre, musicality as well as rhyme.

For a few seconds, the prosecutor stopped firing questions relating to this topic. She moved on to another. As if she had been firing or shooting at the same target but from a different angle, she returned to posing other questions. Aiming her gun at the witness who was standing before us, she wanted to show the judge that he was not being objective and that his testimony had to be discarded by court. How could she not? He participated in left-wing literary evenings in the country, so his testimony was nothing but subjective.

Uninterrupted, Professor Calderon's interrogation went on for two long hours, during which he spared no effort to explain to both the judge and the prosecutor that, in a democratic country, a poet is and can never be tried even if the poem is violent, crass or against the ruling system. He provided a few instances of Jewish poets who composed clear and explicit violent poems, more than mine, in different times, and yet they hadn't been held accountable or jailed since poetry is one of the pillars of art. It shouldn't be censored, especially under democratic rule. Again and repeatedly, the prosecutor claimed that I was not a poet and that what I wrote was not poetry, while pretending to have forgotten about what she had said during one of my previous hearings. She, herself, said that I, being a well-known poet and a recognised one in the Arab world, would be extremely threatening since I influenced many people with my poetry. Once more, the professor reiterated that what I wrote was a poem indeed since it contained poetics and that whoever composes poetry is a poet.

After the professor's testimony was completed, he stepped off the witness-stand. Next witness. The specialist translator, Dr. Yonatan Mendel, took the stand.

Questions were posed. The prosecutor called up the terms and words I employed in my poem but were translated by a policeman, and she labelled them an incitement to violence and terrorism. She presented them to the translator and waited for his response: Who is the martyr? What does "resist" mean? What is "resistance"? No matter what he had to say, the witness was still accused and suspicious in her eyes if the answers didn't suit her or the police's definitions. This was all it took for her to consider Dr. Mendel as subjective. She brought some of the written work he had published and in which he had expressed his left-wing opinions as well as opposing the occupation. She didn't like that either, and in her opinion his pieces of writing were enough to deem his testimony unreliable and to question his credibility. That specialist translator was there to present a full translation of the poem, yet the prosecutor asked him about one line only: "And follow the caravan of martyrs." Dr. Mendel stressed that the word "martyrs" obviously referred to the victims I had mentioned in the poem: Ali Dawabsheh, Mohammad Abu Khdair and Hadeel al-Hashlamoun.

Five hours. The questioning of Dr. Mendel lasted for five hours during which the definitions of some of the terms I had used in my poem were discussed among the team which conducted the hearing and knew absolutely nothing about the Arabic language or its concepts, starting with the court reporter who had to type up the transcription of those terms in Hebrew, the judge and ending up with the prosecutor. The judge and the prosecutor both admitted they didn't know any Arabic. Bitter reality.

How could a discussion about an Arabic poem be held in Hebrew by people who didn't know the slightest thing about Arabic as a language, let alone its literature, old and contemporary poetry? That question drained my mind. Had they all mastered the Arabic language to begin with, and had the proceedings of the court's plenary taken place in Arabic, no translator would have been required. Dr. Mendel wouldn't have taken the trouble of answering all of those questions, either.

Five hours went by without even discussing the whole poem with Dr. Mendel. The only discussion was about the meanings of some of the terms. Those were proven to be translated inaccurately by that policeman and also reaffirmed his errors and points of weakness. His mistakes were grave. Consequently, and after a seven-hour round of questions, we were provided with new definitions of many terms including 'a poet', 'a poem', 'translation', 'martyr' and 'system' from their perspective. This represented their mindset only. Any definition from the opposing side would be considered wrong and would be rejected. Whoever dared to say it or adhere to it, would be deemed an outlaw, an inciter and accused. Most importantly, she came to an irreversible decision: I was not a poet and what I wrote couldn't be classified as poetry even if the poem contained all the required contemporary Arabic poetics and aesthetics. It all was insignificant. All that mattered was being obeyed. She was adamant.

For seven whole hours, the hearing continued. Had it been possible to film it, it would have been the most paramount absurd theatrical work of the century, or it could have been adopted as an ideal university lecture titled 'Surrealistic Polemics in the Science and Art of Poetry: Approaches to the Imprisoned Poem in the Corridors of Israeli Courts.' How couldn't it be when calling experts in poetry, literature and translation to discuss such topics was a first?

CHAPTER 19

I was done with the hearing testimony stage and moved on to a new one – the writing and submission of the summary judgment of the defence and the plaintiff – yet I remained under house arrest. All my requests were still denied, and so were my defence lawyer Gaby Lasky's attempts to gain release for me from all the restrictions. They would continue to be imposed until the end of the legal proceedings. With every request, I faced more intransigence yet some easing of restrictions.

With more than thirty hearings, I became more certain that the Israeli Security Agency was in control; it was the one making decisions and commanding the judges to give their rulings at the end of each hearing. There were seven judges in total, three of whom were Arab, but from my perspective they seemed to have no authority or say in the matter. The judge was nothing but a pro-forma in such courts, particularly in Israel. After my arrest, things became more apparent. As if everyone in court had been marionettes on a set of strings, the security agency was controlling every aspect, especially when it came to we Palestinians. The cowardice and weakness of the judges, and the security forces' control of them, turned into the most significant issue of my trial, as those judges played their roles and followed the scripts which had already been written for them by the country's security agencies.

The restrictions were further loosened after nearly two years of my arrest. The court had endorsed a permit allowing me to leave the house any time between 9am and 7pm, yet I had to be accompanied by one of the custodians. The rest of the restrictions remained unchanged, yet the time during which I was allowed to leave the house did not suit any of the familial custodians around me as each of them had their own work, house and family to attend. My struggle with not being able to go outside persisted until I was offered a suggestion: utilising this mitigation by increasing the number of custodians, and so my lawyer filed to add the names of three of my female friends, who followed up on my case, as potential custodians. In fact, they kindly volunteered to undertake this daunting task; they did so with all of their hearts. Although the prosecutor rejected the request, the court approved it after the three of them were questioned by the prosecutor and the judge. They made sure that they would be able to guard me, hinder me from publishing any of my poems and reduce the risks my poems posed. Those three friends were Ofra Lyth, Bilha Golan and Edith Breslauer.

The fact that Ofra was one of the three custodians was, to me, the highlight of this development. It was also the most effective change with regard to a significant mitigation of my arrest conditions. Right after the hearing, she gave me some of her time. She allocated me a set time each week, i.e. Tuesdays, to get me out of this house prison.

A year and ten months had passed since I was first arrested. I didn't see the outside world except through my bedroom window or the vehicle's windows whenever I was on my way to the courthouse in Nazareth for my hearings. Throughout this period, I forgot what the sky, the sea, the streets, people and cars looked like. I forgot how it was to feel cold or hot outside the house. Outside my bedroom window, I would look longingly for the world; it was as if I had never seen it before.

It was Tuesday, August 8, 2017, when I first left the house with Ofra after my arrest restrictions were eased. It had been a while. I woke up at nine o'clock and got ready to head out for the first time, and not to the court this time. At that moment, around nine o'clock, Ofra knocked on the door. We hugged. We were not allowed to leave the house before nine, so Ofra and my mom had some coffee before the clock struck nine. Ofra and I left the house and headed to the car. Moments before we got in, I stopped Ofra and said: "Are you sure you're giving a lift to a threatening woman like me? You still can change your mind." She laughed and I continued: "Well, that's your decision and you're responsible for it. Just be wary. Make sure I don't write a poem while we're on our way that would put your life in danger." Once those words left my mouth, Ofra couldn't hold herself back. She burst out laughing. We set off towards Jaffa.

She took me to Haifa; spending time with her for the first time on that day, I explored my surroundings as if for the first time. Everything I saw or came across had some new definition and meaning, different from the one familiar to me before my arrest. On that day, I was completely different. I rolled down the car window and felt the air blowing against my face as though I was a curious child exploring the world for the first time ever. Eyes closed. Air drawn down deep into my lungs. Oh how much I missed the scent and taste of fresh air! Ofra didn't like travelling with the windows rolled down; I learned that from our back-and-forth trips to the courthouse in Nazareth when I was under house arrest in Kiryat Ono. I didn't want to bother her so I rolled the windows back up a few moments after truly living in the moment, a moment for which I had longed for so long. The image of the women political prisoners was still stuck in my mind; I still saw them before my eyes no matter where or when. Despite all the joy I experienced at that moment, my heart was breaking; all of a sudden, a wave of sadness engulfed me. Oh how difficult it was for me to be able to breathe in this fresh air while they were still shackled in al-Damoun and Sharon Prisons. I tried to run away from my thoughts but couldn't. They had become an integral part of my life.

I stared at everything I saw around me, everything within my eyeshot: the ground beneath my feet, the sky, the clouds, the mountains, the cars, the drivers' faces, and though nothing out of the ordinary passed, I felt as though it was my first time ever to see those things. Time passed as I stared at the clock. I wished it would stop so I could stay outdoors. Time turned into some devil that was haunting and chasing me. When we passed by al-Jalameh and I read the sign at the entrance, I felt suffocated. The information sign read 'Kishon Checkpoint,' and as I read those words I felt as though an arm was wrapped around my neck trying to choke me. My anger built up within me and memories came flooding back. All the moments in that place. I relived the moments of my arrest, each and every one of them. On the sign, and adjacent to the Hebrew lines, there was a translation into both Arabic and English. I laughed at the mistranslation I had been suffering from. For a moment, I wanted to get out of the car and change what was written into something that would reflect the reality: 'Kishon Detention Centre for Torture.'

We continued walking and passed Shatta Prison. My eyes were glued to the walls surrounding that prison. Traffic jam. We drove by it at a snail's pace. I scrutinised all the visible axes and angles of that prison. Everybody moved past it and merely saw the walls. I, on the other hand, saw it and knew it inside out; I knew what really went on in its locked, shut cells and within its huge metal gates. I saw the bosta parked in the prison parking lot; I felt as though my body started shrinking like a piece of cloth. That same bosta was yet again right before my eyes! Once we got very close to the prison, I called loudly to Ofra to sound the car siren. She asked: "Why?" "Maybe the sound of the siren will reach the cells where the political prisoners may be able to hear it. This sound will make them feel that something is coming in from the outside." And so she did. Meanwhile, I was thinking to myself and praying for all the political prisoners, women and men, to be granted peace and freedom.

We arrived in Jaffa and Ofra parked her car in an old parking lot located in the old city. My eyes darted from one old building to another; those buildings which attested to the history of that ancient Palestinian city. My camera and I had been there many times. I photographed those alleys, neighbourhoods, the street and the blue windows. One day I came here to take photos for a friend, a journalist and refugee who lives in Jabalia Camp, north of Gaza – he and his family are originally from that city but were displaced in 1948. With the help of his grandfather and father who described it to me, I managed to reach his house which was still in existence and robust despite the disaster. Now, a Jewish settler lived in that house. I took pictures of the house and sent them to my friend. I had a video call with his grandfather and empathised with him. I felt his tears; I couldn't help but sob when he showed me the key to that house on the camera. Until this very day, I don't seem to be able to wipe that moment from my mind; I can never forget the tears that old man shed or the longing that spoke through his eyes. In 2014, when Israeli terrorists and the Zionist occupation bombed his house, I lost my friend. He was a martyr along with his family, eight of them. In one second, they were all martyrs. I tried to escape from those harsh memories. A tear was about to roll down my face. I wiped it. I continued looking around Jaffa, the bride of Palestine. As much as I loved that city, as much as it pained me.

I walked along with Ofra until we arrived at the entrance of the port. There, we went to 'Basma' ('a smile') café. It did not take long for my heart to be filled with warm feelings as I entered it. I loved everything about it: the smell of coffee, the food, Palestinian old tools which reflected their heritage and were gathered then hung on the walls to decorate the place. Old pictures of Jaffa.

On that day, I met a group of friends who supported me and my case, including Mohammad Kundos, Khaled Jabarin[16], Alma Cats[17], Shosh Khan, Einat Weizman[18] and Maysaloun Hamoud[19].

Einat sat next to me. She introduced herself: an artist and a director. She also told me she was preparing for a support soirée that would take place at Saraya Theatre, Jaffa, on the 30th of August. Without further ado, she she turned to me and said she was working on a play called The (Political) Prisoners of the Occupation and would be pleased if I told her more about prison and my experience as a whole. The moment she uttered the name of the play, I remembered I had already heard about it and how it was banned during the 'Acco Festival' that year; that was what I'd read in the newspapers not long ago. During that meet-up, some of my friends came over to me and asked me to fill them in. I tried to ensure that everyone got my undivided attention and I left no one out, yet for some reason Einat took it further. Our conversation was different, and from the bottom of my heart I wished I could continue our discussions. Meeting her gave me a sense of peace and comfort. Another woman whose voice they had been trying to silence because her art was concerned with Palestinian political prisoners. I had a feeling she understood me. I talked to her as much as possible, gave her all the time I could and told her a little about the women political prisoners. How I wished our conversation could keep going but she had to end it. "If you don't mind, could we email one another?" she asked before she headed out. "Not at all. It's a pleasure," I replied. "Texting, though. I have a non-smart phone," I continued. We smiled at each other. She said: "Then we'll stay in touch." I gave her my phone number in the hope that soon enough I'd receive a call from her.

Returning home was too hard for me after that nice, emotional encounter, especially as I knew well that I would be returning to the house where I was confined and would have to wait until the following Tuesday to be able to leave and breathe.

The next morning, I woke up at 8.20am to the sound of my phone ringing. I looked at the screen and realised I'd received a text message from an unfamiliar number. It read: "Hello, Dareen. How are you? This is me,

Einat. It was a pleasure meeting you yesterday. I'm still organising my schedule so as to pay you a visit soon. I will keep you posted and will let you know if it will work. I hope you enjoyed our encounter yesterday." I read the text. Twice. I did so because I was deeply moved. I had no clue what the secret behind my sudden, extreme happiness was. Why her? Throughout my life, I had never got along so well with anyone else before and in such a short time. I replied instantly to her text message: "I honestly feel extremely happy that we met. Detention is tough and harsh, yet I owe to my detention the reason we met in the first place. I met you and I met everyone else because of it. I will forever treasure becoming acquainted with you all. You can come over at your convenience and I will truly be happy. I'm eager to meet you. Thank you for everything."

Einat's face was very familiar, yet it took me some time to remember where I had seen her before. Then I recalled that I once saw her performance in a play called The Saturday Worker in Haifa's al-Midan Theatre. I didn't like the play, as it was an awful story with a weak plot; it didn't reflect reality. I still remember those negative feelings. I wasn't certain whether Einat herself was that actress or not. Sadly, I could not connect to the internet to verify it so I waited until our next meeting to ask her and to confirm what I'd just remembered. On August 12th, she texted me again and told me she would pay me a visit to hear all about prisons, my experience and my story. At 5pm, Einat arrived along with her husband, Yoav, and Iris. She sat right next to me and struck up a conversation. At the end of our meeting, I gave her a copy of my latest book, The Last Invasion, and on the title page I wrote my dedication: 'Poetry is the only thing that is left in this world to keep humans human.' Right before they left, I asked Einat: "Are you that actress who was the main character in The Saturday Worker play?" She said: "Yes, but how did you know that?" I told her: "I saw that play but I did not like it at all." My straightforwardness put me in an awkward position, yet her smile relieved me as she didn't get angry. We walked to the car. My dad accompanied me because I wasn't allowed to leave the house without being under supervision. I said goodbye and we hugged each other. She walked away. Standing a few steps away from me, she turned around, looked at me and came back. She gave me another hug and, before I knew it, I hugged her back and, oblivious to it and for no reason, tears rolled down my face.

The support I received, whether international or from the Israeli community, was still ongoing and broadening, yet that of the Arab community was weakening little by little. Despite this, from time to time, some interesting and unexpected events would take place. One day while I was sitting in my room, I heard a man calling out my name: "Dareen!" I looked outside the window and saw an old man leaning on a wooden stick. "Yes, Hajj (a title given to an older man to show respect)," I shouted back. Immediately, I asked my father to go downstairs to help him upstairs. With excitement written all over his face, he came in and looked at me then said: "I am so proud of you, so proud of your position. I came here for one specific reason which is to show my support. I would like to have a copy of your poetry collection." We sat in the living room, I went to my room to fetch him a copy of my collection The Last Invasion and gave it to him.

Out of his pocket, he fished a paper envelope, asked me to take it, and said: "I read about your case and I want you to keep fighting against the occupation. This is not a charitable donation: it is my duty. I know that you still have a long way to go. Yours is a thorny issue and in order to be able to keep up the good fight against those institutions, you will sure need a pile. This is small amount of money; giving it to you makes me feel that I have helped, even if a little. You should know that you are not alone. You have many people supporting and standing by you." His words touched me deeply. He brought my soul back to life and gave it hope. His words were like a pump that injected more strength, defiance and persistence into my heart. I thanked him for his words, his support and the strength he had given me. I wrote my dedication on the title page and gave the book to him. As he was leaving, he exclaimed: "Keep writing and annoy them all. You're the free one among them in their prison. They are the prisoners. You are fighting for us all; you're defending us all as well." His words filled me with some inexplicable strength. I had felt that long-awaited justice, the justice I wanted to hear about from my people. The pressure of support for my case was enough to break all the chains and restrictions were imposed on me and to defy the oppressive powers and authorities. It was also a clear message that poetry was not a crime; no-one should be convicted of writing poetry.

Einat came over to my house two more times; she kept in touch with me by text messages. Besides some of my court hearing transcripts, I also gave her tons of information which was an asset in her work. She would always update me on all the developments regarding the evening gathering, for which she had set a date, August 30th, and which would take place in Saraya Theatre in Jaffa.

The details of my hearings, the discussions, conversations and questions which took place in the court, the testimonies of Prof. Nissim Calderon and Dr. Yonatan Mendel, in particular, as well as the testimony of the policeman who translated my poem, turned into a source of inspiration, creativity, art and writing. The 'script' of the hearings' protocols, to my surprise, was adapted into a stage play by the director and actress Einat Weizman. It was decided that the play would open and be performed at al-Saraya Theatre in Jaffa with the contribution of a group of supporters. It was an evening gathering dedicated solely to supporting my case. The play was titled Dawalt Israel Ded al-Sha'era Dareen Tatour ('Israel Against the Poet Dareen Tatour').

On August 30, 2017, the evening gathering took place, yet due to my home confinement and its conditions I couldn't attend it. My father, little brother, Ahmad, together with my seven-year-old nephew did, though. "I want to go and film Dodo's evening gathering," my nephew insisted. Those were his exact words; he had always liked to call me 'Dodo'. He took along the camera I had given him as a birthday present two months before my arrest. Over that two-month period, I taught him about photography and how photos are taken. He loved it; "I will film the whole evening gathering so you can watch it." Bittersweet.

Anticipating the end of the evening with mixed feelings, I was passionate to hear all about it. The gathering included my dad's speech as well as Lasky's. It also included readings of my poems which were translated into Hebrew. Art and poetry interventions by artists, poets, Arab and Jewish activists took place as well. In fact, they constituted most of the theatrical play as readers of some of my trials' protocols and in presenting my convicted poem to the audience.

162

The clock struck 11pm. Phones ringing non-stop. Calls kept pouring in. The phone calls I received from my friends who had attended the gathering evening did not cease until late at night. Many words of support after a remarkably successful event. Through it, our message was conveyed; it surpassed all expectations, including mine. Many people had attended. The reading and the presentation of the protocols were artistic and professional. The performance was dramatic. The truth of my trial was highlighted and exposed. Einat told me about the biggest surprise: my poem won strong applause and had built up support.

After midnight, my father, brother and his little son, Tawfiq 'Tootoo', returned home. My father was exhilarated and astonished at the amount of support he'd witnessed. Eminently touched, Tootoo approached me. With a voice filled with sadness, he told me, quietly: "Sorry. The memory card is full. I couldn't film the whole evening gathering. I forgot to take an extra one." I hugged him tightly, gave him several kisses and told him: "You did a wonderful job! Thank you, Habibi, I will watch everything you've filmed."

Three days had passed since the evening gathering. Unexpectedly, my case started taking a new turn. Miri Regev, the Minister of Culture and Sport, published a new translation of my poem on her page. Her translation was filled with mistakes and misconceptions. She demanded that the government sue al-Saraya Theatre as they approved of presenting my poem which was accused of spreading terrorism and incitement to violence. She also demanded that the funding for the theatre stop and that the ministry's budget allocation be cut. It was accused of putting on performances which supported terrorism as well as other political performances against Israel under the pretext of breaking the so-called Nakba law[20].

Within a few hours, my poem's number of views on Regev's page reached up to seventy-five thousand, and it was reposted three-hundred-and-thirty times. Not to mention that her page was liked by thirty-one-thousand two-hundred-and-eighty people.

Those incidents didn't simply go unnoticed. They affected the course of my case and my hearings too, as my defence lawyer used this incident, as well as the fact that Regev had posted my poem, in court to back up my defence. In front of the court, she presented this as evidence to prove my innocence and to refute all the accusations against me. If the poem was

163

threatening and called for incitement and terrorism, as the police and the Israeli Authorities claim, Miri Regev should be punished as well. She did exactly what I had done.

As my lawyer, along with the Public Defence Office, were writing a summary of judgment, and through their research they came on the picture which was captioned "I'm the next martyr", which I posted back in 2014 on my Facebook timeline. It was not removed. The lawyer asked to include it, together with the poem posted by Regev on her page, as evidence in the defence file. The prosecution refused. My lawyer set up a special court instead to discuss the request before the judge. The judge, for her part, also rejected including the picture as new evidence which would prove that I posted it more than a year prior to my arrest. Still, she accepted the evidence regarding Regev posting my poem.

On October 5, 2017, I received the most exceptional worldwide support from PEN International since my arrest. Writer, poet and president of the organisation Jennifer Clement, as well as Carlos Turner, the CEO, paid me a special visit to strengthen the position of the organisation. They took up my case and supported me; they, too, were against such an arrest. That was the greatest message I had received during my continued arrest. That honour would remain carved into my heart.

The prison gave me no choice but to fall in love with the experience – despite its cruelty – simply because I wanted to be released with the least amount of damage and loss. With all that support, I felt as if I had been growing like a plant in the soil of new situations. Only time nourished me with vitality. I was reborn. My body was replete with memories. That very visit in itself was like a new lung filled with the oxygen of hope.

Once a week, I would spend time with Ofra. And every time I did, I would cling to nothing but the hands of the clock. The ticks of the clock haunted me; I would hear it ticking loudly and I started to realise, more than ever, the value of time. I would leave and return right on time. I would carefully map out my way from home and home before leaving, regardless of where I was going. Clocks triggered my anxiety.

After spending two years under arrest, my feelings were still chained despite the fact that I, every now and then, spent time outdoors. I still couldn't be my own company. What hurt me more was that I could not indulge my passion for nature photography. Two years had passed. I could not embrace my camera which I missed dearly; my fingers missed its touch and my ears missed the sound of its clicks with every picture I took. Two years. My poetry and pieces of writing were prohibited from publication. For two years. I was banned from taking part in any political or artistic activities. I was forbidden from working and making a living. Two years with no access to the internet. Deprived of meeting my loved ones and going outdoors with them whenever I wanted for two whole years. I was deprived of it all, things that I used to do before my arrest, for two years. Repeatedly violated by the Israeli authorities over the past two years. Suffering. My conviction was simply thinking outside that patriarchal box. They had attempted to rape my identity and take it away from me. They tried to seize my name, poetry, art and writings just because I was a woman who stood up for herself and dared to say "no". No to human oppression. No to injustice and violations. No to rape. No to occupation. No to male domination. No to silence. Yes to freedom. Yes to the freedom of our Palestinian people and to social justice.

Until proceedings are over, every imprisoned person is not solely in captivity inside a prison, or under the restrictions imposed on them, but is a captive for a time whose end is unknown. In reality, all I knew was that I am imprisoned. Counting days without even knowing when this sentence would come to an end or how many days left until it did. Time was the unknown under the circumstances of my imprisonment.

Four walls, a blue door, a small window and iron bars – that is what makes a prison cell. My home confinement, though, turned all of those into loose terms. Everything that surrounded me was similar to the walls, the shut doors and the bars. The whole household, in my eyes, was nothing but a grey prison. I learned patience and hope. The letters became like a spiritual window with a view of the writing oasis, my escape from all of those chains and restrictions. It was where I sought refuge and it helped me breathe true freedom and endure the hardships of the experience. Writing, alone, opened my heart to horizons worth contemplating. Writing charged my blood with determination; whenever I felt weak and felt the harshness of the world around me, I would speak to myself. I would shout at myself until I was encouraged to get my pen back and get inspired. My reality was bad, but without writing it would be far worse.

Oren Ziv, the photographer, had started coming along with Ofra for Tuesday visits to document my home confinement. Einat, on the other hand, dedicated her Saturdays to pay me visits. During that period of time, we grew closer to each other and became best friends. We would go on talking for hours; I felt as though I could talk to her about everything I experienced and felt. Yoav and Iris visited me regularly too. Similarly, Hanin Zoabi came over to pay me a visit and check in on me several times. Alma, together with her husband, Yoav Birash, and two friends of theirs, visited me for the first time. She was nine months pregnant; I laughed a lot at her belly. We spent that evening in the house, talking. I felt the love that connected us all; it was a nice feeling. After Alma had given birth, she, together with her husband, Yoav, and daughter, Tamara, paid me another visit. I cradled her baby and we laughed so much. Alma was extremely thrilled. I told her: "When Tamara grows up, tell her that she once visited a detained poet. Tell her that she fell asleep in my dangerous arms. I stitched an embroidery piece, as I would normally do for those whom I love and appreciate, and gave it to Alma. As for the singer, Danielle Ravitzki, who visited me several times – she asked me to give her some of my translated poems, both into Hebrew and English, so she could write new pieces of music, compose and sing them. Those included 'Resist, my people, resist them,' the poem that led to my detention.

Tuesday, January 2, 2018

Tuesdays were the only days when I was allowed to spent time with Ofra. A typical tour of my neighbourhood. We didn't decide on a place; we were walking aimlessly. On the spur of the moment, we decided to go to Haifa. On our way to Haifa, using her phone, Ofra checked which films were on; she also checked what time each started. Letting out a laugh, she suddenly told me: "What a coincidence! One French documentary will be on at 4.30. It's the only one. Would you like to go see that movie?"

I smiled and felt as if I had won a precious prize so I agree immediately agreed and said "of course". I had no expectations for that day, and all I could think of was that I would get the chance to breathe some fresh air outside my bedroom for a few hours. Last thing I know, we were at the cinema watching a film. I didn't even ask Ofra about that film, I didn't even know its name or what it talked about. Ofra mentioned its title, yet I didn't really listen as I didn't concentrate. The thought of seeing a film at the cinema was the centre of my attention. It had been a long time and the idea took over my heart and mind. After all this time, I longed to be in a seat in front a big screen and in a dark auditorium. That feeling reigned over my emotions as if spending some time in that hall had become my main goal of the moment. Nothing else was of importance then. We bought two tickets. The auditorium was nearly empty: Ofra and I, along with four other women who were sitting in the same row of seats.

I started contemplating the auditorium and its tiniest details, corners and colours. It was almost entirely covered in red, which caught my eye. I recalled at once that most of the cinemas and stages which I had visited before used red in particular. Then I started asking myself questions I had never wondered about before. I asked myself questions without even trying to answer them. Why were the seats red? Why was the colour red used in most of the furnishings of cinemas and stages worldwide? What was the secret connection between that colour and the cinema? Was there a specific rule or was it just a tradition? When I was a university student majoring in media and film directing, those questions never crossed my mind. I didn't even think about reading the history of that colour or the secret behind it being chosen as the standard colour of cinemas. Lights dimmed. Background music began, announcing the start of the movie. I lost my train of thought. The film was shown on a giant white screen right in front of me. My emotions kept up with its scenes.

The 'Faces Places' movie turned the coincidence of that visit with Ofra to indelible memory. Watching a movie which discussed photography, murals and the effects photographs have on people's lives, especially during those difficult times under arrest and the strange, harsh circumstances, was a beautiful twist of fate and an exciting one too. I myself was not allowed to do what I loved most – photography – but that coincidence summoned many meanings and sensations.

167

How I needed to live a collective human life, with all its social strata and different cultures, a life where the individual's social harmony was evident and society was connected to the individual, so that all burdens and concerns were shared by everyone! How I needed to witness those experiences which emphasised the existence of true human beings and humanity, especially now. The film gave me that chance.

For an entire hour, I felt as if I inhabited every scene of that film, and it was enough to prove that I did the right thing by considering the camera a lifelong friend and to stay loyal to it. I was not wrong when I once wrote: "Until the day I die, the camera will always be my most valuable friend, and my pen will always be my dearest love."

With Agnès Varda and JR, with all those faces and places, I had come to discover the creativity within the soul of photographers. I also learned that such energy was only manifested through the stories of the people we met and photographed, those whose stories we circulated and whose emotions we captured in photographs. That film made me long to hold my camera again and hear its clicks. I felt as if I had done my camera wrong by abandoning it through this period due to my arrest. I returned home energised and deeply moved. I took the camera out of the bag, hugged it and gazed at it. I blamed myself a lot, but then I let out a long laugh, probably the longest in my entire life. I felt a genuine link between my laugh and creativity, and as if the camera had been sending me a message saying: "Let's start redecorating this room and its walls." So I took out all the camera equipment from my bag and cleaned the lenses and started thinking to myself how I could transform my arrest in this small room of mine and between these walls into a message which would grant others a chance to think and contemplate. I started thinking about how those moments I lived under arrest would be turned into concrete ones whose pain would be felt and whose face contemplated by others.

I studied the pictures I'd hung on the walls of my room before my arrest. A lightbulb moment. An idea sparked: taking photos which would tell about my confinement, documenting those scenes in artistic photos and channelling the feelings I was experiencing under this confinement to whoever might see them in the future. With these photos, I just might prove that, to an artist, home confinement would be the most cruel form of punishment inflicted by one human on another and the most hideous way of suppressing an artist's freedom and right to live and express themselves.

Talking to myself, I said: "Yes. I will take photographs so that my eyes will have their own voice too, they will be loud enough for everyone to hear. Through this voice, I will express the pain of my arrest as well as that of many other political prisoners from my country. Our screams shall remain stuck in people's minds and they will see them and hear them wherever they are."

Many photography ideas rushed through my mind one after another. I turned one corner in my room into a small studio to help me take the photos I wanted. Doing so liberated my thoughts. I got back to photography and destroyed yet another chain that smothered me. With every thought, the difficulty of my arrest grew less and less. Then I would transform the idea into a photo that would portray one of the painful feelings I had to endure under confinement.

With every photo I captured, I would look at it and smile; my smile was a mixture of happiness and pain since the pictures depicted a prison and expressed my experience. I would smile while I was expressing my gratitude to my camera and to Ofra for giving me that chance to restore the spirit of photography within me.

This prison that stifled me also set me free; I broke free from many other psychological constraints. It unleashed my dreams and emotions so that I turned them into a lyric to be sung or a story to be told. With the birth of each poem under this arrest, I would discover a new ability to be pleased and inspired. I would then become more creative than I had ever been before my arrest.

Although I had been under arrest for two years, it was not over and I could not see its end around the corner. During those two years, my perception of freedom had changed; the prison had become my freedom. In it, I was able to realise my dreams of writing, so I devoted myself to it. It couldn't be denied that such a road was imposed on me and I had no control over it. However, I was able to be productive, and so I put my words out on paper. I created a timeline and I stuck to it despite the unknown I had yet to face. In this prison, I found solutions to all the problems I had been facing and all my emotional conflicts. I came to realise that imprisonment and the very few options an imprisoned person might have, as well as time constraints, made me more focused, determined and daring. I was able to go beyond all limits of space in which I was placed. I was placed in a tiny spot and I was expected to isolate myself in one of its narrow corners. It came as a surprise to everyone, including myself, that I was able to feel more free. I simply learned that during the time period that was determined for me – and which was expected to be nothing but very dark and strict – I became freer than I had ever been in the past.

The prison in all of its forms as well as the experience during all of its stages became a solution. It ricocheted from one conflict to another with unimaginable emotions. At first sight, the prison might have been no more than a waiting point, yet in reality it was an endless war. I would never forget any moment of it. No political prisoner resumed life the way it was before the arrest. Having to live under arrest was a transformative experience.

Over those years, I fell in love with my solitude away from my family. I was more attached to writing. It was not because they didn't keep me up to date, but they didn't provide me with any beneficial information in the first place. With my isolation, and despite my deprivation and the constraints which opened doors to despair, I discovered new sensations which strengthened my relationships with others, especially my friendships. I realised that deprivation, absence, longing and suffering were pillars to strengthen relationships and lifelong progression. Such relationships were opposite to those that began when life was easy and fun and which eventually wilted and dried out when first put to the test. From my arrest, I learned that the reason why those relationships ended was that they were relationships built on meaningless compliments and apple-polishing. My new friends, however, were my true friends. With them, I knew what genuine emotions were. I had missed and yearned constantly for them. With them, and with full conviction, I realised the true value of living, loyalty and sacrifice.

As in a football game, I was waiting for the whistle of the judge, a whistle that would announce the end of my home confinement or my new beginning. The final sentence was to be passed! Afterwards, I would enter a new qualitative game, an outstanding one. This match would be different from all the others I'd taken part in before. It wasn't about the thrill of it but determination and decision-making. I was waiting to receive the final sentence. I was certain I could still go on and win, regardless of the outcome, whether I had to serve a longer sentence or be set free.

During that waiting period, Land Day as well as the Nakba Day 70th anniversary were being commemorated. The national authorities had decided to extend the protests and events starting from March 30, Land Day, until May 15, the Nakba Day anniversary. The most vehement of these were in the besieged Gaza strip where the protesters were oppressed by the occupation's army by every means. That led to the martyrdom of one-hundred-and-twelve people and the injury of thirty-thousand-and-nine-hundred just because they raised the Palestinian flag and called for the end of the siege and their return to the hometowns from which they had been forcibly displaced in 1948. They were guilty of that.

Journalists, paramedics, people in wheelchairs, children, elderly people and artists were martyred. The occupation's army left no one unharmed; those innocent people were shot. There was no deterrence either locally or globally. Killing those innocent people publicly, directly and brutally, was not deemed a terrorist act for which the criminals had to be held accountable. On the other hand, my poem was the definition of terrorism, according to Israel's apartheid regime. I had to watch those scenes and ache over the pictures of those martyrs in order to express how I stood by my people through my poems, drawings and pieces of writing. That would be one of the ways I could defeat the helplessness I was going through during my arrest.

CHAPTER 20

My sentencing hearing was continually adjourned for various reasons. Sometimes an adjournment was requested by the prosecution, at other times it was called by the judge. On a very few occasions, however, it was at my lawyer's request. Adjournment, to them, was a snap. Why wouldn't it be? They weren't the ones under experiencing arrest; they went about their lives without any constraints or conditions. For me, an adjournment was the toughest of all the news I received. It bothered me a lot, but the more my hearing was adjourned, the more patient and adaptable I became. I had to escape from my circumstances, as if by some emergency escape route to avert the fires of despair and frustration.

Every time I got news of the hearing's adjournment, I would go to my room. Headphones on. Classical music turned up. Heart and soul, I would listen to it. Music was the only way to absorb my anger during that time. It had become my only breathing space during amidst mental, social and familial pressure. Besides writing, music – though strangely – was capable of taking over me and helping me to vent my stress and anger in this grim reality.

I couldn't get enough of it as I immersed myself in its melodies for two or three hours, or maybe more, without feeling bored or tired. After that, I would feel comfortable, secure and refreshed. I would regain my composure, then enter another stage of waiting – waiting for the judge to set a new date.

The fact that my sentencing hearing was adjourned many times only lengthened my period of confinement. It lasted for two years and seven months. May 3, 2018. The date of my sentencing hearing had been set; I would either be convicted or acquitted. I arrived at the Nazareth district courthouse and I was overwhelmed by the number of people at that defining hearing. The national support had expanded in an unexpected way; the courtroom was packed with people who backed my cause; they were from various social and political backgrounds, Jewish and Arab people. Everybody was waiting for the judge to pass sentence. She read it in an almost an indistinguishable voice, so I indicated to her that I couldn't hear anything she was saying. Others did so too. Pause for seconds. She said she was sick and she couldn't speak up. People shouted as they demanded she use the microphone in front of her. Broken microphone. The funny thing was that the pitch of her voice got higher while she was saying those words, her illness vanished all of a sudden. She proceeded with reading her verdict: convicted. As if she had been whispering, she kept on reading. We couldn't make out her words, yet after we had received the protocols we learned that I was convicted of all the accusations against me. The judge set another date to discuss with the prosecution and defence the duration as well as the type of punishment I was to receive. All this barely lasted for ten minutes. I was given fifty-three printed pages in which there was an explanation as to why I was convicted and the points she was keeping in mind before passing sentence on me. From this moment onwards, I was no longer accused of incitement to violence and terrorism or supporting a terrorist organisation. I became convicted. I – together with my poem – still had to wait for the type of punishment and length of sentence, which were to be announced by the end of the month.

The conviction didn't shock me. I saw it coming. What would have shocked me would have been to be acquitted. The logic of occupation. A logic that was characterised merely by injustice and racism and started right when the occupation first set foot in this land and took over it. How could I be surprised when I knew well that I had been subjected to a hearing controlled by the occupier's policy, and in a country that was established at the expense of the Palestinian people's rights? It wouldn't be difficult for an authority and a policy of a country which had been established after confiscating all the rights of the Palestinian people – and was settled in all of this land which was rightfully ours – to seize the rights of a poet, a human being who expressed herself through speaking and writing. My last hope of attaining freedom soon was taken away from me.

Despite all the pain I felt as a consequence of that conviction, I felt happy somehow. I saw freedom approaching me. I heard the sound of applause announcing the end of the play which had lasted for around three years. All the systematic acting and the numerous manifestations of racism and oppression were directed by an authoritarian political system which controlled the country and was disguised by slogans of democracy, justice, human rights and dignity.

That conviction didn't stop me from smiling despite my anxiousness, the deep feelings of subjugation and the enormity of the injustice which I had borne in my heart, whether it was because of what had happened or what was about to happen. I found myself firing a smile like an arrow hitting their faces: it was a smile of daring and power. Keeping a smile on my face in front of them at such moments was a victory. I also smiled at my friends as if I had been asking them to rest assured and remain steadfast. I smiled because I wanted to make them feel my love as well. Smiling at my loved ones was the highest expression of my love for and loyalty to them. Another smile. I sent that to my soul as I was speaking with it and giving it an extra push to remain steadfast and proud. Unplanned, I spontaneously smiled at everybody. My smile carried answers to all the questions addressed to me by media reporters – a large number of them attended the trial. I simply smiled; my smile was enough to encapsulate all that could be said. Through it, I conveyed the most heartfelt message to the waiting world in which I would have to live after the trial. In that moment, my smile was the ecstasy of victory. Suffice as to say that with my simple, spontaneous smile I didn't fulfil the end desired by those who wanted me to feel sad and regretful or to cry. It was a clear message: no power on Earth shall silence my voice, my feelings, my poetry or writing. It was a rejection of all those who attempted to do so, whether the Israeli authorities or my so-called cousin who believed that by playing a role in my arrest and trial he would forever silence my voice. He would be surprised. My vocal chords were stronger than ever; they would keep echoing.

My smile did not express happiness deep within, yet it showed that my poems made me mightier than the circumstances, accusations and authorities. By smiling I was the toughest. Keeping a smile on my face, I walked further away. And with every smile brought to my face, I felt that I definitely was stronger; with that smile and with my poetry, I could go further. The only weapons I carried in that battle were poetry and my smile. With my smile, I turned my defeat to a victory and my conviction into acquittal. Poetry dusted off. Poetry triumphed over the authorities that encircled me. I had a feeling my smile made my enemies cry and lose their taste for the delusional victory they had pursued for all this time. It was as if I had said and proved that my jailers were the convicted and guilty ones. They were the prisoners, not I. My smile proved that.

I read the guilty verdict statement written by the judge; it made her sound as if she, overnight, had turned from a person who worked at the Judiciary Service into a researcher in the fields of language and poetry. It was as if she had become a language teacher or a poetry analyst. She explained the poem from her own perspective, and she interpreted its wording using her own lexicon and according to the positions taken by the prosecution and the police. The most noticeable thing about her analysis, however, was that she adopted the translation of Dr. Mendel, a translation specialist. She said she hadn't been convinced by his interpretation and that she was rather more convinced by the interpretation of the policeman who translated the poem, as he was an Arab and Arabic was his mother tongue; he was also raised in an Arab community to which I, too, belonged. Another reason she was more convinced by his interpretation than Dr. Mendel's was that he would understand those terms and the intention behind them, unlike the specialised translator whose area of study was translation! Still, his first language was Hebrew. Besides, he was born and raised in a different community and environment from the one to which I belonged.

Many times and at different periods, I read and re-read my conviction. Each of which left me more lost, looking for my lost poem among all the interpretations, analyses and mistranslations to the extent that I laughed while I was reading the judge's analysis and what she had based it on to prove her accusations.

My conviction didn't scare me as much as it thrilled me and spurred me to think about what was ahead – the length of the sentence length the judge would determine, and the necessity to plan ahead, no matter what was in store. I would finally be able to see, with my own eyes, the end. It was very close.

After spreading the news of my conviction, the minister of culture and sport, Regev, issued a video statement on her Facebook page where she expressed her joy over the decision of the Nazareth magistrates court. She was smiling. Afterwards, and after she called me a "criminal terrorist," she said that she gave the verdict her blessings as it was a right and wise one. Once again, she incited everyone to turn against me and to sue Jaffa Theatre for showing the play, which included the reading of my poem and the evening gathering in support of my case, even though the prosecution acknowledged that the event was considered artistic work and integral to the right of free speech; the theatre could not be punished for that.

As I was reading the papers of my conviction, I suddenly remembered that one of the local council employees paid me a surprising visit; his visit was an attempt to make me compromise and not to proceed with my case. He wanted me to apologise to the authorities, admit that I was wrong, sign a pledge and submit a written one which stated that I would never compose political poems any more or ever discuss politics in my writing. In return, my case would be closed. One of my brothers who was a friend of his seemed to like the idea; my dad was encouraged too. An irresistible offer! They thought that would spare me and my family anxiety. They thought that with that offer they were helping me. I completely rejected the idea; I didn't want to negotiate it. I even verbally insulted that man, you could say I almost kicked him out after mocking him along with all those who agreed with him on such nonsense. Consequently, that offer to lend a hand, which I rejected, resulted in writing a letter against him, and unexpectedly hit them twice as hard.

When his face turned pale with shock when I refused that nasty compromise, resisted that new offer and refused to give up my rights and abandon my poetry, my family pressurised me increasingly to try to influence my decision. I ruined it all for them, and that didn't affect me the slightest. On the contrary, I clung to my opinion and held onto my rights and resolve until the end, making it clear to everybody that I had endured this entire period of my arrest, oppression and suffering and I wouldn't make a cowardly surrender after all that I had been through. I was determined to carry on. I would finish what I had chosen from the very start. I wanted to continue writing in a language of my choice and employing the words which pleased me. I would use the expressions which perfectly fitted the atmosphere of my own poem until my last breath, even if that cost me years of imprisonment. I would never change my mind or go back on my opinion as I was completely convinced of my right to express myself freely, just like any poet. I was also convinced that this art form should acquire immunity from the claimed democracy.

Thinking back to that situation and reading my conviction file were other reasons to reconcile fully with my inner self again. After that, I felt respect and appreciation for myself. I felt inner peace, which I had never experienced before. My thoughts started flowing, as did my emotions imagination towards more poetry.

The inner peace I felt with each incident during my arrest, and with all the things by which I was surrounded, turned into an inner explosion by itself. It became the theme and subject of my poems. I realised that being at peace with oneself could not be reached unless one's soul heard the war drums beating. Moreover, I realised that for my poetry to remain alive, its genre had to be reserved. It represented me and reflected my reality.

After undergoing many forms of suffering while I was under arrest, I was able to let go of everything that exhausted my soul. I stopped becoming attached to things as I used to do. I shed the fake love of those I'd thought were loyal friends from my soul. I learned what true love was, the kind of love for which my emotional bleeding was worth. I held tight to my dreams. I explored and learned about myself more. I gave myself a chance for introspection. I shed the habit of excessive nail-biting – a habit I'd got into before my arrest as a result of living under stress. I hated it and tried to break it so many times yet had always failed. In the hustle-bustle of it all, and despite the stress and pressure, I did it. That achievement was another victory against myself and my circumstances. I trusted my determination more, and I reconciled with myself. I broke free from all of those constraints and chains. I only had one left: this prison. I didn't know when I would celebrate my full freedom.

CHAPTER 21

May 31, 2018
11am

People packed the courtroom; their number exceeded all the previous times. All chairs occupied. The guards wanted to force people who couldn't find available chairs out the courtroom. Lawyer Lasky, however, asked for judge's permission to allow them to sit in the front seats designated for lawyers. Arabs and Jews, from various political and social backgrounds, they all sat down. A picturesque scene! That image would forever be stuck in the minds of the people there: the faces of people looking, worried and waiting for the sentence to be passed by the judge. That image communicated the true meaning of peace which none of us had experienced before. What made it distinct was that it was a genuine feeling shared and felt wholeheartedly by every person in the room. Not only was that image beautiful on the outside, it also carried a great, higher message. My poem and I were accused of incitement and terrorism according to the racist judicial system, although, in reality, the poem could spread love, friendship and amity amongst us all. That hearing, in my eyes, was like a picture depicting the meaning of love which nobody had inhabited or comprehended except for those who witnessed its emotional moment. My threatening poem and I, the "criminal terrorist" poet, as I was called by Miri Regev, were able to achieve love and peace which would always be remembered.

The prosecution, famous for surprises, as usual, took me by surprise. This time, she surprised me by the fact that, in writing, she had submitted her argument as well as her claims for the type and length of the sentence she requested of the court. We had no idea about the length of the sentence I would have to serve until my lawyer, Lasky, took a break which lasted for more than half an hour, during which she read the papers and revealed they contained. We found out that the prosecution demanded that I serve a fifteen-month to twenty-six-month sentence; she argued that prison would be the only effective deterrent for people like me. Prison was the sole, proper deterrent to limit the crimes I had committed. She also demanded that I pay a fine, but she didn't determine the amount. The prosecution asked the judge to determine it instead, as the court saw appropriate for such crimes. Restrictions would be placed on me after the sentence was served, with a suspended prison sentence if I committed the same violations in the future.

What was funny about her written pleading was the part where she mentioned that I, up until that moment, hadn't shown any signs of regret for what I had done. The proof was that I didn't regret publishing my poem and hadn't apologised for doing so or admitted I made a mistake. The silliest part I read was where she mentioned that I showed no regret as I didn't delete my Facebook posts and didn't take the initiative. Nothing would ever make me laugh more than such statements. I had no access to the internet throughout my arrest. The police had kept my mobile phone and computer since I was first arrested up until that moment.

I laughed harder when I read what she said about how threatening my poem and words were as well as her claims that my incitement to violence and terrorism had not stopped since all of my posts still appeared on my Facebook timeline. Could there be anything funnier than those desperate words of hers? What she wrote only showed how the police and the prosecution trivialised my case from the outset. When the police arrested me and imposed restrictions on my exercise of freedom yet left my threatening poem out there where everyone could read it or listen to it, then by doing so did not put a halt to that purported threat. On the contrary, they contributed to its spread; the police arrested me and encouraged people's curiosity about my 'inciting' poem. One of the most trivial matters I had ever experienced or read about. I don't think I'll ever read or learn anything that surpasses it in silliness. It should be called 'the joke of this time.'

In the written pleading of the prosecutor-general, I also came across the exaggeration of my accusations. Lies and delusions. She included some alleged instances of people who had been charged and convicted for similar reasons, and who had been sentenced. Their punishment resembled that which she demanded for me.

Despite all the laughter, misery and the mixed emotions I felt as I was reading the written pleading of the prosecutor-general, and at more than any other hearing where my lawyer defended my being a poet, my right to express myself freely, and poetry which I loved and mastered, I was deeply moved by lawyer's pleading. It had significantly and deeply affected me; her words and expressions were loaded with genuine amity. She wasn't defending me simply because she was doing her job, she defended me based on her being convinced by art, poetry, language and creativity. It brought tears to my eyes when I heard her saying: "We're standing before a convicted poet. She has been standing in the corridors of this courthouse for more than two-and-a-half years as a result of her creative product. When we ask of the creative artist and poet to betray and renege on their creativity, it would be as if their heart was ripped out of their chest."

Her words were enough to cut right through and sum up my emotions. They silenced the echoes I heard whenever I was blamed and reprimanded by many people, including my family and friends, because of my writing and publishing my poem. Her words transformed me with feelings of life, hope and peace. They made me feel more confident, determined and patient, at least.

The hearing ended. The judge asked me if I agreed to meet the probation officer; she gave me a choice whether to accept or refuse that request. She notified me that my approval would mean it would take at least three months to set a date for sentencing. My lawyer asked me, but I rejected the idea altogether because I realised that doing so would not add anything new to my case; it would only be another form of lengthening my home confinement with extra months which wouldn't count if I was sent to prison, no matter for how long.

The judge accepted my decision, and she addressed both parties: the defendant and the prosecution "Keep me informed if you decide otherwise regarding this matter." Date of case set: June 24, 2018. 11am. Sigh of relief. I would end the inner conflict of waiting that I'd lived through. I'd seen no light at the end of the tunnel for too long.

I lived my whole life despising anticipation. Living in anticipation was difficult and now was more difficult given that I knew what would happen was out of my control. It was all in the hands of another power, an authority which controlled my time. I, sighing with each passing day, waited yet received no calls to let me know that there would be another adjournment.

With each passing day, despite how slowly days pass, my hearing approached. I felt relieved, somehow. My relief was mixed with anticipation, fear and nervousness as the end, which I had been waiting for so long, was drawing near, regardless of the scenario they have constructed for me.

Waiting. How agonising waiting can be! Prison environment. I was just sitting there, in my bedroom, staring into space. Lonely and isolated. My eyes wandered restlessly around the room. I still did my habitual rituals but we were bored with one another – that is, my rituals and I. I played with my Persian cats and I contemplated each one of their movements, their exchanged looks and the way they played with each other one minute and with me the next. I practised and tried everything that came to my mind to pass my time. Waiting was killing me. My bedroom had turned into a testing ground for my thoughts, emotions and sensations. As I stared at the phone, in disapproval, the time dragged by. The names of those I missed were running through my head and I was hoping they would appear on my small, old phone's screen and light it up. Throughout my wait and its anguish, I had lived with my wishful thoughts and my longing heartbeats for hearing my friends over the phone, those friends whose echoes of voices had vanished since the beginning of my arrest. I waited. As I was waiting I recalled my sweet memories of days gone by, and then I woke up to another reality: phantom silhouettes of things that would never be realised. I looked around. I tried to give myself some false hope. Even false hope was fading with each passing day, hour and moment. I decided again that I would not wait for any of them any more. I had made up my mind. I would never look back on my love story and my friendship which no longer existed. I would live only in the present and be with my friends who had been there for me during my dark patch. Those were the truest and the most beautiful. In my heart grew another love story of a different kind, a story that I had not known before.

Waiting was eating me up inside as if it were a flame burning down a candle wick. It melted down, drop by drop. It had weighed me down, together with my heart, especially as I didn't expect anything good to come out of my upcoming court appearance. I tried to make the best of this time in every way possible, but those emotions accompanied me, no matter how much I tried.

Thursday, June 21, 2018

I woke up at 8am. Eyes fixed on the date. I put a big smile on my face as I was telling and reassuring myself that this day would pass, and that since it was the weekend there would be no further adjournment this time; I was not informed otherwise. I sighed. I felt as if I had been approaching, bit by bit, the moment of truth. It would be the end of my battle with waiting. I received numerous calls from people who wanted to attend the hearing as it meant something to them. Those people supported my position and would stand by me during the hearing. They called because they wanted to make sure that the hearing's date hadn't changed; they wanted to confirm the time and the date.

At 3pm, the phone rang. Lasky's name appeared on my blue screen. I took a deep breath and answered her call. The news hit me like a bullet. Case adjourned.

I felt extremely dizzy. The whole world spun around me. I fell on my bed and couldn't wrap my head around that news. It was almost impossible for me compared with the previous times. It was as if a bullet had suddenly hit me while being at a wedding. I felt as if my heart was about to stop any moment. I couldn't speak or hear a single word uttered by anyone. All the patience I had been building and restoring through time had crashed down on me out of revenge. I detested everything around me. I cursed everything, even the thoughts in which I believed. I cursed my patience, my strength, my decisions, my luck and my fate. No place for hope left in my heart. Everything was broken into little pieces, all the beauty and logic I had within. Shocked. It was a real shock which was carved into my heart and mind.

I could not comprehend what was happening; it was as if death had been coming my way. I wished it would take my soul away and save me from that pain. I weakened and felt that everyone was toying with my emotions and kicking them as if they had been playing football; they would kick the ball against a tough wall, filled with pins. They took turns to kick me around mercilessly. They waited until I burst with pain and oppression. I was terrified of my reaction as I was shocked, nervous and angry. I was scared that it, too, would be a curse that would fall on everyone else, including those who had nothing to do with this. I decided not to discuss this topic with anyone because I didn't want to hurt anyone by my words or emotions, just like others had been harsh on my heart. I remained silent and didn't bring the news up in front of anyone, my close friends in particular. I didn't want any word to slip out of my mouth and make them feel hurt. My one and only call. I had to call Ofra and briefly keep her posted. I asked her to spread the news by telling my comrades and friends. Phone turned off.

For a second, I wished that I had the ability to practise my old rituals when I was in distress, as I used to before I was arrested. I used to publish a poem on my blog or post it on Facebook. I would be occupied with following up on the replies. I spent time outdoors on my own and standing still for hours in front of the sea, which I adored. I would do some of my favourite sports, such as swimming and running on the beach, or I would go for a walk in the neighbourhoods and on the streets of Nazareth, all by myself. If not in Nazareth, I would spend time in Acre, its port and walls, with my camera while my headphones were on. I would be listening to my favourite music to cleanse myself from all that pain that washed over me. I wished I had been able to get out of the house on my own to let out all the anger I felt by taking photos, the hobby I was passionate about, my saviour whenever fate decided I was to feel lost. I made so many wishes and then woke up to reality, a reality which imposed the failure of realising any of my wishes or anything that I liked, loved or wanted. Doors locked. Windows closed. Curtains rolled down. Darkness in my small room. Headphones on. Music turned up: Mozart. I had some hope that some of the notes might have the ability to absorb all of my anger just like the previous times.

And just like that, with a few words uttered by the judge, I, yet again, returned to another deadly dull, long waiting show. I had to wait for the sentencing hearing. The reason for adjournment, as it was written in the decision, was: "Upon considering and reading the defence (pleading) of both parties with regard to the punishment, the big picture of the convicted still can't be seen. In order to do so, receiving the report of the probation officer would be needed." The date was set: July 26, 2018. It would be the deadline for submitting the report while July 31, 2018, would be my sentencing hearing date.

After spending a few hours with myself and keeping in mind the new date, I felt more resentful. The judge, by adjourning the trial, in my opinion, was punishing me, just like the system which managed my case.

I felt as if I had been treated like a number or a file. The fact that I was human was completely forgotten; some parties would overlook the fact that a human being had been standing, waiting and had suffered incredibly. The new set date was another anxiety trigger since it was determined after the judicial vacation had begun. During my arrest, two of the hearings which were set by the judge had been adjourned over the past two years – two or three days beforehand – until the end of July, due to the refusal of the prosecution to work over holidays. And if the judge rejected the prosecution's request, she would justify that by making some excuses, including alterations or emergencies, a day or two prior to the hearing. I was scared the scenario would repeat itself this year too. I was almost certain that it was what had actually happened.

These misgivings took over my heart and mind, so I thought of a solution to cut short the torture of waiting. After thinking it over, I made a decision to end that conflict by getting back to prison, instead of staying under home confinement, so as to start my countdown for my sentence. That would make this counterclockwise time pass easier for me. I wanted to end the art of the inhumane torture show.

I could not bear any more pressure. Feeble and fallen apart, I had no power or strength. I thought of other solutions, but lack of motivation hindered me. I couldn't get over the despair of the wait. I felt they had drained all the energy I had, and that the only way to finish the house confinement would be what I first thought of – that period that wouldn't count when the judge passed sentence.

This time, I would write the end; I'd do it my way. This time I had decided not to wait for the torture lying ahead; I wouldn't wait for either the judge or the prosecution to adjourn my hearing once more while they only dealt with my case as a folder left on the shelf or a mere number saved on some dumb computer. I was the only one who was suffering under these harsh, restrictive circumstances. Everyone else was going about their lives freely. I was the only person whose emotions were being toyed with without any humane restraint.

This is how I wanted my case to take place on this day and by my own decision, despite how difficult it was, as it connoted weakness and surrender, both of which resulted from a loss of hope in a fair and just decision by this racist, fascist, Kafkaesque court. I was determined to take action as soon as possible without seeking anyone's consultation. I waited for the right opportunity to tell my lawyer about that tough decision after the weekend.

For three nights in a row, I tossed and turned. Three sleepless nights. An empty stomach, I had nothing but some water. Despite all of the feelings I had, having made my decision, I composed a new poem. That poem alone, one Sunday morning, was able to bring a smile to my face, a smile that had been suppressed and vanished for the past three days.

By doing so, I brought this poem to light, it made me feel at peace and it communicated the message for which I had been waiting; it was the most important of all to me. The message reassured me that, in spite of making that painful decision, I would never stop composing poetry, even under the harshest circumstances. Amidst the stress I was under, poetry was the only thing that retained its special place in my heart and I hadn't lost faith in. It had become more effective during those tough times and given this harsh decision.

On Sunday, June 24, 2018, instead of standing before the judge, I went along with Edith Breslauer, one of the assigned attendants as well as Yoav Haifawi, to meet my lawyer. Some supporters of the case, who were also very close to me, joined us.

I announced my decision in front of everyone. My lawyer didn't agree with me; she was discontented and rejected it. She described it as surrender, especially as we were almost through. She clarified some points and she assured me that this move wouldn't work in my favour. It would cause more damage as it would give the green light to the judge to simply pass her sentence against me, and I would certainly go to prison. Such an impulsive decision ruled out any chance, no matter how small, of avoiding imprisonment. It was still possible and was argued during the decision-making process. I looked into the eyes of those who were present to feel their despair and sadness for me. I realised I was selfish by making such a decision. The stares of my friends killed me and so did the words of my lawyer, as if some arrows pierced my heart deep inside. I cried on the inside. I couldn't hold back my tears any longer, nor could I stop myself from collapsing. I was at my weakest; I was burdened. I took off, trying to escape those stares. For a few minutes, I stood outside the office in tears. I was lost and desperate. Einat followed me. Her eyes tearful, she stared into my eyes and I stared back. Alma joined us afterwards; she came closer to me and took me into her arms. Einat and Alma tried to alleviate the pain. I could never cause them to feel miserable, so I looked at them and said: "I'm fine." I looked up at the sky and took a deep breath. I was sad and desperate.

Yet again, I convinced myself, maybe falsely this time, that I was wrong to make such a decision, and that I had no right to give up at this point. I went back in. Smiling and thinking that a smile might bring tranquility to those anxious, anticipating faces. I went back in and changed my mind. I reversed my decision.

I told everyone who gathered in the office: "I will follow through with this strict house arrest and under the harsh conditions under which I live. But if the hearing is adjourned once more, I will not carry this through." Back to the unjust home confinement. Waiting, anticipating, scared and anxious.

I returned home only to live with the nightmare of waiting again. It was the most difficult of all times since I had to go back on my decision. I had a feeling that I was the one who shackled myself with the ropes of despair, weakness like a triple fisherman's knot after this setback. The first knot was when I decided not to complete my time of home confinement and announced my defeat at that stage. The second knot was when I went back on the decision I myself had made and considered to be a logical one, and a decision that would save me from these circumstances I lived under. I knew all too well that the sentence passed by the Israeli Judiciary would not do me justice. The third knot was when I hurt my friends in one way or another and broke out in tears in front of them without protecting their feelings. During those three situations, I considered myself weak, collapsed and selfish as this case was no longer a personal one. It included everyone who was there for me and showed their support, and those who had stayed and never left me alone throughout my house confinement period. I felt that this time I was my own prisoner; I shackled myself with chains and emotions I had already let go of during my home confinement. Those were the emotions I had fought so hard to escape. Succumbing to this weakness and constraining myself was similar to the Israeli Authority's shackling of my freedom, preventing me from publishing my writing, and living a normal life despite my need and desire, more than ever, to publish and live a normal life. Another chain. As if I had surrendered to society, family and male domination.

I couldn't kill my fear, as I had to begin another journey of waiting. I lost my strength; I couldn't face those tough moments. Time dragged by. This time was a world away from the previous ones. I didn't have enough courage. I started a new battle with waiting and with time. I tried to be in control of time, not let it be in control of me, yet waiting had got longer as my lifetime was shortening. Even by waiting, nothing was guaranteed. I began to doubt I'd survive until the moment the sentence was passed: death might sneak up on me before the sentence, making its word the last in this story of mine. These were the emotions I had started to experience. Nothing was ever guaranteed in this life; my life itself wasn't guaranteed by this home confinement. With all of these feelings, I came back to my attempts to keep myself busy with the things I liked and was allowed to do. I didn't want to waste any of my time, which was still was in the hands of the judge. I wanted to do things of use; things that would add something to my life something and would eventually leave a mark, whether for me or for the others.

Bleak day. At noon I received a call. I learned when the date of my meeting with the probation officer was set: Wednesday, June 27, 2018 at 11am. I was ill-prepared. I didn't prepare for any questions or responses. I hadn't received any preparation or notification from my lawyer concerning that meeting, although she had promised she would guide me through it to get it done with the best possible outcome. She did not. I, for my part, didn't call her or enquire about the matter. I was careless and nonchalant. All I had in mind was that I wouldn't utter a single word of apology or regret for what I had done, no matter what happened and regardless of the outcome. I was convinced I had not done anything wrong.

I sat holding a book in a waiting room. I was reading and I felt at peace. I was waiting for the meeting with the officer to start. Fifteen minutes passed before a thirtysomething man came in, confirmed my identity and asked me to accompany him to his office.

He made a gesture with his hand to show me my designated seat. He sat at his desk while I sat on the chair. I looked around the room and explored each of its corners until my eyes were glued to a big photographic portrait. It was hung on a wall close to my seat and right before my eyes. It was the photo that Steve McCurry took of the Afghan girl, Sharbat Gula. I looked at her glowing, magical green eyes, and I looked deep into her sharp, piercing gaze whose strength and daring were inspiring as they overflowed with pain, anger and agony. There was some interconnection between what I had been feeling and those emotions in the portrait, especially since the start of my 'threatening poem' case. That photo of Sharbat, which was taken in 1984 while she was at an Afghan camp during war and which, later, turned into a symbol of the suffering of Afghanistan under what the West called the Soviet occupation, transformed suddenly into a reflection of my story. My story of a long-lasting battle with the Israeli authorities, who invaded my life, stole my right to express myself and took my right to compose poems and publish them freely.

I left my soul there to have a conversation with the photo. For a second, I felt as if what was standing in front of me had been a friend who was close to my heart, if not the closest. I pictured the photo sending me a message which everybody else failed to deliver. She read to me a line from my convicted poem which went like this:

'Do not fear the fire tongues of the Merkava tank
for the belief in your heart is stronger'

Suddenly, I came to a decision. The meeting would record our victory without giving up my poem, principles or position. There would be no weakness or going back this time. That meeting had been imposed on me and it was taking place in a moment. My job then would be programming it and turning it into a football match. I was the defender and I was about to score a goal for myself and my team, yet it would be an own goal, a well-taken one, during stoppage time, into the net of everyone who'd had had a hand in my torture from the first day of my arrest until the very moment of the adjournment of my sentence and the abominable wait.

To reconcile with myself one more time and forget what had recently occurred, I had to sweep to victory at this meeting, no matter how, and to turn it into motivation to keep me going until my sentencing hearing arrived.

I wore a wide smile on my face and exchanged glances with the Afghan girl Sharbat Gula in the painting; I stood in front of my dear and lovely friend to express that I was looking forward to meeting her. I imagined her speaking to me: "Let your story be just like this painting; it became part of history by chance and without planning." I pictured the moment when McCurry took that picture after being taken by surprise when the girl came up to him and asked him: "Would you take a picture of me?" He took that photo without him stopping to think that it was the photo which chose him and made him yield and would be the photo of his lifetime. The photo he took in 1984 and published as the cover page of the National Geographic magazine in 1985 was life-changing and guaranteed he won the 'Capa Gold Medal', after the photo's aesthetics in the glance of Sharbat were admired by so many. That affection turned to compassion for the girl and the misery of her people too. To this very day, the effect of that photo hadn't vanished. At the time, I thought to myself that my poem and I deserved a photo that would perfectly fit our suffering so it would be etched in our memory. Right away, I decided to take a picture of myself that was not any less beautiful than the beauty that stood steadfast before me for all of those years. A picture of myself that I would never forget; it would live on in my heart; it would be as enduring as the glance that was hung on the wall. A picture that I would gift to my friend who had been waiting in anticipation to hear some news about me; it would alleviate, even only a little, her anxiety and fear for me.

That message marked a decision I had to abide by; I urged myself to implement it to reach my desired goal. In light of it, I promptly initiated a conversation with that officer so he would lose the chance to pose commonly asked questions, and listen to my side of the story – the truth behind my threatening poem, the truth that he hadn't and wouldn't find any trace in my case paperwork written by the prosecution and the court. I wanted to provide him the information I needed to convey my own perspective before he formed an idea of me from what he read in the paperwork, indictment list and conviction record. True victory in such a match couldn't be realised unless the opposing team was manoeuvred to score a goal. Sticking to the plan.

Inspired by my friend and reminded by a line from my poem, I knew that the beginning was about how I really felt. So I started the conversation thus: "Just so you know, I am sitting here in this meeting before you by force. This meeting has taken place without my will or approval. I am here today just because the judge has decided that the report which you will write about me is necessary. My trial has been adjourned due to the lack thereof. She asked me if I agreed, yet I utterly refused. And the reason behind this is my distrust of this system which is managing my case, meaning that it's the same organisation you work for."

Our conversation lasted for three hours. I mainly talked about my relationship with poetry and photography. I also discussed freedom of speech; I had the right to express myself freely through the form of art I mastered. Additionally, I addressed my writing experience, so I talked about how it all came about, i.e., the beginning of my writing journey, the poetic movement with which I identified and to which I belonged as well as the first poem I wrote and its topic. I described my case status, which I referred to as illegal, racist and far removed from the democracy which the Israeli authorities claim. Moreover, I explained to him the support I'd received from all over the globe and gave him the names of the societies that supported my case in several countries. I mentioned some names of writers, poets and artists who signed a petition calling for my release. Finally, I told him more about my case and its political, social and cultural dimensions in addition to the reactions to it from the outset until the news of my adjournment.

As for the officer, he tried to get me to apologise for what I had done four times. He strived to make me utter a single word of regret for writing the poem. I insisted on my position and made it clear that I didn't experience any feelings of regret and I was convinced that what I did was right since all I did was express a feeling that I had experienced through composing a poem. In other words, I transformed my human emotions into a work of art.

Our conversation ended with one sentence on his part. He told me: "I cannot send a human like you to prison. In all honesty, I will recommend community sentence over prison. Prison is not for people like you." I felt I had achieved my aim at this meeting, the outcome of which was still not guaranteed. After what I had suffered for around three years, I couldn't trust anyone in this system. I felt tranquil and balanced: my true victory in this contest that had been imposed on me. The officer's opinion was yet another victory, although I didn't really know whether he would write his report based on what he had told me. However, it was enough for me to feel that I'd been able to introduce a differently-detailed decision to the court.

I cleared up the blurry picture to the judge and kept my promise to the friend I loved. I fulfilled my instinct by interpreting photos and my love for photography. Three factors instilled and inspired me to such an ability and power to stand before that officer and talk confidently to him. I sensed that my poem would win against all unjust authorities and brute force, even if I had to wait for so long. My yearning for freedom was greater and stronger than any tyranny on Earth. Because rights are beams of light, they shine more brightly with every passing day, and they lit up every cell in my body, expelling all gloominess and distress. The three inspiring factors had been: my love for my friend, poetry and photography.

191

CHAPTER 22

Writing was the hope I clung to every time I was about to fall into loneliness, despair and pain. Writing helped me to rise above it all and save me from a certain fall. The poems I wrote when everything inside of me was screaming in despair, were the only hand extended to pick me up and help me out when all my old friends abandoned me and gave up on me. Losing my past relationships was what affected my social life for the most part, especially now that the end was on the horizon. The more the sentencing hearing approached, the more I thought about the beginning of my new life in all its details. This arrest altered everything.

I was certain that after gaining freedom, I would be all alone and would start a new life as if I were a newborn. I would start looking for new relationships and friendships. I would start a new lifestyle since all my old friends and acquaintances, most of whom had vanished after I got arrested, would not be with me. Only three of them were left, yet I didn't hear from them after the verdict was delivered. They'd also given up on me; they didn't call on the phone as much as they used to do. We used to talk on the phone on a daily basis. Now, if I called them, the response was cold, or they would come up with an excuse to end the call as quickly as possible. As time passed, they stopped picking up the phone. I then decided that I would never call them because I didn't want to be such a burden on anyone or to impose myself on them. I decided to respect their decision to keep me at a distance, although it stabbed me in the heart. The Israeli authorities could not frighten me, but they were able to frighten those who around me, my acquaintances and friends from my activism and writing. At the same time, though, these people had widened my horizons and allowed me to see the world differently. As the end was drawing near, my only hope of my beautiful past before my arrest vanished, and everything that connected me to my friends was gone. That arrest caused my ties with them to be cut, yet I couldn't erase them or the way I felt towards them. My longing for those friendships, which brought us all together for a whole decade, would lead me to open our photo albums where I collected all the memories we shared, and to contemplate the love we'd had for one another until this

192

ending. Everything was nothing but a memory. I cried bitterly in silence. Only my heart could hear those echoes with every picture I saw which reminded me of a beautiful memory we had shared. My pain, grief, loss and deprivation tore me up inside. Silent screams. Not even for a moment did I regret the path I'd chosen. Despite my home confinement, I was able to make new, unique friendships, which granted me the true love I needed and had always wanted. They gave me attention, hope and sacrifice. Still, I couldn't deny the fact that this reality hurt me. I couldn't hide my pain from myself even if I managed to hide it from others. The pain of my past memories with my old friends wouldn't leave my memory alone especially during the last days of my wait. I was worried, grieving and longing. The mere thought of my future without them caused pain that squeezed my body and soul so tightly. Sleeping to one reality and waking up to another was very difficult. I was used to that reality but had been completely cut off of it for three years.

Three years had passed and changed everything about my life, no matter how big or small the details were. I still thought my life would undergo further change once I gained my freedom. I had to get myself ready for facing this reality so as not to be shocked or ruin the taste of success which had taken every ounce of energy to achieve. Everything was about to change: my friends, work, place of residence, lifestyle, how I treated others, emotions, feelings, ideas, my economic situation, and so forth. In a nutshell, I would start my life from scratch. I would have to live a life where everything would be different from what I was used to before and during my arrest. The only nice yet scary and exciting thing during this period of time would be that I, now, was a well-known poet; a number of my poems had been published and translated into several languages. Many people were waiting for my next literary work to be published. How should I behave with that unexpected fame for which I had no plan, as it had never been my goal? It was something I hadn't taken into account, especially amidst such difficult and unusual circumstances.

One of the principles I uphold is that I don't let anyone down, particularly when it comes to poetry and art, so I had decided to deal with my new life in a way that would serve poetry, my future and my message as a poet only. The only thing that remained unchanged in my life was composing poetry and being attached to it. That was the life I chose to live on release; that craft chose me as one of her offspring. With poetry and writing, I was revived. Taking this path would make me soar like a bird, but without it I would be lock up in myself, isolated in the cage of a meaningless life.

I had one more thing which was no less important. It had evolved over those three past years of arrest and in all its stages, in prison, confinement under house arrest and in exile: hold tightly to feminism more than ever. I almost held a grudge against the Israeli authorities, patriarchy, male domination and tribalism – those authorities that caused my suffering and I fought against with every ounce of energy despite the lack of available means. I'd faced a multi-framed masculine system. All of those authorities gathered to shut me up and pressured me so as to weaken me and force me to retreat from my right to express myself freely. With my long-held belief in that right, and all the support I had received, I transformed such pressure into an ally which helped me to stand stronger. I held onto my beliefs even more and so my resolve turned into resentment against those authorities which I watched before my eyes become subject to my determination, resilience and decisions. They gave up their position when I refused to be a passing thing after all that they had put me through. I rejected the way they treated me and their ceaseless attempts to ratify and objectify me. That was something I utterly refused.

Feminism became my main concern. I started planning out my life ahead after my release. I even set myself a programme to develop this movement and change it; I wanted to contribute to it so I could make it happen. I decided not to be that female who only adhered to principles and called for them. I wanted to be an effective element for the sake of women and their usurped rights in general, and the Palestinian women and the marginalised women political prisoners in particular, those who suffered from all types of male political, social and familial oppression. I believed I could make a difference in the Palestinian and Arab female communities, and to see through and finish what other iconic women had started, including the Italian Christine de Pizan, the French Simone de Beauvoir, the Swedish Maria-Pia Boëthius, the American Betty Friedan, the Australian Germaine Greer, the Moroccan Fatema Mernissi, the Egyptian Nawal El Saadawi, the

Yemeni Amal Basha, the Tunisian Mongia El-Swayhy and the Algerian Ahlam Mosteghanemi. They inspired me to excel at writing a different history for a group of women, on a national level at least, in this era, and to strive my utmost to record the changes I was looking and hoping, for me as well as for the other women. That is what mattered.

CHAPTER 23

Tuesday, July 31
11am

Surrounded by numerous media figures and reporters, I entered the courtroom with a troop of freedom of speech fighters of various nationalities and from different ages, cultures, social statuses, Arabs, Jews and foreigners. We all sat there waiting for the judge to pass her judgment and read it out.

The judge asked me to stand before her so as to hear the verdict. I took a few steps away from my wooden bench and stood next to my defence lawyer, Gaby Lasky, waiting to hear the end of the final scene of the play: 'Threatening Poetry and its Story'. As usual, the judge started off by whispering the verdict. She used abbreviated words in a shaky and confused voice that the text of the judgment was long, yet she would sum it up by reading the last few lines. Struggling, along with everyone else to make out what the judge said, I heard that I would serve a five-month sentence in prison and I would be jailed for six more months if I had committed the same violation, suspended for three years. She also mentioned another part which I didn't quite comprehend due to her low voice. Inside, I was screaming. Those screams were more prominent than all the sounds that surrounded me. I was not surprised at all. I was sure that I would go back to prison again as a result of this case and this battle. The length of the sentence was what surprised me though: five months with the reduction of the time I spent in prison at the beginning of my detention, i.e. ninety-seven days. That meant I would have to serve a two-month sentence.

The judge asked me about when I would be ready for my prison re-entry. I asked her to grant me one week to be well-prepared and say goodbye to my friends and comrades. August 8, 2018, was the date I chose to turn myself in and go back to prison. I didn't choose that date randomly or by coincidence since it was a date which left a mark on my heart, a mark which I would never forget. It was the day I, for the first time, went out with my close friend Ofra Yashua-Lyth after my arrest restrictions had been loosened a year ago. That date was special to me and moved me deeply, as it stirred feelings of a great and distinctive love. I decided on this day because it filled me with its beautiful memory. On that very day, I also entered the prison. I chose it as someone who was completely confident, persistent and hopeful. This memory would be the day's theme; it would erase the memory of entering the prison.

The judge's decision, in my opinion, encapsulated the trial which had been going on for a good three years. It only proved that Israel, its government and policies were nothing but discriminatory and racist in full view and hearing of the whole world. Especially on this day, the Israeli court proved that it lacked justice, reason, democracy and equality. That was not a new fact yet the media coverage of my case had exposed that policy to all. All masks slipped: the so-called democracy. It proved that democracy only applied to Jews; it was a tiered democracy. It was fake and deceitful, especially against the non-Jews. The democracy of racism was practised even in the simplest and most significant principles of democracy: the freedom of speech, art and poetry.

I left the courtroom after the trial holding a twenty-six-page judgment. On these papers the judge wrote her analysis of the decision as well as her motives. She passed the sentence, wrote it and ended the play's last scene with some other new play when she concluded the trial with her final words: "At last, and after conducting an examination of the length of the sentence and the type of punishment by both parties, and the balancing of all considerations, I find that it is vital to set an appropriate punishment for such crimes, whether on the level of danger, status or existence. Therefore, I will impose the following sanctions on the defendant: The defendant is sentenced to five months with sentence reduction of the period which she had spent behind bars in detention; she is given a six-month suspended sentence; it is conditional for three years should she commit any of the crimes of which she has been convicted."

I started talking to the media reporters and giving my comments on the sentence, until Oren Ziv, a reporter at the court and one of my case supporters, asked: "What is the first thing that you will do after being released from home confinement?" I looked at him and was surprised by his question. Without giving the question any attention or care I said to myself: 'What kind of question is this? I am not released yet,' leaving the question unanswered. I left the interview and started talking with my friends until Oren, again, said: "Where are you going now?" I looked at him again and then I looked around and, with more surprise, I replied: "I don't have anywhere to go except my house to wait until it's time for my prison re-entry." He replied: "But you were set free from home confinement."

I couldn't believe what Oren said at that moment. I hurried towards my lawyer who, after enquiring about it, assured me that I was released from home confinement, only to find me leaping with happiness. I automatically started dancing and at the top of my lungs I said: "I am free now. I was released from home confinement. I am not a threat to the national security any more!"

My laughter made everyone else who witnessed that scene applaud; they were happy for me. I was granted a week of freedom before re-entering the prison. The thing I hadn't been able to hear in court was my confinement release, while everything else remained unchanged, including having no access to the internet, not being able to take part in any political events and being denied entry to the West Bank and crossing the 1967 borders.

I couldn't completely comprehend the sentence – this authority was racist towards all things Palestinian yet the judge had granted me release from home confinement until I turned myself in and went back to prison. Out of the blue, at 11am that day, I didn't pose a threat to the public or to the national security any more. I was allowed to move freely and unguarded under those conditions. At those moments, and after three years of restrictions and claims of my being a danger to the public, security and the world as a whole, and after I had been sentenced to five months, that danger vanished without a trace. The irony was what made me laugh the most during this cynical, racist play, and as the Arabic proverb says: "The one that causes laughter, is the most tragic disaster."

After confirming my home confinement release, I laughed a lot and I was happy. I finally would had chance to taste freedom for just a week after spending a long time behind bars and under confinement. Additionally, the end of the arrest was not obscure any more and neither were the place and time: two months after entering prison. Spending a week in freedom was my opportunity to re-energise and recharge my emotions with the elixir of strength and resilience so as to face the upcoming two months in prison. I knew exactly what was waiting for me there: injustice, loneliness, darkness, restrictions and agony.

The Basic Law[21]: Israel as the Nation-State of the Jewish People was passed and enacted by the Knesset, the U.S Embassy was relocated to Jerusalem, demonstrations and the Great Return March protests took place on Gaza's borders, there were numerous martyrs, and a week later came the end of the story of my arrest of the threatening poem: a five-month imprisonment after three years of home confinement and house arrest, and after that I had remained under the threat of the sentence being lengthened to six months, suspended for three years.

I hugged my comrades, friends and family who couldn't hide their shock, unlike me, so I gave them my smile as a gift to reassure them and send them my calmness and amity. I left the courthouse and made up my mind: I decided not to return home even if keeping some distance would not last for more than a few days, and then I would go to prison again.

Acre was my first station during my week of freedom. There, I embraced the sea which I adored, ate up all my past memories and wrote a new history which I would remember. Afterwards, I went to Tamra village where my friend Sameera Jamaa't lived. I spent a few hours with her before I went to Jaffa where I spent three days with my friends. I walked alone down the streets of Jaffa for the first time after two years and ten months of arrest. I began discovering the meanings of freedom anew. With those meanings, I started wondering and living in confusion more, especially as it was short-term and after which I had to go back to prison again.

I sat on the beach, together with the sea; I was contemplating the significance of the life which had passed me by, and then I started walking by myself. In my head, I had so many unanswered questions. While I was wandering, a guy's voice interrupted my train of thought as he said: "Could we get to know each other?"

And then he tried to capture my attention by saying similar things, so I stopped walking, looked at him, took off my sunglasses and, with a smile, I told him: "Yes, we can. I'm Dareen Tatour." He looked back at me and his facial expressions changed in shock. He said: "You are that Dareen who is talked about in the media?"

"Yes, that's her. I'm the poet Dareen Tatour. On Wednesday, I'm turning myself in and returning to prison."

Confused and frightened, he looked at me and then he took off while stuttering: "Bye... bye... bye."

I laughed a lot as I watched the young man stutter and run off like a flea-bitten man. Fear took over him after he recognised who I was. That funny incident was the joke I needed, to sense some humour after all the stress and pressure I'd been through. From the bottom of my heart, I thanked that man because gave me moments of genuine laughter I was in desperate need as a gift. He granted me true feelings of happiness, as simple as that and without him knowing. I continued my stroll on the beach looking for a new meaning for freedom.

I also met up with my friend Einat Weizman for the first time since we were introduced to each other. The two of us sat in a café. Those moments were beautiful and very touching; that meeting was one of the dreams I had hoped to realise. It was impossible when I was under a long period of home confinement, yet it finally came true without planning ahead.

I stayed another night at Ofra's, yet I couldn't bear spending a long time at her place. For a moment, I felt as if I had been confined to my place. I couldn't really express my feelings to her, mainly because I didn't want to bother her after all she had offered me. I was certain she would understand, yet I preferred to leave her place in silence and leave her a note in which I expressed my gratitude and love. Then I headed to Alma Cats' place. I stayed the night there and tasted a new type of freedom at her place and in the company of her husband and daughter.

I entered the house and sat on the couch. I suddenly heard a strange sound. It sounded similar to crashing waves, a sound I had always loved and missed, so I began to look for its source. At first, I assumed it came from the runwell turntable in front of me. Alma and her husband came in and asked me to go to the balcony. They opened the windows. The sea. The sea came into view and the sound of its waves tickled my ears. It was the sound of the sea, not the music. I laughed at my naivety; my reaction and happiness made them laugh too. The surprise was very unexpected and delicate; they offered it to me for only one night before I re-entered the prison. Falling asleep while listening to the sound of the sea, after a long period of imprisonment and yet another lying ahead, was amusing.

I wanted to return home after my journey of freedom had ended, but some of my friends were worried about my moving around while unaccompanied. They opposed my idea of going back home by myself using public transport so as not to be harassed by Jewish extremists, as I could be identified by anyone after news on my case spread along with my name and picture in print and broadcast media. I was insistent, though. Before anything else, I wanted to challenge myself and my emotions; I wanted to challenge the circumstances under which I had been living as well. Although, to tell the truth, deep inside, I was examining the same fears my friends were, I hid it and defied it. I wanted to live in the present moment without surrendering to any of those fears.

Alma accompanied me to the central bus station in Tel Aviv and, once I got there, I had a panic attack; I had never experienced such an intense panic attack before. All my memories started to rewind in my head. I recalled again the moment when Israa' al-Abed was shot at the central bus station in Afula, especially when I saw a number of heavily armed soldiers standing close to me as they were waiting for their buses. I saw her before my very eyes, lying on the ground and covered in blood. I remembered the instant I was arrested. I remembered the Special Unit members and the police as they raided my bedroom. And my suffering scenes in prison in addition to the mistreatment of the Nahshon Unit started to replay in my head. I imagined those scenes again and again as if I relived them. My heart trembled and I was bewildered, yet I smiled and looked in a different direction. I convinced myself that everything would change. Alma was standing right beside me, so I held her hand and gave her a heartfelt handshake. I thanked her for everything, gave her a hug and said goodbye. I was torn up to the point of crying. I got on the bus and yet again I relived the harsh memories of the bosta experience, that ceaseless struggle which ended only while I was standing in line to buy a ticket and was surprised when I saw a woman driving the bus. That woman impressed me when I asked for a ticket to Nazareth. My heart sank as I saw her gazing at me. I realised that she recognised me and I thought she would harass me. "You're very beautiful. Your eyes are beautiful too," she remarked. I looked and smiled at her, leaving all my worries, fears and doubts aside. I thanked her for being nice to me and gave her a handshake. I sat in the front seat. With love, I contemplated my way back home after a week of freedom. I heard nothing but the passengers' clicks on their smart phones. I alone did not own one.

My freedom vacation was over; I packed my bags. Once I was done and left the room for a few moments, I came back only to see one of my cats, Simba, sitting inside it. He wetted it and spoiled all the clothing items I had packed. That strange act was a first. I laughed but felt so much pain over the message that cat had just conveyed. I was really affected because I had to stay away from my cats, hurried towards Simba and held him in my arms. I petted him and gave him plenty of kisses. I apologised for my absence. I also found out that my cats could understand what was going on; they also refused such a sentence. It wasn't only humans who did so. The cats didn't want me to go back to prison and tried to stop me or delay me. I washed my dirty clothes, cleaned my bag and re-packed. Bag closed. Waiting for the next day. Going back to prison.

My friends and family hosted an evening gathering to say goodbye or to charge me with extra steadfastness as a preparation for my prison term. Numerous friends, comrades and supporters attended the gathering. Artists, too, took part as they sang for freedom. Others played musical instruments to protest against my sentence. There were politicians as well as activists; they delivered spontaneous speeches about my case. On that night, my front yard turned into a stage where many forms of art were performed. I also read some poems I'd written while I was in prison. Most importantly, I read my threatening poem. I read it in front of all who were there to renew my loyalty to poetry, writing and my unwavering principle: I did not regret and would never regret composing that poem or publishing it. We celebrated all the meanings of freedom which the Israeli authorities wanted to lock up and confiscate, and all the support that surrounded me and the emotions which lit up the darkness on that difficult night dispelled much of my pain and the ache I felt about going back to prison the next day.

On the morning of August 8, 2018, some of my very close friends, some political leaders from Balad, along with my family, accompanied me to the prison door. I dragged my bag out of my bedroom and I went downstairs after saying goodbye to my room, cats, books, notebooks, guitar, oud, pictures, drawings and all the things I loved and was going to miss. I put my favourite perfume on; I even sprayed it on my white clothes. Weighed down by pain, I plodded towards the prison. Right before I got into the car, I remembered my blue ring. I'd forgotten to take it off my finger, so I removed it and put it on Einat's and said: "I won't be allowed to keep it in there. Look after it for me."

We stood in a line in front of the door of al-Jalameh Prison Centre. I was already exhausted from what was yet to come. Despite that, my smile didn't leave my face. Keeping a smile on my face wasn't something I did intentionally; rather, my smile and I clung to each other even during the cruellest and most difficult moments. Ofra read my poem again right in front of the prison and addressed all those who were there. She kept it short. Without hiding my smile, I hugged everyone. I didn't want them to be pained if I let out the grimace of someone entering a prison, let alone the pain of parting and that moment's dread. Waving at everyone with both my hands, I walked towards the prison door, said goodbye and let my eyes embrace them. I looked up to the blue wide sky above, looked back at them and again at the sky. I wanted to see their faces; my eyes were glued to them. I started moving backwards. My eyes still on them. The huge blue door was opened; I was escorted inside. Door closed. Behind it, I stood still. The officer re-opened the door; they were still standing in front of it, so I waved at them and glanced at each one of them. Einat Weizman was the last one I glanced towards. The glimpse of goodbye, until we meet again. She was the closest to the door and she was waving at me with both hands. The door was closed again and the warden arrived. She approached me closer, took the duffle bag and put it aside. She took me to a tiny room. Strip-searched. A process as harsh and abhorrent as ever. I drowned in my memories and pain, but this time those were mixed with some memories I'd made with my friend Einat. I remembered the time I recounted my story in prison to her and opened up to her about how I felt. Despite the pain, I could still remember her words to ease the control of that search which no one would understand except me and her in that instant. Hands and legs shackled. Double chains. I asked: "Why two chains each?" to which she replied: "You are a security prisoner and you pose a threat to us and to the country as well." I smiled at her and she escorted me towards the cell. As soon as I entered the cell, I dashed to see whether my wall carvings, which could date back to 2015, were still there. I saw them. I smiled, went to the top bed and held some pieces of writing in my hands. I looked up at the ceiling and smiled at it. I tried to I drown out the recollection of all that had passed. I didn't wake up until the warden and officer both shouted near the door: "Wake up! Count Time!"

EPILOGUE

On May 16, 2019, I was summoned to hear the decision of the Court of Appeal. To my surprise, I was acquitted. I was cleared of all the charges relating to the composition of the poem. Although my charges relating to the poem were dropped, the charge of posting the picture captioned "I am the next martyr" and reposting that news item remained imposed on me. As surprising as the decision was, it was also strange to me. The poem was fully acquitted, but the poet remained accused of terrorism. The poem was innocent yet the poet remained a terrorist!

From my perspective, this decision was a further confirmation that the state was racist, an entity full of rage against everything Palestinian and that the true victor in this case was not me: it was poetry, artists, poets and defenders. But for me, nothing changed since the beginning of my threatening poem trial until the end. My memory was refreshed; all the memories were revived and brought back to me each day as I wrote poetry. My trial had helped my poem yield a new sense of victory which lay in the defeat of Israel, as it is not and has never been a democratic state.

By its verdict, Israel managed to snatch and take away my space and time from me, for three years, by its ruling power and its military authority's superiority over me as an individual. It conducted my trial within equations written from its subjective perspective. When I imagined I was facing my destiny in this trial, when I was almost isolated, reality proved otherwise. By the three judges' new decision, Israel was unable to detract me from my will, memory or poem.

I stood up in Israeli courts for my rights to write and express my opinion until I attained them – despite the attempt by Israel to portray itself as a democratic state through this decision, and to exploit the appeal to its advantage when it told the world who followed up on my case that 'Israel is democratic and the poet is a terrorist.' It failed because I did not give in to its decisions and plans, and I was satisfied with the idea of sacrificing my life for the sake of others. What I did was send a message to all the Palestinians who agreed with me or opposed me, who stood by me and supported my position or those who stood against me, to all the free people in the world who supported me. The message expressed was that for their sake, and so the flame of peaceful resistance does not die down and cannot be extinguished, for the sake of Palestine, and for the air my poetry breathes, I had to fight.

Notes

[1] Moscovia (Moscobiyeh) is named after 'Mascob' which is a name the public use to refer to the Russians. It dates back to the 1857 and was a compound built by the Russians to serve their interests. It featured a hostel for pilgrims, a hospital, a church, courtyard and a prison, all of which had distinctive architecture built from local stones. Al-Moscobiyeh did not remain the same. After the Israeli occupation it was turned into a police station where Palestinian prisoners were subjected to innovative methods of torture.

[2] Yasam Unit is a special section of the Israeli police tasked with maintaining security, controlling riots and performing special operations. Its soldiers and officers are selected from the Israeli army and the border guards. The uniform consists of a pair of pants, a grey shirt and a black cap. This unit, in particular, monitors and controls the movement of Palestinians; its elements have carried out numerous field executions of Palestinians.

[3] The Nahshon Unit is the combat unit of the Israeli Prison Service. It was established in 1973 and was named after Nahshon Amminadab, 'the hero', whose name is mentioned in the Jewish Bible, which states that Nahshon was the first to jump to the sea before it parted, so was known for his boldness and courage - hence this unit's motto: "Nahshon Unit - because we chose to lead." This unit represses and abuses Palestinian prisoners and detainees, raids and searches their rooms, accompanies and transfers detainees and prisoners to various courthouses, prisons and detention centres.

[4] Al-Jalameh detention centre Kishon is located at the al-Jalameh junction on the main road between Haifa and Nazareth in the north of Palestine. It was reopened during the Al-Aqsa Intifada. It has twenty detainees, security is tight and prisoners are held until the completion of their interrogation.

[5] A 'security' prisoner in Israel is jailed for committing an offence that has purportedly damaged the security of the state. The term is an internal management concept used among prison administration. Although it is not defined in law, it is defined under delegated authority. This term is used only for Palestinians. Identifying a prisoner with the 'security' label impacts the conditions of their imprisonment in several aspects: prison location, visits, prevention of holidays, banning phone use, the ability to reduce the sentence period, the prevention of access to lawyers and closed and limited family visits.

[6] Neve Tirtza Prison is the only women's prison located in Israel intended for civilian females who were imprisoned on criminal grounds, Jews and Arabs. It is located between the cities of Lod and Ramla; it is part of the Ramla prison. Its establishment dates back to 1968. The prison contains a section used to isolate women political prisoners.

[7] Sharon Prison: A detention centre which holds number 455, in the Sharon region, south of Bnei Yehuda settlement. It is intended for Israelis convicted of criminal charges. It is one of the largest prisons in Israel and has wings designated for high-risk, powerful offenders. It can accommodate approximately 400 prisoners; it also includes a section for security prisoners and another for Palestinian prisoners.

[8] Sheket is a Hebrew word, an instruction to be quiet.

[9] Fawra, which translates as Yard Time, is a word which has been circulated among prisoners from the outset of the Palestinian Captive Movement. It is a restrained outing for political prisoners who can only go out in the yard at specified times and depending on the mood/temperament of the prison administration.

[10] Al-Barsh is a term used by the political prisoners in occupation prisons to refer to the beds in which they sleep. These are different from regular beds.

[11] Mivar is a Hebrew word that is common among political and criminal prisoners; in Arabic, it means 'the passage'. These places are not intended for long stays. Rather, they are places where many prisoners and detainees meet in order to appear before the courts. The most notorious of them are the Ramla and Jalameh transit centres.

[12] Damoun Prison: This prison is located in northern Palestine in the forests of Carmel in Haifa. It was built during the British Mandate and used as a tobacco warehouse, so it was constructed to ensure it was humid enough to preserve tobacco leaves. After 1948, Israel took over the building and turned it into a prison. The prison has a section for women Palestinian prisoners and a section for young prisoners, i.e. 'cubs'. The rest of the prison is intended for Palestinian workers from the West Bank and Gaza Strip who were arrested in the occupied territories of 1948 for not obtaining a permit.

[13] Yoav Haifawi, a political activist in Hirak Haifa, has been a member in Abnaa el-Balad Movement (Sons of the Land or Sons and Daughters of the Country or People of the Homeland Movement) since 1984. He has also been a blog editor of 'Haifa al-Hurra' (Free Haifa) since joining a left-Marxist movement (Workers' Union) in 1972. Haifawi fights for the return of Palestinian refugees and the establishment of a secular, democratic and free Palestinian state all over historic Palestine. [1]

[14] Ofra Yashua-Lyth is a political activist, journalist and writer. She is the author of the book Politically Incorrect: Why a Jewish State is a Bad Idea. She is also a member of the Secular Democratic State in Historic Palestine Committee.

[15] Gaby Lasky is a Jewish human rights lawyer, feminist, social and political human rights activist. As a lawyer, she documents torture cases in prison as well as police brutality in Israel, Gaza and the West Bank. She is one of the most forthright defenders of the children of the stones in court.

[16] Artists and political activists.

[17] Poet and political activist.

[18] Actress, writer, theatre director, and political activist.

[19] Director and political activist.

[20] The Nakba Law, which was endorsed by the Knesset in March 2011, authorises the Minister of Finance to reduce government funding or support for institutions which carry out any activity that opposes the definition of the state of Israel as 'Jewish and democratic,' or which mark the state's independence day or the day of its establishment as a 'day of grief and mourning.' Palestinians classify and commemorate Israel's official independence day as the national anniversary of mourning and, thus, they organise various memorial activities. The law affects/violates the rights of Palestinians, restricts their freedom of speech and damages cultural and educational institutions. It also entrenches discrimination against Arab citizens. The Nakba Law undermines the principle of equality as well as the rights of Arab citizens to maintain their history and preserve their culture. This law deprives Arab citizens of their right to commemorate the Nakba anniversary, which is an integral part of their history.

[21] A law enacted on July 19, 2018. The Israeli Knesset passed the law by a majority of 62 for, 55 against and 2 abstentions. This law defines Israel as a 'national state for the Jewish people.' According to this law, 'the right to self-determination is guaranteed only to the Jewish people,' which excludes 1948 Palestinians and marginalises their political and social roles in the country.